Choice and the Legal Order
Rising above Politics

(

Law in Context

Editors: William Twining (University College, London) and
Christopher McCrudden (Lincoln College, Oxford)

Ashworth: *Sentencing and Criminal Justice*
Barton and Douglas: *Parents and Parentage*
Bercusson: *European Labour Law*
Birkinshaw: *Freedom of Information: The Law, the Practice and the Ideal*
Cane: *Atiyah's Accidents, Compensation and the Law*
Collins: *The Law of Contract*
Cranston: *Legal Foundations of the Welfare State*
Davies and Freedland: *Labour Law Text and Materials*
Detmold: *Courts and Administrators: A Study in Jurisprudence*
Doggett: *Marriage, Wife-Beating and the Law in Victorian England*
Dummett and Nicol: *Subjects, Citizens, Aliens and Others: Nationality
    and Immigration Law*
Goodrich: *Languages of Law*
Hadden: *Company Law and Capitalism*
Harlow and Rawlings: *Law and Administration Text & Materials*
Harris: *An Introduction to Law*
Harris: *Remedies in Contract and Tort*
Lacey, Wells and Meure: *Reconstructing Criminal Law – Text and
    Materials*
Moffat: *Trusts Law – Text and Materials*
Norrie: *Crime, Reason and History*
Page and Ferguson: *Investor Protection*
Picciotto: *International Business Taxation*
Ramsay: *Consumer Protection: Text and Materials*
Richardson: *Law, Process and Custody*
Snyder: *New Directions in European Community Law*
Stapleton: *Product Liability*
Turpin: *British Government and the Constitution – Text, Cases and
    Materials*
Twining and Anderson: *Analysis of Evidence*
Twining and Miers: *How to do Things with Rules*
Zander: *Cases and Materials on the English Legal System*
Zander: *The Law-Making Process*

Choice and the Legal Order
Rising above Politics

Norman D Lewis
Professor of Public Law,
University of Sheffield

Butterworths
London, Dublin and Edinburgh
1996

United Kingdom	Butterworths, a Division of Reed Elsevier (UK) Ltd, Halsbury House, 35 Chancery Lane, LONDON WC2A 1EL and 4 Hill Street, EDINBURGH EH2 3JZ
Australia	Butterworths, SYDNEY, MELBOURNE, BRISBANE, ADELAIDE, PERTH, CANBERRA and HOBART
Canada	Butterworths Canada Ltd, TORONTO and VANCOUVER
Ireland	Butterworth (Ireland) Ltd, DUBLIN
Malaysia	Malayan Law Journal Sdn Bhd, KUALA LUMPUR
New Zealand	Butterworths of New Zealand Ltd, WELLINGTON and AUCKLAND
Singapore	Reed Elsevier (Singapore) Pte Ltd, SINGAPORE
South Africa	Butterworths Publishers (Pty) Ltd, DURBAN
USA	Michie, CHARLOTTESVILLE, Virginia

A CIP Catalogue record for this book is available from the British Library.

ISBN 0 406 05050 3

Typeset by Phoenix Photosetting, Chatham, Kent
Printed and bound in Great Britain by Redwood Books, Trowbridge, Wiltshire

Preface

Many of the themes which are touched upon in this book will almost certainly become increasingly visible in the world order in the years to come. Already futurologists are forecasting the more socially responsible global company, greater co-operation between governments, a burgeoning international, worldwide, upsurge of community, grass-root organisations, greater attention to sustainable development through concentration on job creation with a slimmed-down world energy or infrastructural base, etc. It is clear that knowledge and individual power is capable of growing enormously in the multi-media super-highway of the future with heaven knows what results for the influence of governments and corporations.

None of this should surprise us; the fact that the world is altered and shaped by human action means that the generality of human needs and aspirations will have to be satisfied or there will be a total breakdown in social systems. That is always assuming that we envisage a democratic future rather than a dictatorial world order. However, human needs are such that no other than a loosely democratic outcome is bearable or sustainable.

Correspondingly there should be little in what is said about the UK and its partner democracies that will not have a striking resonance for the world community over the years to come. It is almost certain that important aspects even of the UK experience will have been misrepresented or inaccurately projected so that there would be little point in expanding the analysis outwards at this time. However, on the assumption that global trends are as imagined, the least an island like ours can do is to attempt to set itself on the path which most likely represents common beliefs. The bargained interrelationships between the UK and its allies, the European Union, GATT, UNESCO, CSCE etc are left over for the imagination at this time. That is for the future. The task for the present is to re-examine our own legal order to help reinstate the conditions for choice to be presented as the leading face of citizenship. If what follows is regarded by some as insufficiently internationalist or is one-dimensional that is understandable. However, for the time being at least, the nation state and some conception of sovereignty remain firmly on the agenda. If there is no vision of the kind of social and legal order the British wish to cultivate, then they will have little to contribute to the larger groupings to which the country is inexorably drawn.

Another large omission must be explained. Although a great deal is said about reconstitutionalising our affairs and the need for administrative law reform to accompany that process, little that follows deals either with the present law of judicial review or a more satisfactory and comprehensive review of the area of individualised justice and the state, except for innovations which are incidental to the larger aspirations. This is not because this area is unimportant; on the contrary. The author's thinking on these matters has been recently explored in company with Patrick Birkinshaw and is published as *When Citizens Complain: Reforming Justice and Administration* (Open University Press, Buckingham 1993).

I should like to thank Butterworths for their speed, courtesy and general helpfulness. I should also like to thank William Twining for justified criticism of the first draft and for helping to improve this book. Perhaps most of all I should thank David Campbell of Sheffield Hallam University for his patience and detailed criticism in finally helping to put the book to bed. The usual sentiments as to ultimate responsibility naturally apply.

Norman Lewis
February 1996

Contents

Introduction

Choice has become the ruling political sentiment in recent years, being primarily, but by no means entirely, associated with the New Right. It has informed the rhetoric of politics and yet has not been adequately analysed at a more profound level. Moreover, it has been treated as an ideology which belongs to a particular brand of politics when in reality it goes deeper into the heart of the constitution and the legal order. Choice relates to human beings and their true identity, matters often discussed by philosophers but rarely these days by either political scientists or lawyers. Choice rings political bells but politicians rarely debate its inner meaning; philosophical debate is unalluring to the electorate. However, the debate is crucial if a nation is to offer equal opportunity to all and to be ultimately cohesive. Correspondingly, the ties that bind a nation must find expression at a level beyond politics; in the constitution and the larger legal order. The argument is that the constitution is bigger than politics and any particular generation of politicians. The task, therefore, is to engage in discourse on the kind of legal order which gives centrality to choice as the guiding principle. This will involve going beyond the traditional radicalism of recent suggestions for constitutional reform and calls for a settlement which marries necessary changes in political structures with a statement of belief about citizen entitlements over and above the new orthodoxy of a Bill of Rights, extending to the social and economic sphere and guaranteeing opportunities for participation in all forms of political and social expression.

The argument is set out as follows. Part I seeks to assess the scale and nature of contemporary political developments across the developed world while searching for a vision of the human personality which keeps these developments under the control and direction of human agency. Chapter 1 analyses the concept of choice which is normally taken as self-evident when in fact it challenges the assumptions of ruling political philosophy head-on. On examination the analysis dissolves into a discussion of human rights which in turn needs to treat the question of what it is to be human more directly than is normally the case. The analysis takes on board the relationship between choice and 'New Public Management' (NPM) or re-invented government and the commitment to markets as an expression of human freedom. It extends the argument to the larger notion of economic and social well-being, and introduces the relationship between these various concepts and the notion of both accountability and entitlement under the law.

Chapter 2 develops a discussion about the contested concept of human nature in political philosophy and in particular counterposes man as a bundle of market appetites – as the classic consumer – and man as the restless seeker of his own identity searching to discover his own soul in communion with others. A collective order which ignores anything so fundamental risks producing alienation and dissonance. Again, it is argued that the higher law in the shape of the constitution cannot remain indifferent to these issues.

Part II contains a series of chapters, mostly short, sketching out a number of themes for which the earlier discussions have relevance and which the legal order must ultimately address: they are the social dimension, the federal state, community and society, associations and labour, and markets, regulation and competition.

Part III addresses the significance of the earlier chapters for the legal order broadly conceived; this embraces not only the constitution in the terms which are normally understood, but also what are later described as 'sub-constitutional or directive principles' capable of educative, persuasive and developmental effects. Law is seen as essentially co-terminous with legitimate institutional power rather than as the narrow *gesellschaft* concept associated with Dicey, Hayek and others. Its potential for liberation and self-expression in particular is explored and the conclusion reached is that earlier arguments point to the need for a social market constitution within a social market economy being sufficiently flexible to accommodate the inevitable challenges of the next century.

---

1 *Gesellschaft* is normally used as shorthand for a historically-specific form of law comprised of broad rules having generalised application which guarantee clear rights and impose corresponding duties. Infringement of the rules is accompanied by equally unambiguous sanctions. Crucial though this version of law is, it by no means exhausts the species.

Most of what follows is a (belated) response to the pace of change being forced in public administration. The rush to market, the impulse to embrace NPM, the farming out of public purposes, all demand a constitutional re-examination which was, in any event, long overdue. Newness is not opposed, going with the global grain is perfectly attractive, but as the world changes so must our perspective on it. It is extraordinary that the quiet revolution worked in governing institutions over the last decade or so has been largely unaccompanied by legislation. The British legal order has long been behind the times as far as the pace of politics is concerned, perhaps nowhere better illustrated in terms of its failure to lend democratic help to the policy-making process, which is notoriously elitist. This too is re-addressed.

THE CENTRAL THEMES

A number of the central themes running through this book can be foreshadowed. Brief mention has already been made of the social market economy which has, at its core, the conviction that market institutions are always embedded in other social and political institutions which shape them. This economy is predicated on the belief in the compatibility of the free market with a socially-conscious state. It seeks to promote a unified political economy based on the principles of freedom and social responsibility. But the freedom of the individual and the responsibility of the state are constrained by the constitutional framework within which the economy operates.

A commitment is made to 'the virtuous triangle' of individual, state and community which the constitution must seek to assure. The case for the autonomous individual is clear and unassailable yet it involves self-discovery and communion with others since human beings live in social settings sharing their lives with others (ideally) of their own choosing. This is a recognition of the need for the encouragement and maintenance of collective or associational outlets. It is clear that only the state or more properly the constitution can ultimately provide these guarantees. The state must allow the individual to flourish; it should be enabling and not directive, but to guarantee both the private and the collegiate life it cannot be anorexic. State, individual and community constitute the virtuous triangle and the constitution must be shaped by this understanding. In particular, the community aspect of living has been too long ignored by the political system so that it is now necessary for the larger legal order to come to its assistance. Forms of fellowship at the level of local politics and welfare need constitutional backing if paternalism is to be diminished and associationism is to be encouraged. This is where the 'directive principles' of the constitution, referred to especially in chapters 8 and 9, come into play. In similar vein the right to form associations, not limited to labour associations, has enormous regenerative potential.

Choice involves adopting JS Mill's plea for 'experiments in living'. Choice is in part a celebration of pluralism, but it is also driven by the recognition that the human mind is never in possession of perfect information, that following Weber and others, it has to be accepted that rationality crises will recur so that it is only possible to learn through experiment and freedom from prejudice. Correspondingly, the heavily centralised state can never be logically defended since, among other things, it tends to nullify alternative sites of disagreement. Moreover, in the absence of perfect information, the social ecology, including the economic, must be open, transparent, experimental and encourage as much innovation as possible. An entrenched right to 'participation', political, social and economic, can provide a valuable stimulus to pluralism in civic affairs.

The argument also emerges that freedom and choice are only possible within a framework of relative economic and psychological well-being. The negative theory of human rights associated with Berlin as well as Hayek, Nozick, Von Mises and others is rejected in favour of the establishment of a basic floor of material well-being that makes free-willing action possible.[2] The iron law of the division of labour means that humans can only exist within systems of social support for the provision of material and psychic goods.

Citizenship and community are not simply contemporary chic currency; they emerge ringingly from an effective analysis of choice. There is an overwhelming case for encouraging bodies intermediate between the citizen and the state in order to foster the existential need for social association. With the rejection of the centralised state and equally of the 'atomised' individual, there will be increased emphasis on forms of civic and political participation which history indicates are linked to caring and belonging to

---

2 The negative rights philosophy has been justly criticised as making 'peremptory' assertions which, being intuitionist positions, 'are impotent in the face of conflicting intuitions'; Alan Gewirth *Human Rights: Essays on Justifications and Applications* (University of Chicago Press, 1982) p 198.

informal membership groups. There is also abundant evidence that both the state and the market operate most effectively in civic settings where trust, common standards and networks facilitate co-ordinated action and help to foster partnerships. Bringing all these things together requires paying attention to political and legal institutions, not least at the local level. It is here that there is an increasing clamour for more effective enfranchisement and participation and it is here that increasing dissatisfaction with the contemporary form of the local state can be found.

In order to provide a balance between the settled nature of certain basic human rights and the flexibility necessary to adapt to unpredicted change, a new constitutional shape is called for which provides for three separate categories of 'law': ordinary laws which Parliament passes in the traditional fashion, primary human rights, undisturbable save by a special procedure, and 'directive' or secondary constitutional principles. This middle range of laws would reflect the uncertainty about how the nation gets from one place to another at the same time as being committed to settled philosophic principles, such as the right to a clean environment and to active participation, for example, in economic life. The prescription is for a legal order broader in scope and function than has been traditional, but one which is more normative and purposive. There is a great deal to be learned, for example, from the Indian project of 'Social Action Litigation' which invests the courts with something resembling auditing functions instead of being limited to a Medes and Persian rigid interpretation function. This allows them to appoint fact-finding commissions to monitor the progress of government action in pursuing the obligations laid down by the constitution, and to monitor the response of government to its rulings. It represents a different sort of law which redefines its relationship to the political order, which itself needs radical reform so that the two, working in a restored partnership, enrich each other in fulfilling the nation's purposes.

Finally, there is the issue of 'legal autonomy'. The relationship between law and politics requires careful redefinition in a UK setting both to entrench choice and human rights and to liberate the art of politics itself. However, politics is ultimately subordinate to the higher law of the constitution which is part of the claim for judicial autonomy. A linchpin of the seventeenth century revolution was the concept of judicial independence given the most prominent expression perhaps in the Act of Settlement, and amounting to the simple proposition that an independent corps with entrenched status depending, in the final analysis, on their reputation for disinterested scholarship and authority must retain the final say on the parameters of the collective settlement. Nothing that has occurred in the more than 300 years since that event has diminished the force of the argument. As has been well-stated:

> 'In the regime of autonomous law, the actions of the organised political community are not self-legitimating. The political elite may make decisions and deploy resources, but the question of whether those acts are lawful requires a separate assessment.'[3]

In spite of much anti-law passion in the UK, few will dispute this assessment. However, the difficulty arises when an argument for constitutional reform is made, not least in the area of human rights, for at this point the bailiwick of the judiciary becomes almost inevitably expanded. This dilemma, if that is what it is, is unavoidable, for although considerable constitutional power can, and no doubt should, be invested in ombudsmen and other 'legal' institutions, ultimately the judicial power is the one which must have the end authority and the ability to trump political cards. The power of the judiciary around the world's democracies has been growing, a trend which will almost certainly continue and gather pace, not least as a result of internationally entered obligations. An expanded catalogue of human rights seeking to guarantee genuine choice inevitably raises the profile and the importance of the judiciary. This is a situation which will be charged with interest and controversy in the coming century.

3 P Nonet and P Selznick *Law and Society in Transition: Towards Responsive Law* (Harper and Row, 1978) p 59.

Part I
Political developments and human rights

Chapter 1

Choice and the legal order

This book is impelled, as much as anything, by changes in the way Western governments in general and the UK government in particular have been conducting public affairs over the last 15 years or so. The analysis will hopefully transcend the life expectancy of this cycle, if such it is, but it gains resonance from contemporary developments which presently appear likely to occupy the high ground of politics for some time to come. It is not informed by a commitment to any particular political persuasion, but it may appear to be especially directed to politicians of a centre-right cast of mind. This is because they have usually formed the governments of the major nations of Europe and North America during the period when the changes under consideration have taken place, and they have had, without wishing to sour the opposition, the best tunes. Australasia's governments have been more politically varied, but the language which they have also used to justify the new ways of governing resound with declarations remarkably similar to those of a clearly 'conservative-radical' pedigree.

   Changes in the perceptions and practices of government have moved almost unilinearly; they have been 'anti-state', they have favoured individualism, have extolled market solutions and, significantly, self-expression, even if the preferred language has been self-help. Particular empirical clusters of political preference have emerged, often mirrored in jurisdictions with similar histories, and appeals to the regenerative power of individual responsibility through free-willing endeavour have relegated paternalism to a footnote in history. The state might be a little more than nightwatchman, but its functions in the waking hours are primarily of a benign and conciliatory nature. People must be encouraged to create their own lives, something which is impeded by an intrusive state presence. This brief résumé is a faithful attempt to replicate the credo of the political times, even if the occasional philosophical benefit of the doubt has been painted on. What, however, is manifestly lacking is a theoretical manifesto which jump-starts the fashionable clusters and which conveys a sense of vision. Theology has not yet put in an appearance. What follows is an appeal to those who are forcing change to examine the inner logic of these developments and to assess the nature of the social enterprise. In so doing it will be argued that there is a need to renew the ancient commitments to legal order as a necessary condition of making sense of the compacts which are struck in order to build a collective life.

Choice is the theme which runs through the history of recent political events as a consuming passion. Because choice has dominated the rhetoric of the period, it is used as the focus of the argument to be adopted. However, on reflection, it will be seen that choice is a generic concept which can only attach to basic human needs. Those needs are themselves substantially subsumed by the categories of fundamental rights which have recommended themselves to the world's democracies since at least the end of the Second World War. More often than not the expression has been used as shorthand for a conviction in the superiority of economic markets but it is also the justification for a reduced or minimal state, not least in the sense of weakened state legitimacy to deprive citizens of their wealth and thereby of the choices which they would have made with what is, at top and bottom, their own. It is, in other words, one of the most frequent justifications for a reduced burden of taxation; at least of direct taxation.

It will be argued that choice is the most satisfactory label for the bundle of primary or fundamental rights which have been almost universally adopted in the West and which, of course, bind the UK government. An examination of the politics of the dominant Right will reveal the logic of a clear commitment to a corpus of rights, emanating in and ultimately enforceable through, international law. The 'atomic' nature of choice and its incidents will be considered later, but a little needs to be said about human rights. First of all, the UK is an original signatory to the European Convention on Human Rights (ECHR) and, although so far it has not sought to introduce the terms of the convention directly into domestic law, there is no official suggestion that its terms should be flouted. So also the preamble to the North Atlantic Treaty Organisation, the Committee on Security and Co-operation in Europe (CSCE) and other texts to which the UK is a party, speak with the same voice. It is safe therefore to assume that the UK under any conceivable political stewardship in the near future is unlikely to abandon its commitment to fundamental human rights as a central part of its political philosophy. Indeed there is presently detectable a considerable body of right-wing opinion which sees the very expression of human rights as a polar counter to the failed collectivism of the former Eastern European states, whose new credentials for membership of the world order are both a commitment to human rights and a kindred preference for market economics. As a matter of fact, voices are being raised for the first time in perhaps two centuries[1] to the effect that human rights and a commitment to a market philosophy are, if not two sides of the same coin, at least intimately related.

One source, normally thought of as being on the radical right of British politics, makes the connection quite clearly. In 1993 the European Constitutional Group sought to pre-empt the UK's position on 'a coherent constitutional settlement for Europe'. Several of its guiding sentiments will be quoted together since they not only underline the present phase of the argument but contribute to the broader picture being painted. Thus.

'A decentralised Union provides the only structure in which individual and civil liberties can flourish;'

'Liberty is not conferred by government....[it] rests on powers flowing up from the people.'

'The starting point of the Treaty must be a clear declaration of principles.'

'The market provides a more effective mechanism than political processes for individuals to realise their unique preferences and human aspirations. Political processes have a legitimate role in the Union and in Member States in attempting to redress perceived "market failures" and in providing collective support for those who do not succeed in a market setting.'

'Membership in the Union shall be open to European states that are members of the Council of Europe and signatories of its Convention on Human Rights, that pursue market oriented economic policies and respect the rule of law and political pluralism in a democratic framework.'

---

1 See eg Adam Smith *The Theory of Moral Sentiments* (Arlington House, New Rochelle, New York 1969).

And lastly, to store up a point for later development:

> 'Member states agree to respect the aspirations of the
> European Social Charter of the Council of Europe and may
> avail themselves of its provisions.'[2]

What is as important as the specific content of the main con-
tentions is the call for a clear declaration of principles. Since the
raison d'être of this book is the construction of a vision for those
committed to markets, choice, individual freedom and pluralism,
this is to be welcomed.

CHOICE AT A JUNCTION

So far little, hopefully, has been contentious but the argument
needs to be developed further. Individuals choose in social settings; there is no alternative scenario available. This means choosing in a context of otherness. This simple formulation will have
profound implications for what manner of social construct is
regarded as acceptable according to any prevailing political philosophy. On one thing agreement can be assumed; to use the Kantian
claim, people are ends and not means.[3] Although choosing takes
place in a context of otherness, it does so within a framework
where each 'other' counts for the same value. This is part of what
has sometimes been termed 'the moral heritage of the West'[4]
reflected in a corpus of texts, instruments, claims and rhetoric that
is essentially human rights based.

The language of political change in recent decades has been
choice, especially in opposition to bureaucratic or statist solutions.
This has presently attained the status of a received wisdom, especially in the field of consumer affairs, and even more especially in
the field of state consumer services. However, when unpacked,

---

2 'A European Constitutional Settlement', Report by the European Constitutional
  Group 1993, European Policy Forum, London. However, it should be added that
  the Final Report, December 1993 was somewhat more ambivalent on the social
  rights issue.
3 Kant *passim*.
4 G Poggi *The Development of the Modern State* (Hutchinson, 1978). However, this
  account draws heavily on categoric philosophy; eg Alan Gewirth *Reason and
  Morality* (Chicago UP, 1978).

choice is a multi-layered, fecund concept, attached as it is to the unique status of the individual *qua* individual. What follows is that those who argue for various forms of minimal state, let alone those who argue for a minimal-minimal state,[5] possess a concept, often not positively expressed, of the nature of the human personality. Disagreements at this rarefied level of argument can be anticipated but at bottom it is this step of the argument that has to be addressed if subsequent political discourse is to have any meaning. This issue will be developed in Chapter 2.

THE STATE/THE CONSTITUTION

Except where is otherwise apparent, the constitution and the state will be used interchangeably, with a preference expressed for the former. The constitution is the collective compact. This, surprisingly perhaps, concedes a great deal of the argument which the minimal statists or indeed those who search for the holy grail of 'core' government are ordinarily reluctant to concede. Acceptance of a constitution, of an organised state, follows from a recognition that conditions must be put into play at an ordered level to allow free expression and self-discovery to flourish. Discussion must then take place as to how extensive this ordering must be. It will be argued that the core propositions for potential social being and action necessarily must be provided to ensure what is unharmoniously often referred to these days as a 'level playing field'; in any event, to ensure consistency. But the intermediate structures to facilitate choice and well-being have to be optimally chosen by pushing decision-making in like-minded groupings down to the lowest level where choice can effectively occur. Mutual experience and the dynamic processes of human interaction can be expected both to create new realms of choice and opportunity, through experiment and self- and mutual discovery. The 'state' then will be naturally diffuse, not to say 'federal'. Cognitive deficiencies will often result in central government being unable to make rational decisions about the lives of ordinary people so that intermediate associations will be an inevitable requirement for choice in a complex society. It needs to be underlined that accessible information is a precondition for choice to be effectively exercised. This is

5 Eg Robert Nozick *Anarchy, State and Utopia* (Basic Books, New York 1974).

recognised by the fact that it has become practically an axiom of modern conservatism in relation to consumer choice in schools, medical care and a range of other services.

At this point a caveat must be expressed about rationality as a ruling good. It is that if 'perfect' information is not available 'perfect' choices cannot be made – or at least cannot be made in the full knowledge of their consequences. Indeed, living in relative states of ignorance is one of the great justifications for a market order. Thus a strategy for minimising ignorance must implicitly involve both experimentation within settled belief systems and an attendant, 'competitive', set of social institutions to invite comparison and assessment. This will have implications for the 'diffuseness' of the state apparatus and for encouraging associative conduct of various sorts in order to maximise the range of 'possible societies' and therefore possible choices. Although the point about the diffuseness – or 'federality' – of the state apparatus is widely remarked upon, 'the implications for associative order have perhaps been silted over by the modern tides of welfarism'.[7] However, diffuseness will require the rebirth or reinvention of the state, the parish, the co-operative, self-help groups, self-management styles and much else besides. Some of these ideas will be developed later, particularly in Chapter 9.

THE GREAT EMPOWERER

The constitution is the agreement citizens make and remake with each other to live out their lives in freedom both in isolation or tranquillity and with others of their choosing, bearing in mind the correlative duties which ensure mutuality.[8] British constitutional debate has had little to say on the matter of mutuality, but in recent times political discourse has been charged with periodic moralising and occasional rage surrounding the issue. Yet the discourse has largely been devoid of patient calculation and has rarely been

---

6   See eg John Stewart *Accounting to the Public* (European Policy Forum, London 1992).

7   Though see eg David Green *Reinventing Civil Society*, Institute of Economic Affairs (1993) and more generally TH Green. See eg WD Lamont *Introduction to Green's Moral Philosophy* (Allen and Unwin, London 1934).

8   There is of course an enormous philosophical literature in this area even if there has been relatively little recent discussion in the legal and political science literature.

accompanied by a systematic analysis of the co-incidents of rights claims, of the inter-dependent mutuality of freedoms which requires their social interplay. In fact, demands are made on the basis of rights; the nation is a reciprocal rights market with duty the flip-side of human nature. This is 'the golden rule'; to do unto others; an old, indeed an ancient, insight which reveals the purity of first principle which is the proper replacement for rage and indeed for moralising. Political cant has painted duty as either a hair shirt which the unenlightened must wear from time to time or as the necessary incentive to enterprise; the language of indignation to justify tax cuts. In reality, if rights are universal then clearly they must exist for the benefit of all; for one's neighbours as for oneself. And it would be strange indeed if people were not specially charged to be active in caring for those whom they brought into the world or indeed for those who did the same for them. Duty to family is not a Victorian fad nor a device for lightening the revenue burden for the captains of industry; it is a moral and logical requirement to love one's very closest neighbours as oneself.

It will be useful to revert to the 'state' terminology for the moment since what follows is normally conducted in 'statist' language. It is probably fair to characterise most writings about the nature of the state as arguing that the state is either:

(1)   a set of institutions; or
(2)   a set of beliefs (although a third possibility is a combination of the two).

Now institutions are clearly bound to be involved though many of them are 'contingent'; that is to say it matters little what they are or how, as a matter of mechanics, they operate. For example, institutional discourse must take place to oil the constitution and keep it in repair but its form is not overly important. There will need to be periodic elections, there must be recallability, there must be freely accessible information plus a range of intermediary institutions and practices to ensure that choice is regularised at the political level and is not merely periodised. But the precise arrangements will be culturally-specific, save that there must be a separation of powers as a matter of principle, certainly between the legislature and the judiciary for the purposes of proposing and disposing.

Thus, minimum, though flexible (contingent) institutions are necessary to constitutionalise social territory, but above all the state represents a set of ideas. These ideas, it is argued, are compressed into the notion of 'choice' but that concept is multi-layered and when it is opened out it will be seen to be both richer and more fertile than appears at first sight. In any event, although choice will comprise the dynamo of the rights claims being made, there is a commitment by UK governments to an apparently broader spectrum of rights under collective compacts and obligations.

For the purpose of clarification it should be stressed that the constitution is to secure and guarantee human rights 'proper' and also to enforce the rules for debate about choice elsewhere, both in the political arena and in socio-cultural life. This has several facets. First and most obviously, human rights will be formally guaranteed and enforced; including all 'choice' aspects. Secondly, the choices that individuals make in the form of reciprocal arrangements will also be guaranteed. And finally, morally-optional (that is to say anything that is permitted within a context of upholding human rights) political decisions will also be enforced. In other words, the constitution guarantees the core values while politics, necessarily subordinate to the constitution, debates morally optional measures.

Choice attaches to free-willing individuals; to social agents. Individuals are constituted by certain properties; the need to maintain/sustain life and liberty; freedom of action; freedom to act in an unimpeded, if untainted, fashion. Individuals, to put it another way, are constituted by uniqueness within a homogeneous species. These items alone help to extract almost all of the traditional civil and political rights as logical extensions of these properties, even if those who base the core of their political philosophy on choice normally fail to develop the implications of their position.

Core human rights statements are, inevitably, encapsulations of essential facets of the human spirit and will turn out to be shorthand for *bundles* of rights, aspirations and duties. Unger has shown, for example, that prohibition on discrimination in racial or gender terms is logically embedded in the requirement to treat all people as equally free agents, providing they espouse mutuality, so that what the common law of the UK regards as 'taking improper considerations into account'[9] is an implicit, though ill-remarked upon, recognition that 'discrimination' against untainted actors is improper whatever its source.[10] The same may be said of the unexpected inner nature of other non-contested rights to advance identical propositions. Thus, for example, 'the protection of life and

9 The classic exposition is to be found in *Short v Poole Corporation* [1926] Ch 66.
10 *Critical Legal Studies* (Harvard University Press, 1986).

personal liberty'[11] is perhaps, predictably, the most hugely preg-nant requirement in the taxonomy of human rights discourse. It is the *sine qua non* of being human and, given the sensitivities and sensibilities to which human beings are prey, its ramifications are more than brute. Thus the right to life is more than 'mere animal existence',[12] so that in some jurisdictions the claim has been seen to have associations with the opportunity for dignified labour and even for a clean environment. What will have to be grappled with is whether this most central of all assertions of human value is com-plied with by mere negative restraints; ie the holding back from habits of barbarism 'both punitive and processual'.[13] This line of development is central to philosophising about the nature and being of modern states and constitutions and its treatment will occupy attention throughout the text.

AND SO TO MARKET

Market economics saw their greatest triumph of the century during the 1980s. Quite apart from the fact that market-driven economies[14] have been consistently more successful than planned or command economies in creating and sustaining growth rates, the odd and occasionally prolonged recession apart, the multitude of individual transactions which comprise the market (infinite numbers of signals being transmitted just waiting to home in on receivers) is quintessentially an exercise in large numbers of peo-ple voting for their choices in the market-place. There is an ele-ment of the libertarian high ground in the very description of the market-place. This is an ideal-typical place. Nevertheless, the justi-fication for markets is not simple efficiency since efficiency is a means, not an end. If markets are efficient in maximising people's wants, then they are justified because expressing wants and having them delivered is a choosing exercise. And choice as freedom is at the heart of the human condition. The justification for markets is a human rights justification, based primarily on freedom of

---

11 See s 21 of the Constitution of India, though, of course, this is a common enough formula.
12 *Olga Tellis v Bombay Municipal Corporation* (1985) 3 SCC 545, at p 555.
13 Ibid.
14 Though *quaere* the 'sunrise economies' of South East Asia.

speech.[15] In 'voting' for what they want people are saying what they think. These claims, and their qualifications, are considered in Chapter 7. However, the justification for markets is a human rights/choice justification so that where markets impede effective choice then it follows that the constitution is obliged to restore choice and freedom; to regulate markets, especially where competition, and therefore choice, is impeded. How this is done is information-dependent. To restore markets is to restore choice, not to restore economics, except as an instrument. However, it is interesting that the emerging regimes of post-Iron Curtain Europe are commonly attempting to combine in their constitutions a commitment to human rights alongside faith in market economics, complete with respect for property rights, et al. These new entities have emerged out of seething social and political cauldrons, and it may be some time before a measured assessment of their progress can be made. Their constitutions have mostly been drawn up in collaboration with the Council of Europe and the European Commission for Democracy through Law. The Council of Europe, in particular, may be seen as expressing an implicit opinion as to the way modern constitutions should be drafted.

A commitment to human rights and choice is not a commitment to equality, which is incompatible with a market economy and equally incompatible with the differential drives and appetites of individual human beings, as rich in their diversity as they are homogeneous in their humanity. Nozick is right to point out that starting from any preferred pattern of distribution of material welfare, dramatic disparities will appear over time simply as a result of individuals exercising their freedom to choose. If each has X amount of money at the outset and 70% choose to spend X-Y to see their favourite football player, then in no time at all he will be richer than most others; and more importantly because people have chosen to make him so. This is not the system; it is man's choosing nature.

Furthermore, although a competitive economy is likely to maintain or even increase inequality in various measures, it is not at all unlikely that, operating as neutrally as a market must when it is truly efficient, it will alter people's perceptions of traditional social hierarchies. Such an economy should, for example, alter the significance of gender and race. In the context of changes that it is

15 Norman Lewis, 'Markets, Regulation and Citizenship: A Constitutional Analysis' in Roger Brownsword (ed) *Law and the Public Interest* (Franz Steiner, Stuttgart 1993).

likely to produce it is important to keep in mind the distinction between equality and universality.

> 'Where equality and inequality are concerned, it is impossible in such a society to disregard differences of ability and performance, and the need to relate them to income, esteem and authority. By contrast, the principle of universality demands access to certain basic things irrespective of ability or performance. Drinking water, food, shelter, and also elementary education and primary health care should be universally available to all, and in their case questions of merit do not arise.'[16]

Only a limited number of things can be made universally available to all. Beyond that, a regime of scarcity determines that certain things will be available to some and not to others. This leads to very different kinds of inequality even where the claims of universality are acclaimed and protected. The thrust of social policy should be to make basic rights and facilities available to all. An obsession with salary differentials or positions occupied in social hierarchies is a distraction from pursuing equality of opportunity and ensuring that oligarchies which challenge the possibilities for genuine action and choice are contained.

A NEW WAY OF GOVERNING

Developments in public administration, and particularly in relation to the delivery of public services, have marched in roughly the same direction in the advanced Western economies over a period of more than a decade. Privatisation was perhaps the watershed, but was quickly followed by contracting out, partnerships between the public and private sectors, market-testing, what has become known as the 'New Public Management' (NPM), market-mimicking experiments in the retained public sector and an emphasis on 'customer' or 'consumer' choice, sometimes elided into 'citizen' choice. Although an invisible libertarian hand may be assumed to be conducting these strains, no clear considered intellectual analysis can be obviously said to be at the root of these changes. The First Report on the Citizen's Charter in late 1992 contains most of

16 Andre Beteille, 'Equality and Universality; the Best-off and the Worst-off' *The Times of India*, 8 March 1995.

the policies which inform the present Conservative government which gave birth to it and, *mutatis mutandis,* could serve as a manifesto prototype for almost any centre-right government in the Western world. Even so, it is conspicuously lacking a ringing theology. Even at the level of political sociology, it appears to have taken Osborne and Gaebler[17] to identify the paradigm shift in political function.

Osborne and Gaebler's deservedly influential work, while never utilising the expression 'a new way of governing', nevertheless takes it as a given. They believe that in a 'rationality-crisis' modern economy where detailed planning is a cognitive impossibility, the role of the state is to set broad strategies and mission statements and to encourage multiple competitive providers to determine delivery mechanisms and provide innovative solutions to problems. The role of the state, to borrow their memorable phrase, is to 'steer, not to row'. Among the many claims they make for this preferred mode of expenditure of government energies is that a process of socio-political fusion will take place whereby a given quantity of government energy will be able to unlock forces many times greater than that needed to operate the trigger mechanism. Putting to work the capacities, energies and powers of invention of the market-place, social and community bodies, not-for-profit organisations and sundry forms of hybrid social organisms, will release productive forces and methods of innovation inaccessible to the state machine itself unaided. That state machine, radically trimmed in bulk, will act as a facilitator or empowerer. On occasion in the UK the expression 'enabling state' has been used in a similar though less grandiose context, not least in terms of separating 'purchaser' and 'provider' functions for the delivery of public goods.

Osborne and Gaebler make clear that this role-change does not imply the withering away of the state, nor even necessarily its retrenchment. Less government perhaps, they say, but not less 'governance'. In an open appeal to politicians of any given stripe, they claim that these insights and the attendant steering function are value-free, or at least politically neutral. It appears that the helm can be made of any timber and that the charts and compass will be fit for almost any voyage. Their insights are many and they have made a major contribution to modern political science, as well as providing an explanatory theory for much contemporary public administration. But in spite of this, they claim both too little and too much.

17 *Reinventing Government* (Addison Wesley, New York 1992).

If, instead of taking the authors at their own estimate, the concept of 'reinvented government' is subjected to 'an immanent critique' – if, in other words, the substance of their claims is examined in order to find a common thread running through those claims – the concept will be seen to be more than a mere vessel which can be steered to any port.

Their analysis has much in common with a generally familiar body of sociological and political science literature concerned with 'cognitive deficiency'. Sometimes this is expressed as perhaps the central conundrum of the social sciences: a 'rationality crisis'. Public administrators in their turn have spoken of the 'limits of administration';[18] Hayek, Von Mises, Polyani and others[19] have spoken of the impossibility of planning and remarked that command structures are ultimately incoherent. What unites these claims is that there is no available system of perfect information from which a central command structure, the state, can effectively order choices for individuals, even if that were morally permissible. This is another way of pointing to the superiority of the market as a 'discovery process' or learning curve. Even if public administrators were clear as to the ends to be pursued, they will face the wall of 'the limits of administration'. There are simply too many contingencies, too many imponderables, too many different needs and preferences to be expressed by the 'recipients' of services at the sharp end of their lives. It is true that governments will sometimes be able to make 'strong' political choices as a result of signals consistently sent out over a period of time through the medium of economic and political markets, but this is only to say that the real choices of countless individuals will validly feed into the role of state/government as ringmaster of the constitutional compact.

Part of Osborne and Gaebler's new way of governing amounts to recognising the relentless contemporary pressures which render a hands-on style of government instrumentally self-defeating. But there is more to the analysis than that; at least twice as much. In the first place, the new way of governing concedes the moral authority of the individual as chooser. After all, it would matter less if a central apparatus got things wrong or failed to maximise selected policies if the individual preferences did not count or counted for less than some abstract collective. But it is precisely because only individuals count, because they are autonomous, that they wish to

---

18 Christopher Hood *The Limits of Administration* (Chichester, Wiley 1976).
19 Generally see John Gray *The Moral Foundations of Market Institutions* (Institute of Economic Affairs, London 1992).

experiment in new settings, making new choices with each suc-
ceeding wave of opportunities that it does matter. The centralist,
hands-on state is not capable of choosing for free rational agents.
Its primary job is to defend individual autonomy and help to create
the conditions under which self-discovery can occur. Even the currently fashionable preference for the 'contract state', for separating
purchasers from providers, is a recognition that a multiplicity of
providers offers not only choice but innovation and experimentation, which are prismatic facets of choice itself.

The second sense in which there is more to the analysis is that it
identifies, in sloughing off tasks which are better performed elsewhere, the 'core' or strategic role of the state in governance. This
truly *does* identify the moral responsibility of government to act as
the ringmaster for making choice possible. This is a Herculean task
in a complex twenty-first century society which would test the met-
tle of the most Periclean of statesmen. To fiddle is not only to interfere unjustly; it is to leave Rome to burn.

There is one further seam of the analysis to be tapped. In
Osborne and Gaebler's work there is reference to 'another half of
the equation'; viz the empowerment of communities. This empowerment requires a revised compact between central and local
government and between all levels of government and the citizenry. Wherever possible, that citizenry should be encouraged to
be part of the management of public services; where that is not
possible, their experiences and preferences should be brought
institutionally to bear on the process of the formulation of needs
and ends. Collectively, they should be encouraged to work with
market processes for the greater prosperity of all. But when governments push ownership and control down into the community,
their responsibilities are not at an end. Even if they no longer, or
rarely, provide services, they remain responsible for ensuring that
needs are met. And if markets are to work effectively, they need the
highest quality inputs they can get in terms of trained workers,
research, infrastructure and accessible capital. This makes government's roles as educator, trainer, research funder, regulator, rule
setter and infrastructure operator far more important than they
were 30 years ago. Furthermore, governments must learn to take
their budgets apart and reassemble them painstakingly to reaffirm
or alter their policies. There is no point in cutting public expenditure if it is unclear whether fat or muscle is disappearing. So also,
there is no point in throwing money at failed systems, which is,
after all, an almost universal temptation. The other side of
marketising services is to be good at governing; to be good at
strategy; to produce policies that people want and policies that

relate outputs to outcomes; policies that work.[20] In short, the tide of public administration is moving in a direction which should cause governments to concentrate on the arts of statecraft; to affirm the constitution and to free up the life choices of the people.

Both Osborne and Gaebler's *Reinventing Government* and the Citizen's Charter are defensible at profounder levels of political thinking than first meets the eye. Their houses stand on firmer foundations than they know. However, it is necessary to dig deeper than the rhetoric. For example, not only has the concept of 'duty' not yet been adequately treated, but the full range of responsibilities of the constitution and the legal order have yet to be examined.

'DEBATE' AND 'INFORMATION'

As part of the argument surrounding accountability it is important to develop the innate relationship between choice and debate or discourse and freely available information. It should already be clear that choice and freedom of speech are fused within each other. Speech is the main vehicle of communication between individuals and is how beliefs and aspirations are registered with 'other minds'. The corollary is that human beings grow in the context of otherness, a fact which obsessions with economic markets has sometimes disguised in recent times. This is, nevertheless, the subject of extensive philosophical literature among which the most influential has perhaps been Habermas's construction of the 'ideal-speech situation'.[1] This nicely combines the requirements of freedom, integrity and information. For speech to be 'pure' or untainted (and therefore to avoid deceit and the entrapment into false or forced choices) participants in the dialogue must be honest. Information must not be hidden nor tampered with. These are the preconditions for action taken on the basis of discourse to be free-willing. This should, in a nutshell, lock together choice, discourse or debate and information.

Moving from face-to-face situations, where these simple precepts are easily assumed to operate, presents greater complexity. In the modern world, dealing with others frequently occurs at one or further removes, whether in the social, economic or political realms.

20 Norman Lewis *How to Reinvent British Government* (European Policy Forum, London 1993) p 33.
1 J Habermas *Communication and the Evolution of Society* (Heinemann, 1979).

To take the economic first. Consumers daily trade with long-distance partners (where, in English law, for the most part, there is no contractual relationship) in the purchase of goods in particular. This is primarily through retail outlets. These consumers shop in the markets, but it should be appreciated that to make free and effective choices price is not the only information needed. Price is crucial, but to choose in a real sense is to know *what* is being bought for the price. The 'ideal', long-distance, speech situation requires that the seller as manufacturer, or the seller as retailer in substitution, must make available to the purchaser all the relevant information in his possession. Otherwise choices are partial, forced or even fake. This necessitates information of a 'constructive' nature on safety, quality, durability, servicing, repair and replacement costs and the like. Here is a clear role for the state: to 'regulate' the market into existence. The market is a moral concept whereby exercise of choice is queen. It is to ensure this which is the very *raison d'être* of the constitution. These are insights which are partly understood when the law spoke of 'merchantable quality' and 'fitness for purpose',[2] but they are the mere outrunners of a larger imperative. Legal systems regularly (and quite properly) oppose monopoly and cartelisation and dignify and encourage competition. But this is to move only against the most evident obstacles to free markets without announcing a programme to assist in the establishment of markets in their classical or fully realised form.

Before speaking to the implications of debate or discourse and information on the political process proper, some current initiatives occurring as part of the new way of governing need to be connected with the present analysis. This should serve to illustrate that much of the programme of the political centre-right, articulately expressed but inarticulately grounded, can be best located within the philosophical tradition being expounded here. Managed or 'ersatz' markets, 'internal' markets within existing state service regimes, and other market-mimicking contrivances will illustrate the claim.

Education and health services from the late 1980s are cases in point as illustrations of how discourse and information operate as adjuncts of limited choice, no classical markets being in existence at the time. The catalogue of change directed, eg to secure choice in education, has been made elsewhere.[3] These proto-choices have

2 Now *satisfactory* quality.
3 Mike Feintuck *Education and Accountability* (Open University Press, 1993).

been nurtured by controlled bodies of information being made available in such matters as the comparative academic achievements of different schools, truancy league tables, student reports and the like. With minimum common standards set and monitored by an 'independent' inspectorate (OFSTEAD), a concerned parent should be empowered to make a more rational selection of school than would otherwise be possible. Note that the freedom to choose a school through 'open enrolment' antecedes these developments which thereby support Habermas's argument, even if at a tangent. Choice without a full discussion of the qualities of different schools accompanied by the hardest available 'data' available is to buy a pig in a poke. Similarly with the health reforms since 1990. The internal market has been accompanied by statistics on waiting times, patient throughput, various levels of costing and so on which afford the Department of Health, Area Health Authorities and budget-holding practitioners as the 'agents' for consumer choice better information with which to exercise their judgement.

Perhaps less needs to be said here about information than in other realms since Freedom of Information (FOI) has occupied centre stage in many theatres across the free world for some considerable period of time. Information in the public realm is *ex necessitate* public information, and the touchstone of all political choice, the periodic opportunity to recall and replace governments, is incoherent in the absence of FOI *at the systemic level*, and not merely arbitrarily at the moment of general elections, a point which has been made many times before.[4] This statement is so self-evident as to be axiomatic. However, a rider is needed for this pedigree horse. Conceding FOI is to concede its 'best evidence', to use a time-honoured legal expression. That is to say that summaries, abstracts and epitomes are no substitute for public documents, except in clear cases mandated by the constitutional order itself as a result of extended public discourse. Pale imitations cut real choice to the marrow.[5] The test for all exceptions has been well stated by Sir John Laws in a related area.[6]

It is necessary to develop discourse and debate in the political realm, where again FOI is crucial. Not all information, however, is expressed in documents. Much of it is in people's heads. The concomitant of document availability is calling public actors to give

---

4 See eg Ian Harden and Norman Lewis *The Noble Lie* (Hutchinson, London 1986).
5 As in the recent Government White Paper, *Access to Information* Cm 2290 (HMSO, 1993).
6 'Is the High Court the Guardian of Fundamental Human Rights?' HMSO, [1993] PL, 59.

evidence subject to the rules of discourse. The UK House of Commons, to take a cardinal sin, scarcely qualifies *qua Chamber*, regardless of the 'validity' of the election of its constituent members. The Committees of the House are closer to a state of grace, for all their impediments.

Too little is traditionally made of discourse in the political realm, certainly in the UK. Yet accepting that state institutions operating under the constitution are the ringmaster for collective and individual decision-making, they will need also to be instruments for the fullest debate in order for acceptable choices to be made throughout the polity and the community. Elections for recallable Parliaments are the ultimate touchstone of a polity of free-choosing citizens, but they will require reinforcing techniques of discourse for the intervening period if any political choice is to be real. These reinforcing techniques should probably be of the following kind, though contingency once more is the order of the day: given the need for relative centralising abstention, then *at the lowest level of citizen impact* there must be the opportunity for bottom-up choice at a local point of delivery; this will require discourse techniques for intermediate institutions which provide this delivery capacity where self-help is not possible, and those intermediate institutions will in their turn need to be able to communicate with the central decision-makers who will also need to 'loop back' to affected citizens on the ground.

To a large degree these techniques or institutions or both, provided they are systemic, are not for *a priori* determination but will yield to culture, history and local necessity. Yet typologies of discourse arrangements can be usefully illustrated. Thus there is a need to institutionalise active debate at the level of the local community, where many decisions will have a real impact. Nor is it realistic to expect community-level discourse to plug directly into a central apparatus without mediating forms or institutions. Representative politics to refine community opinions is a compelling intermediate stage, whether at the regional or sub-regional level, in order to make sense of the task at hand. There is a need, in other words, for a geography of cognitive capacity. The link between these intermediate stages and the centre will require close attention to optimise the discourse leading to informed choice, just as the centre's reinforcing processes of consultation will need to be nurtured. The implications of this claim for the shape and extent of political institutions and accountability regimes will occupy attention in Part III. However, it is important to stake out at a more abstract level the case for choice involving 'ideal-speech-in-decision-making', informing the total institutional life of the nation rather than a central apparatus necessarily confined by imperfect information about citizen wants.

CHOICE, HUMAN RIGHTS AND ECONOMIC WELL-BEING

There is presently something of a divide between those who believe that government should be in the business of protecting social and economic well-being, as well as the traditional civil and political rights, and those who contest such a claim. It is, for example, frequently argued that affording such protection interferes with market economics. This appears on closer examination to suggest that a regime of social rights will impede economic growth. This may or may not be true but if the justification for markets is choice/human rights, the claim is of subordinate interest. The real question is whether affording protection for the purposes of social and economic well-being impedes choice and human rights or enhances them.

The UK has been a signatory to the European Social Charter of the Council of Europe for upwards of 25 years. Furthermore, the Council itself takes the view that human rights are indivisible and embrace both the traditional civil rights and those of the 'second generation'. Even some influential right-of-centre thinkers are tentatively prepared to reaffirm their commitment to this generation of rights. What, however, of the waverers or opponents? How, if at all, does a commitment to choice affect the stand to be taken on these issues?

The first point to note is how diverse opinion is on these matters, even though there is a wide range of agreement on the duty to ameliorate the worst excesses of underprivilege.[7] Few are prepared to defend the state turning a blind eye to starvation, homelessness, illiteracy and the like. Few are prepared to adopt a Nozickian line on non-distribution and leaving love for thy neighbour purely to voluntary alms-giving. Where that is the case, it is incumbent on those who preach even a limited degree of state duty to explain the reasons for the stand they take. What is the *principle* which motivates them? There must at base be some view of the make-up of what constitutes unflawed human behaviour? Nozick, most clearly

---

7 See eg John Gray *The Moral Foundations of Market Institutions* (Institute of Economic Affairs, London 1992) and David Green *Reinventing Civil Society* (Institute of Economic Affairs, 1993).

associated with the 'minimal-minimal' state, for example, expels certain needs from the catalogue normally assumed to describe basic defining characteristics of human beings, yet the ultimate reasoning for this crucial decision is difficult to follow. So, in a different but still unspecified way, those who resile from an Olympian fastness over supervising abject poverty, reinstate both basic needs and basic duties without a compelling framework of argument. It would be helpful if political debate recognised that there is more to pragmatist humanitarianism and knee-jerk sympathy than meets the eye.

There is a wide spectrum of political attitudes on these issues ranging from 'full' welfarism through to minimal welfarism with all the usual stopping places on the way. One difficulty in confronting any of the positions adopted on the spectrum is in asking *why any requirement of a non-negative nature is justified.* In other words, one is thrown back to asking what features are necessary for free-willing action to be taken. Such a question is normally met with pragmatism or emotionalism; a 'natural' repulsion to starvation, disease et al. Yet such concerns must necessarily be grounded in principle even if those principles remain too frequently undefined. Defining those principles, *per contra,* will yield answers to cases more satisfactorily than can otherwise be expected. Starvation is a case in point. It might be asked what the objection is to people starving, always assuming of course that they do not wish to. The answer will presumably be 'because they're human beings', which in turn raises questions about the characteristics of human beings.

This is not intended to represent a conclusive position so much as a statement of the problems; a likely response to the needs question is 'food, shelter, clothing and the ability to participate in the life around them'. This statement clearly disposes of few of the difficulties, but it does at least indicate the extended implications of assuming *any* redistributive position. Thus, participation in the life around them includes, most evidently, voting in parliamentary elections. In order to exercise choice in this area there must be the ability, at some level, to understand the issues confronted and the ability to impose that understanding on the available materials. Literacy, therefore, is a prerequisite of exercising the right to vote. Now even accepting that each individual has a duty to help themselves, it is not really possible for most people to educate themselves so that the provision of education appears immediately to be a necessity for the exercise of choice. This does not of itself close the argument about who should pay for that education, but clearly not everyone will be able to pay for their own education unless a major redistribution of resources takes place to facilitate this. Either way, some form of redistribution is necessary if choice is to be meaningful. The somewhat vexed question of taxation immediately imposes itself upon these propositions.

It is arguable that at one level taxation is a form of robbery and a mechanism for reducing the freedom of choice of individuals to spend their own money as they see fit. However, a counter argument needs to be posed. It is that most will agree that human beings must be treated as ends in themselves and never as means to ends.

> 'Persons are not treated as mere ends when they are taxed in order to help persons who are starving or are otherwise in dire need of basic goods ... the principle underlying the taxation of the affluent to help the needy is concerned with protecting equally the rights of all persons, including the affluent... it manifests an impartial concern for any and all persons whose basic rights may need protection ... [it] involves treating *all* persons as ends, not merely as means.'[8] (emphasis added)

Another, more terse, way of expressing this is to say that taxation is justified by the contribution it makes to the whole mutually supportive system of the equality of generic rights.

It is possible to approach the issue of redistribution/second generation rights in another way. It may be assumed that there are no obligations owed to others save the obligation not to harm. Thus there would be little in the way of duties. This would mean that there would be no responsibility to keep alive the collective of rights; no duty to keep alive the mutuality of commonness. It is unlikely that many accept that proposition. However, most will presumably accept a duty not to impede others; a duty not to stand in the way of self-development. But is this restricted to a duty not to harm? If so, it is a fairly low-life claim. However, if that is indeed the claim then it means that there is no responsibility to pull another human being out of a hole or trap, so that they may be left to be pounced upon by a wild animal. Yet is it possible to watch the destruction of another with equanimity? Must caring for individual survival imply care for others? Species survival means humans saving and helping other humans. Since no-one can exist without others (except in the most primitive state and even then only for a

---

8 Alan Gewirth *Human Rights: Essays on Justifications and Applications* (University of Chicago Press, 1982) p 213. Gewirth develops this argument through what he terms the principle of generic consistency or PGC. The principle is too complex to be developed here.

very limited period) it is irrational to watch others disappear with equanimity. This amounts to more than not harming. It amounts at the least to pulling out of the bear-pit. The alternative is that bears live and humans die. In consequence, the survival of the species is necessary for each to live the life of choice as the only form of being presently available. The preservation of the social ecology is imperative; the remaining question is how much? At one level the answer is that humans expect and are entitled to mutuality. This says little about the content of that mutuality but much can be gained from looking at the attempts of the Council of Europe to put flesh on this particular model. One thing, however, is clear: beggars cannot be choosers.

CHOICE AND ACCOUNTABILITY

Choice and accountability are inextricably connected. Accountability is necessary in the sense of having to account for the decisions which are made by those in authority. If the context for choice is not maximised, or if the conditions which are created by those in authority contestably do not liberate, then they have either no or a contestable authority to act. It is inherent therefore in the nature of choice that those in authority should render an account to those who chose them in the first place.

If governments maximise the conditions for individuals exercising choice then at one level their task is done. Individuals become responsible for themselves and account to themselves, though also with and through others with whom they choose to associate. However, there is a considerable residue of power left with government whose actions are surrogate choices for the collective of individuals. Those actions rationally must take into account the views of the citizen and seek to absorb the best information available in order to make choices. Several points flow from this. The first is that the widest possible trawl of view and opinion is mandated, but this is merely part of the logic of choice requiring the best information. At the institutional level, however, it means that governments need ancillary devices for legitimating their action; that is to say, ancillary to periodic elections.

Law is the cement of the social order; its most sublime expression is the constitution which has to take the strain of the expectations which are engendered. From all that has been said, this means that a fully developed enabling framework of law needs to be constructed in order to facilitate a society that is characterised by interactive choosing. In the British tradition law has not been centrally placed. Much is made of 'the rule of law' but it is insufficiently analysed and even then usually in the context of the criminal law whereby loose congeries of expectations exist which are often little more than opposition to Kafkaesque nightmares; of the rejection of the mailed nocturnal fist at the door. Not that this is to be sneezed at. Many good men fought and died to produce a level of fairness in the criminal justice system which, for all its manifest imperfections, is a considerable achievement. But it is a long way short of a vision of society. There is little in the way of architecture, little in the way of constitution-building.

During 1993–94, the Treasury and Civil Service Select Committee on the Role of the Civil Service heard evidence which began to identify some of the themes raised here. At the outset the response was to changes taking place in the nature of the civil service, mostly produced ad hoc by a series of government interventions. However, after a while it appeared that the government might indeed have an agenda for change; a change that recast the whole perception of the public service and the core features of state action. It is at this point that the committee began to ask questions that have rarely been asked by British politicians. Questions about the potential of law for the enlargement of politics. This is something very unusual in British political life given the traditional hostility to courts and to lawyers. This is not to say that a constitutional cathartic is yet clearly in place on the political agenda but rather that there is a rumbling somewhere in the hills.[9]

This has taken a number of forms. Individuals have suggested to the committee that some form of legal regulation might replace the traditional understandings; a Civil Service Act for example might have something to say not only about the parameters of public life but also about its ethical standards of conduct; freedom of information legislation has been more commonly canvassed as might be expected, while several other witnesses expressed the view that greater justiciability than heretofore would signal not only the seriousness with which certain values were held but that executive convenience and discretion should be more publicly curtailed. The committee itself was even heard to ask questions about the nature of the state and the constitution. However, there is still too uninformed a debate about the contribution of the legal order to the larger system of politics and civic expectations. There has

9 TCSC, 'The Role of the Civil Service', Fifth Report (HMSO, 1994).

been too little questioning of law in the round to see what it can contribute to active citizenship.

It is time to enliven and inform this debate and to seek to categorise different forms of law and not just court law, important though that remains. Law can contribute to the political process, not simply in architectural terms, but also in encouraging policy communities to broaden their sweep and to empower communities and community experimentation. Two major themes will emerge here. The first concerns the use to which law has been put in promoting choice and experimentation, and the second concerns the replacement of discretion by law.

As to the first, it is necessary to ask whether the laws which already exist foster and promote choice or instead impede it. Secondly, it will be argued that too much discretion inheres in public officials who ought to be constrained by a larger set of legal obligations. This is not to accuse public officials of abandoning their professed beliefs or wishing to contain choice but rather it is to argue that discretion allows the possibility of more relaxed standards than might be compatible with genuine civic empowerment.

Choice, inhering in free-willing, human-rights-possessing individuals, invokes both rights and duties. Contrary to much speculation that the spheres of rights and duties are distinct, they are in fact interdependent.[10] This gives added force to the unity of the moral and the legal order. Law in its generic form, encapsulating claims about, for example, 'the rule of law', is a second-order institution in that it legitimately provides a kind of regulation of other institutions as well as non-institutionalised activities. The rights applying to each are protected ultimately by the state and in this narrow sense the state takes precedence over the freedom and well-being of individuals in cases of conflict in that its duties are to all. However, this is perfectly consistent with the duty of the state to infringe the rights of individuals as little as possible, and only then when it is necessary for preserving and supporting the system as a whole.

Choice requires markets but when choosing is impeded then the state needs to regulate choice back into existence; yet such regulation must be based upon rights and not upon narrow notions of economic expediency. What is needed is a 'republican' regulator – one who upholds the values of the republic which UK citizens expect to inhabit. This necessitates a broad constitutional debate and settlement and assumes that oligopolies be not allowed to impede the republican enterprise. Choice has to be available at the

10 *Gewirth*, p 243.

collective as well as the individual level lest individual choices become a mere will-o'-the-wisp. If there are no real economic and political choices – if people are faced with a monolithic politico-economic programme – then the very business of voting becomes devalued. This has implications for the regulation of 'fiefdoms' – industry, the city and other major players. This may be obvious but is frequently side-stepped; not least by writers on the constitution. It is time to expand the debate, to expand the frontiers of the constitutional enterprise and to engage the implications of choice at a systemic level. One example is afforded by Will Hutton, who argues that British notions of sovereign and autonomous action for shareholders as much as for workers are borrowed from the Westminster model of the state: the democracy in British corporate law is the democracy of owners, who vote at a parliament of annual shareholders on which directors will be the custodians of their interests.[11] The constitution is a seamless web running from top to bottom. It is a lesson slowly learned.

11 *The State We're In* (Jonathan Cape, London 1995) p 87.

Chapter 2
Choice amongst equals

The political programme of the New Right (NR) is coming to be seen as less than philosophically coherent, although choice as an informing concept is one which most people can rally around. Confusion and contradiction are not surprising in political programmes and they can be found in almost any political enterprise which has been launched in the post-war years. However, it is important in a democracy that critical analysis should not be suspended.

To take a simple illustration:

> 'Reporting on Company Investigations, the House of Commons Trade and Industry Committee in 1990 found a mismatch between, on the one hand, the objectives of promoting efficient and honest markets and maintaining the integrity of the United Kingdom as a financial and business centre, and, on the other, a system of company law which focuses almost exclusively on the duties of directors to their companies and the rights of shareholders. On examination, almost any area of company law will be found to be shot through with inconsistencies and even conflicts in its objectives.'[1]

As with company law, so with a whole swathe of governmental policies. Although choice comes near to identifying a consensual belief system, it has yet to be elevated to the status of a coherent ruling doctrine. It is not, to stretch the argument, formalised after the manner of, say, the British Labour Party's celebrated constitutional clause four. Because of the absence of transparent and rational constitutional mechanisms, either at the level of the nation or of the Conservative Party, it is relatively easy for such confusion to

---

1 Judith Freeman, 'Accountants and Corporate Governance: Filling a Legal Vacuum' (1993) 64 Political Quarterly 292.

occur. Clear foundations and symmetrical architecture are absent but this is largely unremarked in a polity where pragmatic power conveniently exercised within conflicting agendas has become the governing habit.

A government committed to choice would produce pluralistic and extensive institutions to encourage rational discourse rather than assume that the dominant executive, as in the British system, automatically knows best. Quite apart from anything else, secretive centralism flies in the face of what is part of the hard-core belief of the NR; namely that government rarely knows best. Centralism is the breeding ground for paternalism. If the least government is the best government, it is unacceptable for the executive to engineer seismic changes without consultation. This is nothing less than government arrogating to itself the power to choose for people rather than allowing them to do it for themselves – an undermining contradiction. Yet a number of seismic changes have been occurring without adequate information and without full debate. Privatisation, de-regulation and contracting out and, above all, decisions on what constitutes 'core' government activity, both overall and in such functional areas as policing, are of this magnitude.

The inconsistencies and lack of clear vision have to confront the basic question of what it means to be human[2] if a rational political philosophy is to emerge. Choice can only inhere in human beings and there have, for many centuries, been crucial debates and disagreements about the essential attributes of the free or complete human personality. Such debates have been driven into the background in recent years both in the UK and across most of the Western world. Yet they need to be readdressed in order to make sense of a world which is changing faster than in any period of human history. To shape this changing world, and to create appropriate institutions for its governance, it is necessary to ask elementary, elemental questions about the very human nature which social and economic structures exist to serve. This is the most basic question of all. What kind of animal is the human animal?

BACK TO BASICS, NOT BACK TO FRONT

It would be valuable to stake out ground which could attract most people at the level of non-party political debate. That might make

---

2 The arguments are essentially 'ontological'.

it possible to work out where there is common cause and what are its imperatives; what kind of political world is tolerable and what not. This should lead eventually to the nature of an acceptable constitution and legal order.

There is general acceptance of the contents of the European Convention on Human Rights, and probably on the United Nations Covenant on Civil and Political Rights. Free speech is central to those accords and is an open manifestation of the choosing aspect of human nature. To recap: free speech implies access to all available information; it assumes good faith in conversation and debate, especially at the political level, and it implies the freedom to choose among options on the basis of mutuality.

Traditionally the link between human rights and markets has not been made apparent, yet to choose in free and open markets is an instantiation of freedom of speech and choice. This point has already been touched upon in the opening chapter. To play the market is one form of choice which is a generic concept attached to free human beings who may expect to live in democracies under rule of law constitutions. Choosing in both economic and political 'markets' appears on the surface to be unproblematic. Choice here must relate both to goods and to services, public and private. A floor of social and economic rights is generally also regarded as crucial, though more controversy rages here.

PHILOSOPHY AND THE PHILOSOPHY OF GOVERNMENT

Choice as a concept is meaningless without application to human activity. This may seem banal but nothing can be more important, whether at the political, psychological or spiritual level, than determining the inner needs and nature of human beings. All organised life, to be properly directed, must aim at liberating those needs and that nature. If there is uncertainty or incoherence about what constitutes humanness, then organised endeavour is of necessity labouring under enormous constraints. However, it seems clear that 'elemental' issues do not seriously affect the thinking of most politicians so that if they get things right it will be by instinct or accident, and it is much more likely that there will be confusion and major contradiction. For choice in politics to work, the elemental issues need to be settled at the outset. Perhaps that is too much to ask and, in any event, it may be heard that any agreement forged will come apart at the seams as soon as the detail of social or economic policy is discussed. Perhaps so, perhaps not, though that is no excuse for not taking the most important exercise of all as seriously as it demands.

Since the constitution embodies the ties that bind,[3] it is bigger than political parties and bigger than parliaments. Self-evident truths and irreducible presuppositions cannot be compromised by the small change of political disagreement. Naturally, free men will will a free society and the room for dispute and difference of opinion will operate within very wide margins indeed. One experiment will also be replaced by another in the face of experience which shows it to be inhibiting, or that it undermines free-willing action in spite of the best intentions. This leaves enormous scope both for organised politics and, more importantly, for each individual to find their own peace and their own excitement within social contours which have been drawn up precisely to facilitate that process of self-discovery.

However much disagreement occurs some way down the road of experience the ground-rules must hold; otherwise there is the danger of someone attempting to use power to cudgel right and entitlement. This has been recognised throughout the ages in the rhetoric of slogans such as 'the rule of law'; but slogans do not make constitutions and constitutions must make peace. All of this may seem elementary and it is. However, the NR, in striking out on bold ventures about the shape of public life and its incidents, has rarely paused to reflect on man's inner nature and how that should be reflected in legal institutions.

DICTATING CHANGE

The past decade or so has seen a rupture in the consensual understandings of politics in the post-war period. Changes have been radical in a number of directions; old power structures have been dismantled or seriously enervated, while whole social programmes have been called into question and frequently replaced.

The move from public to private provision has been central to political developments over the period in question. This has a number of important repercussions. First, where state institutions have not actually been abolished, their functions have dramatically

3 This is without prejudice to the argument that humanity cannot be confined to state boundaries and that all constitutions ought therefore logically to be merely cultural variants of a universal theme.

changed. Local government, health and police authorities, the civil service, the nationalised industries, the BBC, the changing face of welfare, and so on; even Parliament itself has been challenged under the Deregulation and Contracting Out Act 1994. This has resulted in constitutional understandings being challenged or swept away without a grand public debate. Several fundamental initiatives have emerged from tightly-knit semi-secret conclaves of the executive and their placemen. One relates to the discussion on what constitutes 'core' governmental activity; what can be privatised or contracted out and what needs to remain in the public domain. Think not what can go but what needs to remain has been the acid test. This has even affected the nature of policing; what tasks are central to the state apparatus and what performed by, eg, private security firms. The issues here are so visceral that ancient alliances have been sundered. The increasingly rapid erosion of local government joins the list. A view of what the public is and wants has been inarticulately adopted in circumstances where objections will not be brooked. Moreover, given the systemic nature of the changes, much of this alteration appears irreversible.

The second issue is intimately connected with the first. The nature of the state, its size, shape and functions, speaks to a view of what constitutes individual needs and how much collective and/or constitutional support an individual requires. So great is the rethinking currently underway, that epic challenges to the nature of both citizenship and human need are being posted. Most of this has been occurring as the result of little more than middle-range thinking or philosophising. True, there are a few hard-bitten supporters of Nozick whose philosophical foundations are clear, if desperately pessimistic. However, there are few on the political scene who openly espouse these views. They are much more likely to be supporters of the likes of Milton Friedman. Controversial and influential though those authors have been, they have been coy in disclosing the atomic crystals which make up their nostrums. They have urged crucial courses of action without ever embarking on a journey into the human psyche.

No opposition to change *per se* is being made here. The objection is that change is being dictated rather than debated. The constitution is being altered or even disfigured by mere politics and it is a politics without scholarship, as if a fashion lightly adopted on the basis of some insights and some half-truths was entitled to challenge nature. Exclaim that man is a bundle of appetites, that man is a consumer and material-maximising and there is an end to the riddle of the sands. These truths are self-evident. Yet it is passing strange that when other democratic nations sit down to worship at the ark of their covenants, brutal market materialism has not been given the authority to trump all other aspirations. The time is over-due for recent insights to be subjected to more detailed scrutiny.

AUTONOMOUS MAN?

Western liberal democracies have been described as veering between two maximising claims as far as the human personality is concerned. The first relates to the maximising of individual utilities, and the second to the maximising of individual powers. The first is particularly associated with nineteenth-century political theory, not least in its Utilitarian form. The second, most clearly identified perhaps with John Stuart Mill, focuses on the potential of each person's uniquely human capacities. This claim is based on a view of man's essence not as a consumer of utilities 'but as a doer, a creator, an enjoyer of his human attributes'.[4] These attributes have been variously described as the capacity for rational under-standing, for moral judgement and action, for aesthetic creation or contemplation, for the emotional activities of friendship and love, for religious experience et al. These attributes are seen as ends in themselves and not a means to consumer satisfaction. 'Man is not a bundle of appetites seeking satisfaction but a bundle of conscious energies seeking to be exerted.'[5] The essence of man, in that characterisation, is as activity rather than consumption. This is an old assessment, challenged only by the emergence of modern market society. Still purposive and rational, he was nonetheless held to be dedicated to unlimited individual appropriation as a means of satisfying wants.

The democratic movements of the second half of the nineteenth century saw an attempt to revert to the older tradition, but as Macpherson points out, utilitarianism was by then too entrenched to be easily ousted while patently too inadequate to explain the human condition. The result was an uneasy compromise – 'an unsure mixture of the two maximising claims made for the liberal-democratic society'. The 'liberal' society was encapsulated by the notion of contractual relations between free individuals who traded

4 CB Macpherson *Democratic Theory: Essays in Retrieval* (Clarendon Press, Oxford 1972) p 4.
5 *Macpherson* p 5.

their powers, natural and acquired, in the market with a view to maximising returns. This society produced crass materialism, gross inequalities and massive human indignities. An uneasy compromise has existed for most of this century, although in recent years the pendulum has swung back to the material-maximising end of the spectrum. However, this is a fashion impelled by external forces and not an insight into the human condition.

The absence of a written constitution in the UK reflects a traditional national opposition to thinking through first principles. To paraphrase Holmes, the life of the British polity has not been logic but experience. 'Common sense' and continuity are the British watchwords, and this has coincided with a reluctance to embrace natural law doctrines or indeed anything resembling a philosophic faith. Hence, no doubt, the pre-eminence for much of this century of logical positivism as a contribution to human philosophy. There was perhaps a blip in the 1960s and early 1970s when more overtly humanistic concerns were being expressed, but that period also coincided with an increasing disillusionment with any form of central planning. It represented a recognition of the limitations of the nation state, of administration and politics, so that by the mid-1970s the almost inevitable coronation of market economics took place. Those who had been nominally in charge of affairs in the preceding years were accused of heresy, of ingenuousness and a serious derailment of the national enterprise.

The overblown claims of the state to plan the nation's affairs have become increasingly apparent. The limits of the possible in terms of collective action are only slowly becoming understood and there is likely to be a long learning curve before confidence returns. In these circumstances, the market was bound to come back into fashion, even if some 'markets' are merely the dignifying of extant non-governmental power configurations. Yet 'pure' markets are or should be instruments of human freedom and are much more likely to produce economic growth and some version, at least, of efficiency than anything else on offer. The danger is that they, rather than man's innate, though often suppressed, capacities will become ends in themselves. God's finest creation and an economic instrument thereby become coterminous.

The market maximising 'tendency' view of man is a relative newcomer to the pages of history and the uneasy accommodation of opposing tendencies is also a discrete product of Western history:

> 'It cannot be too often recalled that liberal democracy is strictly a capitalist phenomenon. Liberal-democratic institutions have appeared only in capitalist countries, and only after

the free market and the liberal state have produced a working class conscious of its strength and insistent on a voice.'[6]

In other words, there is no evidence whatsoever that 'unbridled' capitalist or market systems are capable of promoting freedom and well-being for each and every citizen. As Handy remarks, unfettered market forces carry the seeds of both dynamism and disaster.[7] It is not possible to fathom the motives and the strategic impulses of those who were persuaded to concede political democracy to the masses, but there was clearly no balancing historic force contained within the mode of production itself. The untethered market whose moral justification is individual liberation has shown no sign of delivering on that promise. It has always had to be modified, ie softened. This is a lesson to be learned well if all citizens are to be afforded genuine, if unequal, choice. The choice comes first as a prerequisite of according individual respect; the market not only comes second, as an instrument, but has to be shaped in order to conform to universal expectations.

The problem with almost any version of the market in its unobstructed sense is that all wants tend to be seen as equal; if there is a demand which the market can meet, then one utility is as good as another. This is clearly an unacceptable proposition if set against any version of man's basic inner material and spiritual needs. The merest flim-flam will not and cannot weigh in the great debate against elementary freedoms and basic material welfare. The theory of marginal utility has refined this primitive position by arguing that the more you have the less you want. Yet, as Macpherson swiftly counters, 'to admit this would be to recognise an order of urgency of wants in man, ranging from the most basic necessities to pure frivolities'.[8] The market idolater's reprise is to contest that the satisfactions of individuals can be compared over time. As soon as inter-temporal comparisons are ruled out, the socially divisive implications of diminishing utility are ruled out. By insisting that utility is maximised regardless of inequality the classical liberal market defence is restored.

Galbraith, following Rousseau,[9] sees a moral distinction between original or natural desires and the 'artificial' desires created by a competitive and, at base, unequal society. Answers to these objections are

---

6 *Macpherson* p 173.
7 Charles Handy *The Empty Raincoat* (Hutchinson, 1994) *passim.*
8 *Macpherson* p 177.
9 JK Galbraith *Economics and the Public Purpose* (Penguin, Middlesex 1975) and the general literature cited there.

rarely convincingly made by the NR who can scarcely claim that the primary needs of a man do not constitute the pre-eminent social consideration, and yet continue, at least implicitly, to contest the content of the irreducible values. However, in pressing that activity as a market player is 'core' to a fully formed human being they are, willynilly, eliding the generic concept of choice with one of its mere aspects. For dialogue to be constructive, what is needed is a market model or paradigm which is genuinely open to (more or less) all comers and which identifies the optimum level of playing field opportunities whereby a genuine society of choosers is created. This does not require equality but it does require an approximation to equality of opportunity.

If broad agreement can be reached on the paradigm and the conditions for genuine opportunities, then the task of the larger legal order – of constitution-building – becomes to nurture and promote the social, economic and political parameters for personal liberation and choice. Some assessment of the essential nature of markets may be able to produce common ground among political opponents.

Rejecting a supposed synergy between markets and unbridled capitalism represents a beginning. Again Macpherson's assessment will carry many people with him:

> 'But I find it very unhistorical to equate capitalism with *laissez-faire*. I think it preferable to define capitalism as the system in which production is carried on without authoritative allocation of work or rewards, but by contractual relations between free individuals (each possessing some resource be it only his own labour-power) who calculate their most profitable courses of action and employ their resources as that calculation dictates.
>
> Such a system permits a great deal of state interference without its essential nature being altered. The state may, as states commonly do, interfere by way of differential taxes and subsidies, control of competition and monopoly, control of land use and labour use, and all kinds of regulation conferring advantages or disadvantages on some kinds of production or some categories of producers. What the state does thereby is to alter the terms of the equations which each man makes when he is calculating his most profitable course of action.'[10]

---

10 CB Macpherson *Democratic Theory: Essays in Retrieval* (Clarendon Press, Oxford 1972) p 181.

The position of neo-liberals is even more unstable if it is assumed that market economics is what necessarily characterises the extant industrial world. It is now widely understood that a relatively few corporations transcend the traditional market model by making prices, dominating markets and being more concerned with empire-building than maximising utility. Whether this is labelled capitalism or not is less important than the fact that it destroys the justifying theory that the going economic order maximises social utility. It does not provide genuine choice and it does not allow the average citizen to be a genuine market player.

It follows that the tendency of the system to create the wants it satisfies becomes stronger.

> 'There is no reason to expect that the wants and tastes which it satisfies will reflect or permit that full development of the individual personality which is the liberal-democratic criterion of the good society.'[11]

In other words all the ideologies which have been, over a century or more, competing for the political high ground are at base asserting the same ultimate value:

> '... the development and realisation of the creative capacities of the individual.'[12]

There are now few conservative thinkers who celebrate established authority *per se*; rather they are almost all of the disposition that authority is a means and not an end.[13] Modern capitalism does not fit easily into such a programme. However, the globalisation of the world's market-place has meant that governments, not least the British, are much more attracted to assisting national 'winners' in the international environment than to foster genuine competition.[14] Efforts directed to promoting a national version of economic success are bound to have at heart a set of concerns over and above that of marginal utility. If these national concerns were examined closely and more honestly it might be possible to revive

---

11 *Macpherson* p 183.
12 For this general argument see *Macpherson*, Essay IX *passim.*
13 David Green *Reinventing Civil Society* (Institute of Economic Affairs, 1993) p 22.
14 This is very much the message of *Competitiveness: Helping Business to Win* Cm 2563 (HMSO, 1994).

debate on the kind of a state which should be nurtured and on where individual citizens fitted into the scheme of things.

A CHEQUERED HISTORY

The centrality of the individual may have an honourable pedigree but, especially in the English tradition, it has not occupied centre stage unchallenged. Thus, Conservative thought in the early nineteenth century was virtually unanimous in condemning the appeal to the reason, interests and rights of the individual. As Edmund Burke had said, 'Individuals pass like shadows; but the commonwealth is fixed and stable.'[15] The French Revolution was naturally a catalyst in all this and seemed to foreshadow the chaos of self-promotion. There was 'too much liberty . . . and not enough religion'; everywhere was a frightening growth of individual opinion.

> 'Infallibility was an essential condition of the maintenance of society, and indeed government was "a true religion", with "its dogmas, its mysteries, its priests; to submit it to individual discussion is to destroy it".'[16]

Interestingly, what might be called the counter-revolutionaries adopted their positions by attributing to society the same exclusive emphasis that eighteenth-century philosophy had given to the individual. This is ironic for perhaps two reasons. The first is that the contemporary NR has been so strongly associated with the 'no such thing as society' mentality, while the second is the hostility to the cult of the individual exhibited by nineteenth-century socialists. While opposing the ecclesiastical and feudal orders of the past, they extolled the virtue of the new industrial order with its emphasis on social solidarity and harmony.[17] True, the end of the nineteenth century saw some socialist philosophers fusing individualism and socialism, but this was never mainstream thinking, which tended towards holistic solutions.

Several things are beginning to coalesce. It may not be easy to pin down the ultimate values of the neo-Liberals but there is a general

---

15 'Speech on the Economic Reform' (1780) in *Works* (The World's Classics, London 1906) vol 11 p 357.
16 de Maistre, quoted in Steven Lukes *Individualism* (Blackwell, Oxford 1973) p 4.
17 *Lukes* pp 6–7.

acceptance of the ultimate moral worth of the individual. Although there are numerous social traditions from which to choose, Lukes directs special attention to the Christian doctrine as set forth in the Gospels: 'In as much as ye have done it unto one of the least of my brethren, ye have done it unto me.' The clear implication, as Lukes points out, is that national and other social categories are of secondary moral importance and that with the coming of Christ, 'there is neither Greek nor Jew, circumcision nor uncircumcision, Barbarian, Schythian, bond nor free: but Christ is all and in all'.[18] The Christian ethic was elaborated by some of the most influential thinkers in the history of modernity, but within the context of the present discussion the words of Thomas Paine strike a chord:

'Public good is not a term opposed to the good of individuals; on the contrary, it is the good of every individual collected. It is the good of all, because it is the good of every one: for as the public body is every individual collected, so the public good is the collected good of those individuals.'[19]

If that version of the relationship between man and society is adopted then much NR thinking would have to be revised as it will if Kant's insistence on treating each human being as an end in themselves rather than a means for someone else's will is endorsed.[20] Kant believed in innate, universal and natural sentiments which inhered in each human will. Few will find a mere commitment to market economics and marginal utility in these remarks any more than they will find them in the desire of John Major, the British Prime Minister, for 'a thriving artistic and cultural national life'.[21] Whatever contribution the market is capable of making to the nation's artistic and cultural life, no-one in their right mind believes that it will deliver a range of choice for a multitude of tastes in this area. There is considerable leverage both for state intervention and for the voluntary sector.

Macpherson states the case in terms from which few in current politics would demur:

'Since every exercise of a man's capacities is an exertion of energy, such exercise requires that a man should have energy,

---

18 Colossians 111: ii. Quoted with approval by *Lukes* p 46.
19 Quoted *Lukes* p 49.
20 And see Alan Gewirth *Human Rights: Essays on Jurisdictions and Applications* (University of Chicago Press, 1982) p 268.
21 *Competitiveness: Helping Business to Win* Cm 2563 (HMSO, 1994) p 3.

and therefore that he should have a continuous intake of the
material means of maintaining his energy. Since it is not just
physical energy but also psychic energy that is required, this
calls for a supply of the material prerequisites for his taking
part in the life of the community, whatever the level of its culture may be, as well as for food and shelter. Lack of this is an
impediment.'[1]

Most in current politics would agree with the view that 'no one
should be allowed to starve or suffer severe privation'.[2] Even so,
there has been a tradition of hostility to a material base for individual autonomy and self-fulfilment, often associated with Sir Isaiah
Berlin, whose concern that redistribution by the state could turn
into an engine of oppression is well taken.[3]

On the other hand, Gewirth has argued a categorial or transcen-
dental case for human rights both negative and positive. He terms
them basic, non-subtractive and additive. Basic rights have as their
objects the essential preconditions of action such as life, physical
integrity and mental equilibrium. Non-subtractive rights have as
their objects the abilities and conditions required for maintaining
undiminished one's level of purpose-fulfilment and one's capacities for particular actions. Additive rights have as their objects the
abilities and conditions required for increasing one's level of purpose-fulfilment and one's capacities for particular actions. Positive
duties for him, however, are circumscribed to some extent by the
principle that 'ought' implies 'can'. In interpersonal relations,
where one person's life or other components of well-being can be
saved only by some other person's action at no comparable cost,
the latter has a strict duty to perform such an action and the former
has a basic right to be helped in this way.[4]

None of this is to argue for equality as such since many inequalities stem from the differentially effective use which persons make
of their freedom, but this does not justify the unequal distribution
of civil liberties since that would amount to denying the equal
rights of each person to a degree of freedom and well-being consistent with their human dignity as a potential self-determining
agent. Nevertheless, most actors on the public and political stage
believe that market opportunities will be differentially grasped by

1 *Macpherson* pp 60–61.
2 *Green* p 144.
3 *Four Essays on Liberty* (Oxford, 1959).
4 *Gewirth passim*, but note especially pp 8–9 and 19.

those with different interests and impulses with inevitable repercussions for considerable disparities in material welfare. However, this leaves untouched the search for core human values and the springboard conditions for each to explore their sense of the possible.

SPECULATION ABOUT ACCUMULATION

The moral component of the market is but one which makes up the choosing nature of humanity. There is no inherent conflict between free and open markets as a mechanism for human choice and other aspects of freedom. However, in the present state of knowledge, the market and its derivative imitators also appear to be the most effective engine for economic growth and therefore for making everyone freer choosers than might otherwise be the case. Hence there is a reluctance to tamper with the marketist model, even when it produces results which manifestly hamper the freedoms of particular individuals or groups. This is the claim for it to be the 'least worst' model.

The dilemma clearly confronted Mill, who, for all that he saw the prevailing relations between wage-labour and capital as morally damnable, could envisage no other obvious replacement for it as an engine of material reproduction. The capitalist market is productive, tends to ensure that even the poor are less poor than in other kinds of economy (*sed quaere*) and offers incentives for industry and flair. To dampen the creativity of investors, entrepreneurs and managers would be to the general disadvantage.[5] Few will argue about the general desirability of economic growth, but there are many who argue that it is a necessary but not sufficient condition for the creation of opportunities to escape from poverty. 'Government has a responsibility to create an economic framework consistent with liberty.'[6] In harness with this view is the recognition that many claims for the superiority of markets amount to little more than normative assertions that private property, market institutions, free competition and the like are natural laws.[7]

5 GA Cohen *History, Labour and Freedom* (Clarendon Press, Oxford 1988) p 289.
6 *Green* p 149.
7 See eg Gunar Myrdal *The Political Element in the Development of Economic Theory* (Streeten, London 1953).

MODERN POLITICS

The contradictions outlined above are not merely political; even the economics are cross-grained. Thus, although some competition has been introduced into both electricity supply and tele-communications, privatisation of the state utilities has been char-acterised more by a preference for some version of private ownership than a genuine commitment to competition. Equally, the response to environmental pollution has been ambiguous, whether one looks at energy policy, transport and the like. True the DoE recently published guidance to its suppliers on improving quality while reducing the impact on the environment[8] while it has been left to HM's Loyal Opposition to propose judicial machinery for vindicating individual environmental rights.[9] Even so, nothing has been proposed which goes as far as the revision to the post-uni-fication German Constitution which is set to entrench a clause on environmental protection.

The Citizen's Charter, on its first appearance, pronounced among the principles of public service, information and openness, choice and consultation.

> 'There should be regular and systematic consultation with those who use services, [and] users' views about services, and their priorities for improving them, to be taken into account in final decisions on standards.'[10]

Where choice was limited in some of the key public services, independent inspection would be introduced to ensure that the citizen's voice would be heard. Later documents emanating from the Cabinet Office clearly indicate that the sentiments suffusing the Charter have moved away from being simply an expression of feeling about the means of governing towards a philosophy of government itself.[11] The precise nature of that philosophy may be elusive but the core must be a set of humanistic attributes and an enabling framework.

What seems to inform much of the thinking of the New Right is the concept of 'empowerment'. This was, quite understandably, something of a buzz word during the early 1990s. It encapsulates

---

8 *Competitiveness: Helping Business to Win* Cm 2563 (HMSO, 1994) p 156.
9 See Ingrid Persaud *The Right Environment* 144 NLJ, 22 July 1994.
10 'The Citizen's Charter', First Report, Cm 2101 (HMSO, 1992).
11 Norman Lewis, 'The Citizen's Charter and Next Steps: A New Way of Governing?' (1993) 64 Political Quarterly 316–326.

the necessary dualism of concern for the provision of goods and services with a belief in self-realisation and diversity. The aspect of empowerment which has been accentuated most in recent times is that of offloading service delivery to competitive centres. There is much to be said for this.[12] However, empowerment in the sense of giving citizens and groups a sense of ownership of the state has not received the attention it deserves. The state is more than periodic elections; it is freedom of information, the opportunity to contribute to debate, to share the management of services and a great deal more besides. Although these claims are frequently heard, the action has not always been as loud as the words. When the logical implications of empowerment have been addressed the need for a reformed legal order will become more apparent in order to prevent a reversion to the old habits of executive convenience crowding out real citizen choice.

GOVERNMENT AT THE FRINGE

Minimum government has been a clarion call in recent years, built upon the acceptance of individuals as the masters of their fates. Interestingly, Nozick makes common cause with the Kantians in upholding this vision of the state; individuals may not be sacrificed or used for the achieving of other ends without their consent. Where Nozick parts company with other 'Kantians' is that he rejects the view of an overall social welfare since there is no collective entity which undergoes sacrifice for its own good:

'To use a person in this way does not sufficiently respect and take account of the fact that he is a separate person, that his is the only life he has.'

When Kantians agree and oppose it is perhaps no wonder that politicians, driven by the requirements of compensatory and fudging pressures, drive their chariots through the middle.
Nozick continues:

'The minimal state is the most extensive state that can be justified. Any state more extensive violates people's rights.'[13]

12 Norman Lewis *How to Reinvent British Government* (European Policy Forum, London 1993).
13 *Anarchy, State and Utopia* (Basil Blackwell, Oxford 1974) pp 31, 149.

Those who have followed the plot so far will realise that it all depends on what is meant by rights; back to the contested, unresolved, nature of man. The conundrum is well stated as follows:

'. . . support for competitive markets in economic affairs, combined with a recognition that a free society worthy of the name also rests on civic duty, that is on an ethos of shared personal responsibility for the well-being of our fellows. The challenge is to foster and maintain this ethos of mutual respect with the minimum resort to political action, a realm which today is grievously distorted by the shallow factionalism of modern party politics.'[14]

Although this sentiment may be readily accepted, it contains a number of contested concepts. However, for the time being the notion of limited political action will be pursued, although much of the argument has already been anticipated in the brief discussion of individualism. Spheres of action by society/state should be conceded only by free, voluntary and undeceived consent, though JS Mill would add to this list 'participation',[15] a rider of considerable importance. However, the general sentiment is reflected by Berlin when opposing authority whose natural tendency leads inexorably to despotism. Again, Thomas Jefferson is often remembered for his aphorism that government is best which governs least while the adherents of 'economic individualism', ably depicted by Lukes, raised presumptions against economic regulation in favour of both economic freedom and private property as the essential bulwarks against the overweening state.[16] The concept of private property should not be seen as an absolute but, in this context, as a necessary means of self-expression through personal space. It is an instrument or means for self-reflection, and a space in which potentates and powers can be held at bay. This is an important qualification since even Milton Friedman, in supporting the state's role in enforcing competition, encouraging charity and even intervening to overcome social disjunctions, has made it clear that the 'consistent liberal is not an anarchist'.[17]

Associated with minimal statism is a low tax regime. A stage seems to have been reached in liberal democracies where taxpayer resistance to funding public services, in part based on a concept of

14 *Green* p 4.
15 *On Liberty* p 9.
16 Steven Lukes *Individualism* (Blackwell, Oxford 1973) ch 13.
17 *Capitalism and Freedom* (Chicago, 1962) p 144.

citizen autonomy or freedom, means that the improvement in public services demanded by government and citizen alike must be delivered at constant or diminishing cost to the Exchequer. The belief has been fostered that freedom from being over-taxed is premised on individuals making their own choices rather than having them foisted on them by the state. This impels many to argue for a transference of necessary taxation from income to consumption, since, among other things, this encourages frugality and savings. To this might be added the trend to international freedom of movement of both individuals and capital thereby making the 'residential' tax base more problematic. The UK government's attitude is also that a country's tax regime affects its competitiveness, that that regime must be used to make markets work better, and that revenue must be raised in ways that do least harm to economic efficiency. It also makes strong claims about the privatisation programme having lightened the burden of the average taxpayer, although this claim needs to be treated with circumspection.[18]

A low direct taxation regime is very much a contemporary international phenomenon, and although it fits squarely with many shared beliefs about freedom and absence of state coercion, the balance must be carefully struck. So, for instance, in Zimbabwe, *per capita* spending on health has fallen by a third since 1990 and user fees have been imposed on health care provision. The objective, as in other countries, has been to reduce the budget deficit through a system of what some see as regressive taxation. Yet when it is reported that there has been a sharp downturn in women's attendance at ante-natal centres and an increase in infant and maternal mortality rates among the poorest alarm bells are sounded. The very poorest countries hardly ever manage to emulate the 'Tiger' economies of South East Asia where state intervention has been carefully targeted to achieve some form of social cohesion.[19]

An area of increasing agreement across political ideologies in recent years is the conviction that, where the state is still expected to have a role and to ensure adequate provision, hands-on intervention is unacceptable. Choice is to be assured through multiple providers, a separation between purchaser and provider, competition and an emerging concept of the citizen as volunteer. The multiple providers may be the public sector, the private sector, the third force or voluntary movement and/or public/private partnerships. Even social services may be better provided by encouraging local authorities to become 'gatekeepers' to ensure that need

18 *Competitiveness: Helping Business to Win* Cm 2563 (HMSO, 1994), pp 16, 142.
19 See eg *The Guardian* 20 July 1994.

determines provision. The idea of empowerment or enablement as
the optimum role for public authorities is, as a principle, rightly
becoming established.

CUTTING TO THE QUICK

Although there is considerable agreement, the questions of
what responsibilities inhere in the state and who carries out
those responsibilities are often elided. Note the following:

> 'Cleaning of streets, education of children, treatment of ill-
> ness are all necessary functions in a modern society. That
> these should be carried out is not in question. That it is neces-
> sary for the street sweeper, the teacher or the doctor to be
> employed by the state is increasingly called into question.'[20]

Perhaps there is some consensus around this short list; perhaps
not. Sadly, the most important issue is rarely discussed: ie the
methodology of making these decisions. The UK practice is one of
executive stealth. An example is the so-called 'prior options' exercise. This is the operation whereby government departments, in
conjunction with the Treasury and the Cabinet Office, determine
whether a function should continue to be performed and if so
under what auspices. Whether it should be privatised, contracted
out, turned into an executive agency etc.[21] This has, to date, not
been the subject of any consistent or extensive debate although,
following criticism in a number of quarters, a gesture has been
made to prise the process door ajar, if nothing more. Thus:

> 'This new policy of openness in respect of agency candidates
> ... will provide opportunities for those in outside organisa-
> tions with innovative ideas about how functions can best be
> discharged to put them forward in a timely way.'[1]

This is little more than a gesture and falls far short of the structured
processes of consultation and evidence testing which characterises

---

20 Graham Ward, 'Reforming the Public Sector: Privatisation and the Role of
    Advisers' (1993) 64 Political Quarterly 301.
21 See eg Norman Lewis, 'Reviewing Change in Government: New Public Manage-
    ment and Next Steps' [1994] PL 105–113.
 1 *Next Steps Review: 1993* Cm 2430 (HMSO, 1993) p 5.

US administrative law. As has been mentioned, an even more egregious denial of discourse, democracy and choice was the exercise in 1993–94 of identifying the tasks of 'core government'. In the UK the executive has performed this exercise under wraps and, were it not for the select committee system, the activity would be even more opaque than it already is.[2]

Where change is not driven by principle and moderated by contrary assertions, unfortunate and unintended repercussions are likely to follow. Governance as the necessary condition for creating the conditions for people to choose the kinds of life they wish to lead, the goods to buy, the quality of service to be delivered, etc is not in dispute. There is agreement that the state should be servant and not master but the nature of its functions and the atmosphere in which it performs them require to be determined.

Both in the UK and elsewhere there is a general failure to isolate the conditions for state action, direct or indirect, and for the private and market sphere to operate relatively unimpeded. The qualification to this blanket observation is that many other countries have written constitutions which do half of the job for them. However, how 'hands-on' the state wishes to be is, in some other jurisdictions, the subject of structured legal requirements. In the US, the Office of Manpower and Budget has produced a 'Policy Letter on Inherently Governmental Functions'.[3] This was produced to provide guidance on what kinds of functions may be performed by private persons under contract with the Federal Government. Under US Federal law the government was obliged to publish the letter in the *Federal Register* in order to receive and absorb comments from the general public. This is an exercise which ought to be performed in the UK to take the general public along with the government.

These issues are too important to be left to smoke-filled rooms and represent an argument for a constitutional approach to such matters. This is a lesson which politicians may be unwilling to learn but it is almost certainly the price to be paid for progress. Instead, these enormously important shifts in the nature of the public sector are being taken by the time-honoured executive processes. The mechanisms for considering the hierarchy of options include 'the fundamental reviews of public expenditure, the Financial Secretary's most recent round of bilateral discussions

2 'The Role of the Civil Service', Interim Report (1993) vol 1 p VII and the Deregulation and Contracting Out Act 1994, s 71.
3 Office of Federal Procurement Policy, 'Policy Letter on Inherently Governmental Functions', *Federal Register*, vol 57, no 190, 30 September 1992.

with colleagues on privatisation, the parallel round of discussions by OPSS on market-testing and contracting out,' etc. Processes of consultation are self-confessedly unpatterned.[4] Informal but broad-ranging inquiries have produced the impression that there is no principled clarity in the way the options are being discussed. The minimum state as the guarantor of maximum freedoms needs to be dispassionately considered and subjected to a methodology which allows the maximum of flexibility and experiment so that a public learning process can be undertaken. This is, sadly, not the British way.

A reinforcing argument for a 'demure or retiring state' is the inability to plan effectively; to allow room for the growth of human understanding. Given the uncertain state of collective knowledge, there is a strong argument for allowing people to back their own beliefs at their own risk. At any given state of knowledge, a government monopoly may be capable of providing a limited level of service effectively. But such an arrangement, if it suppresses alternatives, will stifle change and impede the means by which better services than can currently be imagined will emerge. This tendency to cause stagnation was one of the clearest failures of the command economies. Social engineers tend to be irredeemably ignorant.[5] To this, however, must be added the fact that markets too often 'plan' disasters, that they consist of thousands of people backing hunches that might go amiss and that, even with global technology, market actors are also irremediably ignorant. On the other hand, where government decides to contract out it must be aware that contracting is one of the most difficult methods a public service organisation can choose for numerous reasons, not least the unpredictability of new relationships. However, as a general principle there is little doubt that political interference can seriously impede choice. What this says is that the conditions for freedom must be chosen optimally, with open minds, a clear set of principles, even if overlapping or even competing, and a willingness to rectify mistakes and learn by them. Such matters will continue to be the subject of debate as human experience broadens and deepens. Principle and experience debated is as central to freedom as the concept of a limited state.

---

4 TCSC, 'The Responsibility and Work of the Treasury in Relation to the Civil Service', vol 11, p 259.
5 See eg *Green*, pp 119, 124, 127–128.

CHOICE AND BELIEF

At the Committee on Security and Co-operation in Europe (CSCE)[6] meeting which took place in November 1990 a Final Document was adopted in the shape of 'The Charter of Paris for a New Europe'. This committed all participating states to democracy as their only system of government and enumerated human rights and fundamental freedoms which must be guaranteed in a free society. It also recorded agreement to economic liberty and free market economics. The importance of this lies in its linkage of human or constitutional rights and markets as a form of the expression of rights. Furthermore, the organising sentiments which give rise to the belief in human rights and to a series of international obligations to which the UK is party naturally go deeper than the individual articles or clauses of the documents themselves. Thus, for example, art 1 of the UN Universal Declaration of Human Rights 1948 says that 'all human beings are born free and equal in dignity and thought'. There would be little point in talking the language of universal human rights if that were not accepted. Similarly, the numerous commitments to democracy and human rights emanating from the Council of Europe assume a commonality of belief and aspiration within a broader conspectus of the wider Europe.

These, now traditional, rights are all facets of choice which in turn authorise experiments in living even if this dictum is not directly constitutionalised as such. But what must follow is that there is a right to choose how to live as a social being provided that one allows the same degree and measure of choice to other free, unstained, human beings. This in its turn is commensurate with not only 'freedom and well-being' but also with 'equal concern and respect', the concept of equality being capable of bearing considerable analytical weight. The idea of respect lies at the heart of the idea of equality since it amounts to a belief that respect is equally due to all persons in virtue of their being persons.[7] Once committed to equality as a concept then it is irrational, all things being equal, to legislate for equality in one area of life and to ignore another; to elevate race and gender and to float free disability and age, for example. The basis on which anti-discrimination laws are founded is anti-discrimination which is a roundabout assertion of equality.

It is relatively simple to find a catalogue of human characteristics

6 This has recently been relaunched as the Organisation of Security and Co-operation of Europe (OSCE).
7 See eg *Lukes* pp 124–125.

at the broad level, even if the longer the list the more likely the disagreements. Even so, many of the inclusions in the catalogue are so
broad as to leave an enormous leeway for interpretation and dispute,[8] although a dalliance with even generalised first principles
might represent a healthy sign amongst politicians. So might the
opportunity to dwell on forgotten or overlooked themes such as
the notion of man as actor, of doer of deeds, as creator, not least in
the course of engaging in materially productive labour.

The 'Millian sentiment' sanctified reflective, self-reflective, individual freedom against society at large and not just the agency of
the state, whose special vice is railed against by the forces of contemporary liberalism. This would require the state to liberate from
oppressive authority however conceived unless the market is
thought to be legitimated by whatever power configurations exist
at any given time. However, that would be to abandon any moral
claims for the market as a superior social and organisational force.

In an influential recent work, Professor Katherine Newman has
charted the shift in American attitudes from a time when work was
seen as the locus of self-development and a moral sphere to a time
when occupations are too rarely an expression of the inner self or
a means of contributing to the greater social good. The purpose of
work has come to represent the single-minded pursuit of 'freedom'; to consume and build a 'privatised life'.[9] In this view the
moral dimension of work has become endangered by managers
who do not even grasp that their staff may have other purposes
than mere preservation of a salary and a job. In the UK attacks on
academic tenure and muddying of the independence of broad-
casters contribute to this feeling of unease. It is not sufficiently
recognised that the formal institutions of democracy can remain
seemingly intact at the surface level at the same time as the inde-
pendent-minded are marginalised and where people spend their
lives in fear.

SUMMARY[10]

Hollis adopts the view, endorsed here, that language can only be
understood if 'Other Minds' are assumed to use it rationally in the

---

8 Eg see *Macpherson* pp 53–54.

9 *Declining Fortunes* (Basic Books, New York 1993).

10 Most of what follows is taken from Martin Hollis *Models of Man* (Cambridge
   University Press, 1977) *passim.*

main and that the assumption must be justified *a priori*. Rational action is a skill whose understanding depends on knowing neces- sary truths about the rational thing to do. There has to be unity of the judging mind in the ordering of experience; 'bodies are just bodies unless relations among them are endowed with shared meaning'. This is to insist that the social world is constructed out of shared meanings by acts of self-definition and, most crucially, that whatever constitutes human beings is something to be preserved and fostered in action. The advantage of informed philosophy is that it provides the guidelines for a political programme. For choice to be real in political rhetoric or in life the politician needs first of all to 'capture his human animal'. If there are no categori- cal needs, no human nature, then choice has nothing to stick to.

As with autonomy, so with choice. Liberty or freedom is a com- plex idea which, when analysed, can be shown to require or pre- suppose a number of further, more basic ideas, such as privacy and self-development. When does a person behave autonomously?

'A crucial element here is clearly that of consciousness and critical reflection. No less important is that the decisions and choices should be genuine ones – that there should be real alternatives between which individuals make a choice . . . Thus the degree of his autonomy is a function, at least, of the degree of his self-consciousness and of the range of alterna- tives before him. His autonomy will be reduced to the extent that he is unaware of the determinants of his behaviour and to the extent that the alternatives before him are restricted.'[11]

To accept this is to accept a more active role for the state than that recommended by Nozick, Friedman, Hayek, Portillo and most of the marketeers. Identifying human needs produces an obliga- tion on the part of politicians to attempt to construct the condi- tions for humans to play out their personal drama. The main degree of potential dispute is how much self-reliance is possible with what set of minimum assisting conditions being put in place. The answer to that is that nobody knows, but dependency is unac- ceptable and genuine self-discovery personally propelled as far as possible is one of the highest aspirations. Non-damaging political experiments are called for, but within a firm framework of individ- ual entitlement.

One thing is clear, as Hollis remarks: the self is not knowable except in relation to others. An autonomous man acts freely, which

11 *Hollis* pp 127–128.

requires that he has good reasons for what he does, which in turn means acting in his ultimate interests. That in turn depends on what he essentially is. What he essentially is depends partly on what is essential to his being any person and partly on what is essential to his being that particular person.

> 'Autonomy requires a choice of roles in which a man can rationally do his duty. If few men take this course, it is in part because few societies offer it. To create a Good Society in which men can be themselves remains a task not for tinkers but for tailors.'[12]

That is where constitutions come in.

---

12 *Hollis* p 106.

Part II
Facing the challenges of the next century

INTRODUCTION

A modern constitution would embody first principles and create institutions for running those principles through the nation's affairs, its discontents and the contemporary challenges. Political factionalism would operate in the interstices of the constitution or be judged in cases of irresolvable disharmony by the legal and constitutional order which at root represents common ground and, in particular, a common conception of humanity.

Going back to basics ought to produce a wide degree of harmony about politics at the heroic level. At the periphery will lie disagreements, many of which are likely to be the result of imperfect information about what constitutes 'natural' behaviour in conditions of social and existential balance. Where disagreement relates to imperfect information, collective duty requires a social ecology (including the economic) which is as open, transparent, experimental, encouraging of innovation and diversity as possible. It must be an ecology which, within the framework of rights entitlement and duty, celebrates choice. The political and legal orders must reflect this simple truth. Currently they do not. The task of the legal order is to marshal constitutional commitments in the cause of defining national solutions to contemporary problems. High-sounding, beset by pitfalls, but the only available scenario.

The necessity to move in this direction sooner rather than later is heightened by the pace of political change already identified: a change which, in the case of the UK is, at least, double-sided. Not only is the shape, role and function of the public sector undergoing sea-change, but this is happening in tandem with the emergence of a distinct constitutional identity for the European Union. Not only is there no time like the present, there is unlikely to be any other time in the near-to-distant future like the present. An opportunity lost at this juncture in the nation's history may be irreclaimable.

The role of the judiciary too is changing. The law of judicial review in the UK is at a crossroads and the shotgun marriage between the common and the civil law through its membership of the ever-maturing European Union will necessitate clear and principled juridical thinking. The unfolding, while expanding, nature of human rights jurisprudence will post major questions about the shifting boundaries of the separation of powers. Again this will be ratcheted up by the expanded competence of the EU in the field of social, economic and environmental rights, to mention the most obvious. Against this background the judiciary, however constituted, cannot be left without constitutional instruction.

This is the background against which some of the central challenges which will need to be addressed if choice amongst equals is to be promoted have been selected. Some of these are treated more extensively than others largely because moving from first principles to detail is simply easier in some areas than others; the information available is less contested, the 'other worlds' more inhabited. However, each of these areas (and they by no means exhaust the subjects which a revised constitutional settlement would need to address) will need to be carefully attended to if the language of choice is to be given meaning.

Chapter 3
The social dimension

It is perhaps offering a hostage to fortune these days to quote Karl
Marx in support of an argument, but he remains a powerful force
who simply took on too much and was overpowered by the tide of
the history from which he expected ultimate redemption. There
are worse epitaphs. In any event the following is difficult to refute:

> 'Production by isolated individuals outside of society – some-
> thing which might happen as an exception to a civilized man
> who by accident got into the wilderness and already dynami-
> cally possessed within himself the forces of society – is as great
> an absurdity as the idea of the development of language with-
> out individuals living together and talking to one another.'[1]

The claims which have been made about nature now need to be
re-examined in the controversial setting of the social obligations of
government. The greatest current political divide is between those
who believe that self-help is the universal solvent, and those who
believe that the state not only can but should make a difference.
The former position is, as Marx makes clear, a logical absurdity so
that where the line of collective obligation is drawn becomes the
acid issue. John Donne has not been undone, the moral of *Lord of
the Flies* has not been lost on everyone, and the secret of the universe – how to unlock native energies without dictation or conde-
scension – remains the pressing concern. The exercise, however,
can only be conducted in a social or collective setting.

Mutual concern and respect represents a sound beginning.
Without respect being accorded, self-esteem is eroded; when it is
accorded, both social ease and generosity tend to follow. Respect is
obstructed when, without good reason, there is interference with a

---

1 Reproduced by Steven Lukes *Individualism* (Blackwell, Oxford 1973) p 76.

man's valued activities. Stratified societies, whatever their ideological provenance – feudal, capitalist, state socialist – exhibit not only structural inequalities but inhibit the self-development which is the hallmark of the 24-carat human being. The importance of education is crucial and Lukes stakes a strong claim:

> 'A stratified educational system which reinforces other social inequalities and thereby blocks the self-development of the less favoured constitutes a denial of respect to persons ... Similarly, ... if it is possible to make certain types of work more challenging and require a greater development of skill or responsibility, it is a denial of human respect to confine workers within menial, one-sided and tedious tasks.'[2]

This makes the social claim almost as strongly as it is possible to make it. It may be thought that starting from the present state of affairs, it represents a counsel of perfection and that wand-waving is best left to the pantomime season. Yet the contemporary order has to be judged by whether it is moving in the right or the wrong direction. To that extent it is useful to have a map and to have one where the compass recognises the difference between north and south. Lukes appears to support this sentiment in extending the classical defences of the rule of law defences to broader concepts. Thus, in arguing that the formal legal framework of modern democratic societies is the guardian of the abstract individual, he treads the same ground as many others, including, for example, Edward Thompson and Roberto Unger. This claim is of the same order as that already staked out about human rights and markets. Formal equality before the law, and freedom from arbitrary treatment, contain within themselves transcendent values which recognise the social nature of being treated commonly as universal, though unique, phenomena with an identity of hopes and aspirations. Otherwise equality before the law is simply a convention with historical antecedents and little else.

DRIFT OR DRIVE

Nations and communities are the product of history, experiment, failure and fortuity as well as native necessity. Where they are at any

2 *Lukes* pp 134–135.

given time is in part because of invention, individuality and the entrepreneurship of the unguided spirit. But nature and the movement of the planets has played a part while invention, individuality and the entrepreneurship of the spirit have given nudges to war, pestilence and outrageous misfortunes. Any given social world is unlikely to be self-balancing in terms of fairness, decency or even logic. The task of government, however strenuously some administrations deny their ordinances, is to improve the general lot; to take the compass and steer towards a better life. The ancient urge of the state to control production and distribution has been rightly abandoned in the name of freeing up the human spirit. However, any given economic configuration seems to get in the way of the basic task, which is too easily overlooked. Yet, reconciling essential equality with the state's hand on the tiller is as necessary as it ever was. Lukes again:

> '... sociological and social psychological enquiry is an essential prerequisite of egalitarian and libertarian social change. Hence a methodology which ... simply precludes one from examining the deeper structural and institutional forces which constitute the central obstacles to such change must clearly be rejected as not merely theoretically narrow, but as socially and politically regressive.'[3]

Debates about the superiority of markets again make the point, and even at the theoretical level weaknesses are unmistakable. The maximisation of utility by the market can only be demonstrated by assuming a certain income distribution which is not a demonstration of an ethically just distribution of wealth or income. Furthermore, a capitalist market society, by its very nature, compels a continual net transfer of part of the power of some men to others. This is the nature of a system which grants the individual right to a virtually unlimited accumulation of property as an incentive to get the productive work of a society done. Part of this, as Macpherson says, is because a silent value judgement is made about the highest value being a commitment to an endless increase in productivity.[4] In other words, the market moves towards consolidation and exclusion in a remorseless fashion, and true equality of opportunity is a sacrifice society seems all too prepared to make.

---

3 *Lukes* p 157.
4 CB Macpherson *Democratic Theory: Essays in Retrieval* (Clarendon Press, Oxford 1973) p 17.

Attention to principle necessitates redressing the balance in important respects.

The concept of individual empowerment, of freeing up the ability to realise chosen ends, involves recognising not only natural capacities but the ability to exert them. 'It therefore includes *access* to whatever things outside himself are requisite to that exertion.'[5] This state of affairs will not come about automatically. Freedom and choice can only be exercised in an atmosphere of an absence of impediments to a man's developmental powers and an understanding by politicians that they have an obligation to deal with those practical impediments. These are not fashionable arguments in present-day politics, but it is inconceivable to argue for free-willing individuals to explore their inner natures while nailing one leg to the floor. It is possible to argue about the balance between self-help and other-directed help, but a level material playing field of sorts is a prerequisite for choice of action in the context in which most people find themselves.

Social deprivation is unacceptable in a rights-based community which embraces choice as a ruling passion. While technical, methodological, and psychological issues might be contested, the universal nature and needs of man should not be. The very purpose of government, its sole justification, is to ensure the absence of impediments to choice and freedom. Only the political barbarian would deny the obligation to put man in touch with his nature, a matter of infinitely greater value than keeping taxation at the minimum level. This is perfectly compatible with an unobtrusive state which nonetheless remains a central component of the virtuous triangle; of the ideal mix of individual, society and state. But just as the state needs to ensure the autonomy of individual life, including access to a degree of material welfare, so it needs to encourage intermediate society. It should by now be clear that society and state are not coterminous and that the former is constituted by activity in common which is both voluntary and duty-laden, which cares for others and the social system which gives everyone space to breathe. It is part of the duty of the state to recognise this state of affairs and to encourage the social system at the expense of its own power. But that requires it to act, albeit at its own expense.

The ruling imperative in these matters is one with which the NR should feel perfectly at ease. One of the guiding principles of a free society is that the state should not use people as a means to an end

5 *Macpherson* p 9.

of the government's choosing, but that it must provide them with the means to choose. However, that is to concede a great deal; it embodies a commitment to relieve poverty and privation; to ensure adequate housing, education and health. It is the 'alms-length' state:

> 'To accept that the state should maintain a safety net in order to prevent hardship, and thus the potential waste of talent, is quite different from urging that it should use its powers of compulsion to compress incomes until they conform to some pre-ordained pattern.'[6]

There can be no substitute for treating human beings as moral agents capable of moral and prudential choice whose inner resources should never be underestimated. But atomic individualism is the enemy of a society which respects these canons, and it ought to be axiomatic that life cannot be lived apart from others; as strangers and indifferent to their fate. Supporting the cause of individual freedom cannot be costless, but it must be empowering and not patronising, a fact recognised by Milton Friedman who has advocated a negative income tax and giving money to the poor.[7]

NO SUCH THING AS SOCIETY

The main bone of contention in European politics currently surrounding these matters is the EU's 'Social Chapter' which the British government has, of course, rejected. However, the European Social Charter's impetus has hardly been stopped and indeed the Commission's blueprint for European Social Policy over the rest of the century asks whether the time is now ripe for a citizen's charter of social rights. On this view, the pursuit of high social standards should be seen as a key element in the competition formula. Increased confidence can be expected to come only from a reconciliation between economic growth policies and their translation into higher social development with upgraded living standards for all.[8] Whereas there is no universal agreement, even the British

6 David Green *Reinventing Civil Society* (Institute of Economic Affairs, 1993) p 145.
7 Wilbur J Cohen and Milton Friedman *Social Security: Universal or Selective?* (AEI, Washington DC 1972).
8 *The Guardian*, 26 July 1994.

government supports 'Treaty objectives for social, environmental and consumer protection' while also pledging itself against social tension and 'unjust ways'.[9]

Elsewhere there is common ground on the need to regulate for various forms of social improvement. Although, for example, the present British government seems to be in a permanent state of flux in relation to local authorities' responsibilities for the homeless, it accepts that subsidised housing should be genuinely available to all who need it. The National Federal of Housing Associations has called for the integration of housing benefit and employment policies, hardly a view which is consonant with government being able to make no difference to the quality of people's lives. Whether the call is for a greater role for private landlords, the 'third force' or a resurgence of local authority activity no-one seriously suggests that the state can stand idly by in the face of a rising tide of homelessness or ghettoisation. Naturally the optimum solution is one which affords the maximum choice of housing to all and the highest level of accountability for decision-making in this area.

So with education. State education in the UK may be a system of local monopolies; there may be need to restore a greater level of parental responsibility and to allow parents greater choice of schools, but not only must an enabling structure be put into place but the schools must be available in the first place. Some schools will be established as the result of local or community effort but most will transcend the life-cycles of political generations; schools cannot be rebuilt with every passing intellectual fashion and it is no use pretending that the state can abandon its function of encouraging the most appropriate form of pluralistic education. The state may have made egregious errors in this respect in the past but it retains the responsibility; the ideal may be a partnership between parents, children and the state, but a partnership it remains nonetheless. Similarly with health, the most precious of all human needs. Green may be right when he says that the NHS is not the best form of health care, not the most efficient and not the most democratic, but he is clear that essential medical care must be available to all.[10]

The consensual menu is more extensive than this. Infrastructure is a clear example; the benefits to the nation of infrastructure projects – jobs, regional growth, balance of payments, relief of congestion,

9 *Competitiveness Helping Business to Win* Cm 2563 (HMSO, 1994) pp 21, 27.
10 *Green* pp 142–143.

tourism etc – etc can almost certainly not be reconciled with the short-term profit requirements of the private sector. *The Private Finance Initiative*[11] indicates the possibilities for partnerships between the public and private sectors in this area, but early experience already suggests that initial expectations were probably over-optimistic. However, there is no suggestion that the state can withdraw from responsibility here any more than in the field of health and welfare.

The problem of private provision and public need is not restricted to infrastructure and the environment. The wider health of the economy depends upon an understanding and effective relationship between government and industry which has not been reviewed in recent times to examine its fitness for purpose. The institutional context in which industry operates has remained largely unaddressed for some time. Yet there is no logic in advancing and underwriting a system of law and governance which sacrifices the medium- and long-term interests of the nation as a whole to the time-scale of footloose shareholders. The incorporated association or company can take any one of a number of forms and does not necessarily find perfect expression in present UK company law or culture. Ideally it claims to have the capacity to offer skilled labour or cheap capital. Too often, as others have pointed out, it has become a vehicle for buying cheap and selling dear. Yet the success of such organisations depends critically upon the economic and social institutions in which the firm is rooted.[12] Ultimately, governments have a responsibility to ensure that the nation is not depleted either in terms of the qualities of its citizens' needs or of the social and economic environment needed to flourish in late-twentieth-century capitalism. Whatever form of delivery mechanism is preferred – joint projects between the public and private, the third sector, franchising arrangements etc – the social context to which citizens aspire is crucial. To the extent that industry and the economy succeed in advancing collective expectations, choice at the level of the individual will be advanced. Individuals alone cannot refine the total social ecosphere.

On the other hand, individuals can do a great deal with the right encouragement. The Friendly Societies Act of 1875 is a case in point. Sir Stafford Northcote realised that strengthened legislation could help to produce an environment in which associative conduct,

11 HM Treasury *The Private Finance Initiative: Breaking New Ground* (Central Office of Information, November 1994).
12 See eg Will Hutton, *The Guardian*, 8 August 1994.

moral and social responsibility and self-help could flourish. A later generation of politicians failed to learn those lessons well and it is only now perhaps that the advantage of working together in communities to satisfy felt social and economic needs is being rediscovered.[13] Part of the problem is a failure to think through a vision of a just society. This is intimately related to the adequacy of political systems and the more general institutions of governance. Urban regeneration and renewal is a case in point. The devastation of urban areas and social communities has been brought about by a combination of the short-sightedness and greed of earlier industrial adventures and the unwillingness of governments to address their responsibilities to successive generations. These issues have major relevance for government philosophy, government programmes and, not least, for the institutional shape of government. Centralised government, however well attuned to its empowering social responsibilities, is incapable of articulating the needs of local communities, let alone regenerating the community fabric. This regeneration is possible only through an institutional reorganisation which reflects the social as well as the economic aspirations of communities.

WHAT KIND OF SOCIAL SYSTEM?

Any given social order is unlikely to have achieved the level of harmony which adequately satisfies the needs and aspirations of people at large. If, however, some measure of agreement on first principles can be achieved, it may become possible to envisage the general shape of the social, legal and constitutional order which will most faithfully serve those needs. The task of government then becomes one of seeking to move the existing social order in the desired direction. Social obligations are at the heart of government even if the nihilism of recent times has tended to conceal it. Human beings have needs which will not be met automatically by coming into the world armed only with raw desires and appetites. The social fabric needs to represent nature and give it sustenance. How that is done is another matter, but the state bears the ultimate responsibility for allowing individuals to be free. In order to provide the kind of government that is most relevant, there will have to be a comprehensive assessment of need, a specification of standards of

13 *Green, passim.*

service, the development of monitoring and inspection facilities and readily accessible complaints procedures. New tasks must be undertaken to realise old goals. Osborne and Gaebler offer an example.[14]

During the Congressional debate of 1990 on child care, two opposing attitudes were struck. One was to afford Washington the power to fund day-care centres directly and the other was to use market mechanisms such as tax credits and vouchers to give low-income families the power to make their own decisions. The latter view prevailed. But the debate is not restricted to pure markets which, as is well-known, are practically unknown in nature. One of the tasks which government must set itself to achieve agreed public ends is to help create, to intervene in or perhaps structure the market. It is a salutary thought that the only markets genuinely free of government regulation are black markets, which are controlled by force and wracked by violence. There are the examples of the old command economies of the Eastern bloc and the South American drug market. However, if a government can create incentives that affect millions of decisions made in the market-place rather than affecting only those activities for which government pays, it can multiply its impact beyond the wildest expectations. This has clear implications for social welfare – one of the most tortuous of problems facing modern governments, but one which must be addressed.

It is worth repeating that committing the state to responsibility for ensuring freedoms does not entail gross interference, let alone direction of individual lives. As Osborne and Gaebler remark, if the best value for money is to be provided, if the most choice and the most innovation are sought, then governments must be prepared to be flexible. They have provided a rough formula indicating the relative strengths of the public, private and voluntary sector with which it is difficult to quarrel. An evaluation technique is needed which can be regularly if not routinely applied to questions concerning service initiation, continuance, amendment or expansion. The strengths of privatisation, contracting out, franchising, vouchers, user fees, public-private partnerships etc need to be considered as a set of general principles and then applied to particular delivery systems once policies have been determined. Such a model will not be developed here, but, for example, it is generally the case that the public sector is best at such things as policy management, regulation, ensuring equity, social cohesion and the like. The private is generally better at performing complex tasks, delivering services to

14 *Reinventing Government* (Addison Wesley, New York 1992).

diverse populations and services which require rapid adjustment to change. As for the 'third force' or voluntary sector, it is best at utilising voluntary labour, giving hands-on personal attention and being committed to the poor and vulnerable.

Hayek supports a number of these propositions, even though he would feel clearly uncomfortable with much else which is being advocated:

> 'The range and variety of government action that is, at least in principle, reconcilable with a free system is thus considerable. The old formulae of *laissez-faire* or non-intervention do not provide us with an adequate criterion for distinguishing what is and what is not admissible in a free system. There is ample scope for experimentation and improvement within that permanent legal framework which makes it possible for a free society to operate efficiently.'[15]

This suggests, perhaps even mandates, creating institutions which allow wide experimentation with different styles of government; what Green has called a 'competitive market in regulatory styles', achieved by leaving as little as possible to central government and as much as possible to localities, financed with local taxes.[16] Hopefully, a number of the themes which have been pursued are coming together to form a pattern which will advance the possibilities for choice while rising above factional politics.

Macpherson shares relatively little with Hayek in terms of political philosophy and perhaps not that much with Green and yet, since they are all attempting to speak honestly and without partisanship to the needs of the human spirit, there are links and connections which it is important to identify. There is, for example, no real difference between Hayek and Macpherson when the latter says something which perhaps would never have found this particular emphasis in Hayek's *The Constitution of Liberty*:

> 'For it is not entirely an illusion that in a capitalist society men are free from normal social ties except those imposed by the state. There is an obvious sense in which the individual in capitalist society is freer from social ties than the individual in a society based on status. The greater insecurity of men is a measure of their greater freedom. The social ties in capitalist society are real, being largely determined by the

---

15   *The Constitution of Liberty* (Routledge and Keegan Paul, London 1980) p 231.
16   *Green* p 20.

individual's relation to capital, but are not as cohesive as the social ties of other societies. The result is that on the whole a stronger state is necessary to maintain a capitalist society than is needed to maintain a society in which the social relations are obviously more personal, or more obviously purposeful, and so more easily understandable.'[17]

The world is in a state of flux; the movement from one form of market production to another is often referred to as post-capitalist society. However, there is little doubt that down-sizing and devolving the state apparatus is capable of producing conformity with societal and communitarian needs and finding the optimum shape for the virtuous triangle.

Within this changing world, food, warmth, shelter, health and education remain vital to survival. The UK being party to the European Social Charter, the British state is, in any event, committed to ensuring the adequacy of these primary goods. But the modern world is so far from being a primitive society, let alone a desert island, that all things connect and everything depends on everything else. The global community reinforces social nature and interdependence and shows how easy it is for ordinary people with ordinary needs to fall through gaping holes in the new order which is being created, largely by accident if not out of chaos.

All social systems have strengths and weaknesses; so, for instance, although capitalism is a great producer, it is regarded by some as 'myopic'. It ignores the future since with any reasonable interest rate the discounted net value of a dollar eight years from now is approximately zero. But human societies have many things that have to be done on a longer time-scale, including research and development, the provision of systems of education, etc. 'In some sense in capitalism it is the role of government to represent the interests of the future to the present.' Since everyone wants private companies and governments each to do the things they do well, there is a need to ensure that capitalist societies do not simply become consumption societies which fail to make the necessary investments for the future.

> 'Our democratic systems are going to be tested ... At the moment they are failing the test. History will judge us based on our ability to restore the appropriate balance.'[18]

17 *Macpherson* p 249.
18 Lester Thurrow, 'The Global Company: New Game, New Rules, New Strategies (1994) C XL11 RSA Journal, pp 50–56.

The investment referred to here represents the futures of everyone; it relates to such matters as the reproduction of investment capacities, education and welfare.. These kinds of claims ought to be banner-headlined in a nation's articles of government and systems of governance reshaped to restore the balance between individual, society and the state so as to recognise the need for experiment and innovation and to abandon the idea that there is any one right answer to achieve these universal objectives.

Let Gewirth have the final say:

> 'The poverty which afflicts sizeable groups in our society and which drastically reduces the effective achievemental power of their civil liberties in the political process derives from a set of humanly-caused institutions which constitute dispositional obstacles to the ability to act on behalf of the poor. The positive governmental policies . . . should be viewed . . . as attempts to expand the freedom of the poor at a crucial point, for their aim is to remove the impact of these obstacles on such groups' effective ability to participate more equally in the democratic process.'[19]

The urgent task, he believes, is to deal constructively with the pressing problems of the extent and distribution of freedom and well-being.

The discussion in this chapter seeks merely to stake the claim for state action to liberate the human spirit through an unspecific range of interventionist devices. It is a simple point though one which in recent times has fallen on fewer and fewer ears. Simple truths should not only be, but read as, self-evident.

19 Alan Gewirth *Human Rights: Essays on Justifications and Applications* (University of Chicago Press, 1982) p 327.

Chapter 4
The 'federal' state

The absence of preponderant concentrations of power is one of the general characteristics of freedom. The demure or retiring state has already been commended; the logic of celebrating choice is that, whatever the role allotted to the state, it cannot be a heavily centralised state but needs to be one which is dispersed as far as possible to the peripheries or provinces. The case for the state as enabler, using competitive, sometimes experimental forms of provider has also been made out. Hayek too has argued for competition between a variety of local jurisdictions while Green has pointed out that the intellectual leaders of the immediate post-war period failed to understand the value of diversity in allowing room for human progress in relation to the National Health Service.[1] Centrally-located omniscience whereby a single person or group at the hub can hold all the information relevant to social or economic programmes was rightly termed by Hayek the 'synoptic delusion'.[2] This thinking has also characterised government thinking for more than a decade as witness the enthusiasm for privatisation, the shift from direct to indirect taxation, the health and educational reforms and so on.

Another way of expressing support for these sentiments is to say that if human civilisation is to flourish there must be room for the growth of human understanding. It is not possible at any point in time to know the future state of collective knowledge nor who or what institutions may prove the great benefactors of progress. One implication of this is that more attention, certainly in the UK but elsewhere too, should be paid to what may be labelled 'political markets'. Citizens directly affected by decisions at the immediate or local level need to be able to affect those decisions for if judgements about crucial issues are to acquire the consent of the public

---

1 David Green *Reinventing Civil Society* (Institute of Economic Affairs, 1993) p 110.
2 *Law, Legislation and Liberty* (Routledge and Kegan Paul, 1973) vol 1, pp 14–15.

then the procedures for arriving at them must be open. In a free and choosing society, the processes for making decisions can be as important as the content of the decisions themselves.

There are a number of international texts, especially at the level of the Council of Europe, which in effect affirm the doctrine of subsidiarity. This doctrine is often invoked in the UK when claiming that Whitehall sometimes knows better than Brussels, but it rarely extends to examining the reverse side which stipulates that Whitehall does not always know better than town hall. In recent years the powers of local government in Britain have been severely diminished. There is no doubt that part of the reason lies at the door of local government itself, which has not always been responsive to the local citizen's choices and preferences.

Too often bureaucratic and professional interests have suppressed the citizen as customer. But there is a danger of overkill since it is clear that it is simply not possible to govern from Whitehall unaided. It is hypocrisy to condemn the failures of command economies while retaining all political power at the centre. In any event, it cannot be done. Central government can set standards and principles and can operate certain vital services, but it simply cannot and does not possess the information to manage effectively throughout the localities and regions. Indeed, over the last dozen years or so central government has increasingly used partners to effect its policies throughout the country in the form of business and voluntary associations and a disconcerting number of quangos. As Stewart has said, the process of centralisation with the assistance of unaccountable 'partners' has not only created an accountability gap but has placed a cognitive burden on ministers that is beyond their capacity to bear.[3]

There is widespread unease about the 'third party' partners of the state assuming as much power and influence as has been the case in recent years. Empowerment through competing service delivery mechanisms is an attractive and liberating prospect, but it must be mediated through elective politics where clear programmatic choices are offered to the electorate. After all, elected politicians have a long-term commitment to their communities and have to live in them, a consideration which does not necessarily apply to business groupings or unelected quangos. The position in the UK is particularly unsatisfactory and made more so by the fact that public and administrative law does not supervise the behaviour of

3 John Stewart *Accountability to the Public* (European Policy Forum, 1992) and see *EGO Trip* (Democratic Audit of the UK, London 1994).

unelected bodies in as rigorous a fashion as, say, the USA. Where it is appropriate to proceed with the refinement of local government through the empowerment of partners and other agencies, then the reform of administrative law must be accorded a high priority if citizens are to have an account rendered to them and if they are to influence the shape and content of policies adopted. This is developed in Part III.

The democratic game plan must be anti-centralist, except in so far as primary concerns need to be given general application by a body with the authority to enjoin them on the polity as a whole. Economic markets, including the administrative/economic activities of the state, will provide part of the answer but politics/regulation will also have an important part to play. It cannot be right that central government seeks to allow local decision-making to be in the hands of sects or interest groups, thereby excluding the rest of the community. What is needed is an optimum level of democratic decision-making orchestrated by an elected body, though from time to time mediated through other agencies which themselves must be accountable and non-exclusive. Moreover, there is much to be said for the argument that a system of municipalities can provide a degree of decentralisation resembling the market-place. Such municipalities could potentially compete with each other in a quest for efficiency, a principle to some extent recognised by recent UK governments which have prepared league tables of performance for some areas of local government activity.[4] However, this is not the general direction in which UK governments have been moving. Furthermore, in delegating many tasks formerly undertaken through elected assemblies to those with apparent technical or business expertise, there has been an implicit preference for so-called technical outcomes as opposed to choice through political differentiation. This has been a serious concern over recent years, reflected in some ways by the pre-eminent position increasingly adopted by the accountancy profession. The profession, and bodies sponsored by it, have assumed a distinct 'public' role[5] which could not have been anticipated even a decade ago.

Not only has the state become increasingly centralised but it has simultaneously been seriously constrained from both experimentation and creative competition. Although compulsory competitive

---

4 And see eg John Kingdom *No Such Thing as Society* (Open University Press, 1992) p 81.
5 See eg Judith Freedman, 'Accountants and Corporate Governance: Filling a Legal Vacuum?' (1993) 64 Political Quarterly 295.

tendering and market-testing are well-entrenched in the UK, the public sector is not always free to compete with the private as is the case, for example, in New Zealand. Limits have been placed on local authority direct service organisations while many of the executive agencies of central government have not been permitted to develop products which could compete with the private sector. Such restrictions are difficult to square with a belief in genuine competition and, therefore, choice.

Consistency, choice and accountability would require that there should be no 'no-go' areas for the public sector, especially since policies will continue to be set by that sector. Furthermore, such policy setting should take place in conjunction with users, carers, professionals of all sorts in quality action groups or whatever form of wide citizen involvement seems appropriate, especially bearing in mind what will be said later about the need to take a 'hard look' at the nature of the decisions ultimately taken. For genuine choice to be the watchword, then the users of services need to be regularly consulted on their views of the service with a commitment to changes where necessary either in the service itself or in the delivery system where appropriate. Where public bodies deliver services, comparators can be used with other public bodies delivering similar services. Above all, real choice in schools, health and other services should be afforded, always provided that minimum standards are guaranteed. There is a great deal to be done in each of these areas, not least because the deliberative machinery for taking decisions is inadequate. True, advances have been made, not least in terms of grievance machinery, customer satisfaction surveys and the like. However, the nature of constitutional and administrative law needs to be readdressed if the full range of opportunities for critical analysis of proposals is to be explored. A number of suggestions for improving that machinery and furnishing it with ideal-typical models with which to seek the best policies delivered in the most efficient and competitive manner will be presented in Part III and it is important to ask whether stronger legislative support for some of these ideas might not reinforce a commitment to them. In particular, a statement of a competition policy under which the public and private can compete evenly needs to be seriously considered.

WHAT KIND OF GOVERNMENT – CENTRAL OR DIFFUSE?

The following summarises much of what has gone before:

'As a general rule, wherever possible, services which belong in the public sector should be supplied locally by self-financing units of government. There can be no absolute right answer about the necessity for a service to be public or private, or publicly financed yet privately provided, and consequently we should allow room for different localities to experiment, some with more or less public services, others with direct provision, and still others with local finance combined with competitive tendering by private agencies. But units of local government should experiment at their own cost ... It is fundamental to liberty that people should be free to say yes or no to taxation and without full information about the services they are receiving in return for their taxes it is impossible to form a rational judgment.'[6]

Within this statement of preference, it is naturally assumed that central government must still be able to lay down standards of acceptable service and to publicise those standards to ensure that they are understood by citizens at large. However, responding to the diversity of local people and their needs requires a decentralised system; the political version of markets, so to speak. To advance these ends, the UK might ratify the European Charter on Local Self-Government as an underpinning for the process of developing independence. An open and clear definition of the powers of local government would be given some firm form of constitutional status ultimately enforceable by the courts. It might even be asserted that local authorities should be given the power to undertake locally whatever is not expressly prohibited under the appropriate parent legislation (which ought to enjoy a special status) or even to receive a set percentage of the national taxation take from local income tax.[7] Whether this suggestion is acceptable or not, there is clearly something irrational and arbitrary about the current distribution of central government finance to local authorities plagued, as it has been, by manipulation and raw party politics. Some degree of choice in relation to revenue-raising ought to be central to a new federalism, with local government itself responding to the informed choices of its own electorates through reformed methods of consultation. Furthermore, as Allen has

6 *Green* p 129. In a British setting, the Treasury would almost certainly resist such proposals but their prejudices ought not to be regarded as holy writ.
7 See eg Graham Allen *Independent Local Government* (European Policy Forum, 1993). This second suggestion would, of course, be unattractive if Green's earlier argument is found convincing.

observed, the record of financial and economic management under a diversified, 'federal' system responsible to local electorates could scarcely be worse than under the centralist command political economy of the recent past. In addition, public–private partnerships could be expected to flourish in such an environment, freed from the one-size-fits-all obsessions of the Treasury. In this way and others local government could use its freedoms to work for wealth generation, employment opportunities and a crime-free environment. This is the logical corollary of putting local politics to the test in competition with other experiments and forms of innovation around the country. It would also fit snugly into what has already been said about new associative and community forms of action.

Government works best when it is as close to its area of competence as possible. Training, innovation and the regeneration of cities and local economies are cases in point. True, government has experimented with differing forms of local initiatives over the past decade but not within an overall context that maximises the chances of success; the constitutional arrangements do not admit of a sufficient degree of independence. The Training and Enterprise Councils (TECs) are a clear illustration, being based on a tradition of voluntarism, of so-called 'contract' and conducted within a time-frame which makes long-term planning exceedingly difficult.[8] Germany is usually contrasted with the UK in terms of the development of the local economy, where sufficient autonomy is enjoyed to equip firms with a relevant industrial policy supported by a system of local and regional banking institutions committed to the long-term development of the local economies.[9] The social and political system is seen in itself as a major source of competitive advantage with powerful local political figures as linchpins of support and advocacy. Some see a fundamental revision of the banking system as a necessary accompaniment of such a change,[10] together with a revised system of company law dedicated to the recognition of broader stakeholder interests. It is difficult to resist the force of such pleas if there is to be genuine local autonomy and a genuine commitment to the social and economic rights of all citizens. It is almost certainly the case that any revised constitutional

8 See eg Robert Bennett, Peter Wicks and Andrew McCoshan *Local Empowerment and Business Services* (UCL Press, London 1994).

9 Equally this is the case in Spain and, arguably, even more so in Italy. There is a very large body of literature on the subject.

10 See eg Will Hutton *The State We're In* (Jonathan Cape, London 1995) especially at ch 12.

compact would need to dovetail with co-operative developments within the European Union as well.

In so many ways these ideas build on the perceived advantages of both markets and the rediscovery of the 'contract' culture even where the contracts, as in arrangements between one part of the public sector and another, do not exist in the strictly juridical sense. Thus contract can help us to recall that the public service is not the province of one indivisible organisation with ministerial responsibility at the top. Rather it needs to represent the process of agreement between separate aspects of the public interest. As has been well observed:

> '... the contractual approach does offer the possibility of greater accountability for public services, by specifying objectives and by delegating functions to accountable organizations with separate interests. It could also provide the basis for expanding individual legal entitlement by specifying the obligations of the service provider.'[11]

THE DIFFUSE STATE

It seems clear that contracts between different parts of the state enterprise do indeed recognise the necessarily heterogeneous nature of the public domain in spite of the centripetal tendencies of recent years, even if not everyone would approve their use in the NHS. However, if, as a matter of principle, the contractual ideal is aimed for then there should be some justification for not importing it or something very similar into central–local relations. If roles were specifically allocated from the centre to the periphery, it might be advantageous for centrally defined global sums to be sub-allocated for the purpose and to give central government a responsibility for monitoring the outcomes – though preferably advised by some body with a degree of independent status. This process ought clearly to be public as should the preliminaries to the role/financial allocation.

Such an arrangement would encourage local government to be innovative and to use whatever mix of public/private/voluntary partnerships was best suited to the tasks allocated. This would allow discretion as to the delivery of goals (subject of course to legally

11 Ian Harden *The Contracting State* (Open University Press, 1992) p 36.

enforceable provisions concerning consultation), but precision for citizen or customer rights once the particular mode of service delivery was chosen. In short, commitment to choice and to rights requires a revised compact between central and local government and a revised compact between all levels of government and the citizenry. Wherever possible, that citizenry should be encouraged to be part of the management of public services; where that is not possible their experiences and preferences should be brought institutionally to bear on the process of the formulation of needs and ends. And collectively they should be encouraged to work with market processes for the greater prosperity of all. But when governments push ownership and control down into the community, their responsibilities are not at an end. Even if they no longer, or rarely, provide services, they remain responsible for ensuring that needs are met.

Proposals remarkably similar to the ones which are being urged here have been made for various schemes of regional government, not least for a Welsh Parliament. Suggestions have been made for organising the activities of such a body through a series of policy committees which would involve as wide a social constituency as possible in its deliberations. This would be aimed at producing a healthy mix of professional expertise and public accountability. This is also wholly in line with mainstream education thinking in Wales where a new Standing Conference for Education in Wales has been established uniting both professional and parent associations. This coalition emerged in part because of a breakdown in the traditional partnership between schools, local communities and local education authorities and the perceived erosion of local democracy through an exponential increase in the number of unaccountable Extra-Governmental Organisations (EGOs) or quangos.[12]

It is worth remembering that regional assemblies are perceived to be a necessary component of a modern democracy and an innovative economy within the European Union. In fact in recent years Wales has signed co-operation agreements with some of the most robust regions in the EU, each of which has a directly elected Parliament. However, it must be observed that the Welsh Office, which regards these regions as exemplars in the field of economic development, has been stubbornly silent about the political systems of 'subsidiarity' which have been the prime movers in the process. Not only is the logic of federal systems in line with all the

12 Kevin Morgan and Ellis Roberts *The Democratic Deficit: A Guide to Quangoland* (University College of Wales, Cardiff 1993).

arguments in favour of choice and decentralisation but there is a telling body of evidence that central government benefits from having a more positive relationship with localities and regions. However, recent years have seen local authorities finding ever more creative ways of evading central government controls and misinforming Whitehall about their activities.[13]

In other words, the move towards democratic devolution in the UK should not be seen as a zero sum game in which the regions are the only beneficiaries: the benefits of devolution would accrue to both central and sub-central governments. If devolution is extended and a more 'federal' system adopted, not only would this be more likely to empower the people but it would ease the burden of political overload at the centre.

> 'Equally significant, democratic devolution is a form of political education in the sense that the electorate is in a better position to understand that more self-government involves political *duties* as well as political *rights*. In contrast, the over-centralised political system we have at present, in which decision-making is perceived to be too distant and too remote, encourages a one-sided emphasis on rights rather than responsibilities, demands rather than duties. This is a deeply corrosive political ethic and it constitutes one of the greatest threats to social and economic stability because central government cannot possibly meet all the aims and aspirations of such an electorate. Paradoxically, central government, whatever its hue, will have to devolve power if it wants to manage more effectively: the basic maxim of a mature democracy is to trust people.'[14]

Few sentiments could more comfortably fit with all the main themes of this essay. Nevertheless, successive UK governments have been less impressed with these arguments than they might have been. The general trend towards centralisation is clear as is the proliferation of non-representative bodies to replace elected politicians, although the tone of some recent reforms is more compatible with 'federal' arguments than might be supposed. Thus, for example, the institutional reforms in the National Health Service announced as *Managing the New NHS* in late 1993 were said to be intended to strengthen accountability and continue the

---

13 *Morgan and Roberts* especially at pp 31–33.
14 *Morgan and Roberts* pp 33–34.

process of decentralisation. This was to be achieved by abolishing the 14 regional health authorities and replacing them and the existing management outposts with eight regional offices of the Department of Health each headed by a regional director. The management's offices will take on the development of the purchasing function and take over the task of monitoring trusts from the existing outposts. Clear criteria are to be developed to define the circumstances in which central management can intervene to ensure that providers fulfil wider national policy objectives. NHS management will build on Regional Health Authority work in developing networks and mechanisms to assist the Research and Development Strategy, developing clinical audit programmes etc. The new regional offices will also work closely with individual universities to ensure that medical education and research are properly supported by the NHS.

Correspondingly, lip-service is being paid to at least some of the arguments being presented here, and yet there is genuine concern about lack of local representation and the greater secrecy that will surround the work of regional offices. It would also seem appropriate that if the government were serious about decentralising management responsibility, the proportion of the budget spent on management should be left to local discretion. The regional offices will have to accept that health authorities make health policy and that it is only they who can make the trade-offs between efficiency, effectiveness and local needs and preferences. However, having elected members on health authorities is still not countenanced by the present administration so that the only alternative is to explore ways of securing public legitimacy for local health strategies through 'social marketing'.[15] In other words, much of the language of decentralisation and empowerment is adopted at the same time that the over-centralisation and diminished nature of the democratic mandate is pursued.

The record in relation to other public services is equally ambivalent. Education is an example. Although there is broad support across the political spectrum for a national curriculum, the general move towards centralisation has been undeniable while the growth of grant maintained schools has done little to restore schools to the parents and to the teachers. In fact, more radical New Right versions of schooling directed to producing more choice would see parents controlling their own budgets, selecting schools and establishing new ones in partnership with existing schools.[16] The

15 See eg *News Focus*, Health Service Journal, 28 October 1993.
16 See eg *Green* pp 139–142.

outcome is that pushing power downwards has been a half-hearted affair.

Equally, confusion has been displayed by community care policies where the local authority is again intended to be the empowering agent giving the individual greater choice of whether to receive care in residential accommodation or in the community. The choice of the kind of community care is also intended to be given back to the individual, but most research conducted on the reforms indicates the illusory nature of choice in this context. The choices are made more often by the local authority as purchaser than the individual, while it appears clear too that cost-cutting has been the main engine of reform. In the prison service, there has been a recognition that management structures have for too long been overly centrally prescriptive. Moves are afoot to allow governors the power to take more decisions locally. To this end, local development plans will afford senior prison service managers a far stronger basis for assessing the management performance of individual prisons than exist at present together with a mechanism for allocating capital funds dependent upon the quality of local proposals. These developments are welcome even if caveats still need to be entered concerning accountability mechanisms.

ACCOUNTABILITY AND THE LOCAL STATE

On the larger political level contradictions are also evident. In late 1993, the government announced a swing back towards local and regional strategic planning designed to unite and regenerate the urban renewal programmes of up to six Whitehall departments, with a new Cabinet committee to provide clout. From April 1994, the regional offices of four government departments were combined under ten newly-appointed regional directors charged with supervising a combined budget and recommending locally-made bids to senior ministers in London. The claims made by the government for these changes include bringing decision-making closer to local communities and to provide more effective and flexible services. It is too early to know how far these objectives are met yet it is still *ex facie* disturbing that 'pure' politics remains firmly rooted at the centre. This is bound to sow confusion about who is ultimately accountable for the delivery of public services. What compounds this problem is the government's use of the Standing Spending Assessment (SSA) system. Originally devised as a mechanism for allocating central government grants to local authorities, the SSA has been used for tasks such as 'capping' for which it was not intended. This has concerned the Audit Commission which claims that the system has confused accountability for local services between central and local government.[17] It concluded that the logical step would be for central government to take local services under central control, an option which was unlikely because:

> 'Central government would not welcome a more explicit trail of accountability for local service delivery reaching its door and is content to be shielded by the SSA process. But this obfuscation of accountability is inimical to responsible management. SSAs have a future role, not as a substitute for political accountability but as an aid to it. It must be clear where the buck stops.'[18]

In other words, central government clearly wants to exercise more control over local expenditure but it does not want to be held accountable for the problems associated with local service delivery. In consequence, clear lines of accountability are absent and this weakens the ability to improve economy, efficiency and effectiveness in the public service. When central government is responsible for more than 80% of local authority expenditure, what exists is less local government than local administration. However much that administration is devolved, all the main tests concerning choice, democracy and accountability will be flunked.

There is a clear need to redefine the public sector to make it more efficient, more responsive, more democratic and more innovative. It is also crucial to ensure that it co-operates with the private sector through exchanges of various kinds, including information, joint ventures and the like. This cannot be done through quangos and bodies dominated by patronage. What is needed is vision at both the national and the local level. If local government, for example, is to lose its traditional role in relation to service delivery, it must be re-empowered in terms of genuine strategic autonomy. Although government should not seek to replace local communities, it may need to empower them by strategies of support, including revenue-sharing and technical assistance. There is a great need for study and experimentation with creative use of the structures of

17 Audit Commission, 'Passing the Bucks: The Impact of Standing Spending Assessments on Economy, Efficiency and Effectiveness' (HMSO, 1993) vol 1.
18 R Vize, 'DOE Finance System is Slammed by Watchdog' 19 Local Government Chronicle, March 1993.

civil society and public–private co-operation. The argument which is emerging here is beginning to fuse with what will be said about the 'spirit of community' and civic associationism and civic politics. Furthermore, it underlines a larger issue which runs through the whole of the argument being presented. This is well summarised in the following passage:

> 'Generally, no social task should be assigned to an institution that is larger than necessary to do the job. What can be done by families should not be assigned to an intermediate group – school etc. What can be done at the local level should not be passed on to the state or federal level, and so on. There are, of course, plenty of urgent tasks – environmental ones – that do require national and even international action. But to remove tasks to higher levels than is necessary weakens the constituent communities. This principle holds for duties of attending to the sick, troubled, delinquent, homeless, and new immigrants; and for public safety, public health and protection of the environment – from a neighbourhood crimewatch to CPR to sorting out the garbage. The government should step in only to the extent that other social subsystems fail, rather than seek to replace them.'[19]

The logic of choice is the logic of constrained autonomy, of responsibility, of action based on the most accessible knowledge and of experimentation and diversity. The political system of the UK is out of kilter with these objectives by some considerable distance. A revised compact, embodying both the legal and the political, would be bound to address this dissonance. To be market-players is to be freed from the tyranny of political centralisation.

---

19 Amitai Etzioni *The Spirit of Community* (Touchstone Books, 1994) p 260.

Chapter 5
Community and society

FAITH, HOPE AND CHARITY

The makers, or at least the inheritors, of modern politics seem until recently almost to have forgotten that human beings are social animals, finding meaning in shared understandings and ultimately depending upon each other for survival. Living reality is the division of labour, co-operative endeavour, social solidarity, defending the hearth and the larder while wresting shared livings from nature and from the vicissitudes of the seasons and the epochs. Survival depends on healing and nurturing, fighting common causes and common enemies, celebrating (notoriously difficult for the unaccompanied), praying and giving thanks; sharing and caring with others of the species.[1]

Some of this is dimly perceived by the purveyors of market exchange, at least on those occasions when their consumer needs fall to be satisfied. But this is typically viewed as mere long-range exchange with one service buying another and everything having a calibrated value; calibrated by the accountant rather than the priest. It has been argued that beggars can't be choosers and that the social world ought to be so constructed as to allow everyone to choose. There must, it will be recalled, be a level material playing field if opportunities are to exist for all. There is, however, more to it than this. Ensuring the removal of the grossest inequalities and the availability of opportunities is an utterly worthy aim and a necessary precondition of human association, but is not of itself human association. The generosity has to be of spirit as well as of provision. Perhaps the fact that, until recently, political fashions were not congruent with people's inner needs explains why citizenship has

1 For the most sophisticated treatment of this subject see Ernest Becker's admirable *Denial of Death* (New York, Free Press 1973).

returned to some level of fashion alongside a yearning for lost identity in the shape of community and kinship.

In asking what purposes the constitution exists to promote, the list will need to include the banishment of poverty, offering genuine choice to individuals and also cementing group understanding and encouraging a life shared together. It has been noted that the social responsibilities of government are keenly contested, but the case for positive rights has had the better of the argument. The state has a strategic responsibility for clearing beggars from people's consciences as well as from the streets even if there can be genuine debate as to how best this is to be done: through workfare, self-help etc. By mapping similar attempts in the course of the nation's history it will be seen that the impetus has normally been more than charity since charity of itself is not enough.[2] Nevertheless, charity has been ever-present, regardless of its frequently mixed motives. And from time to time, the concept of shared community has broken out.

FROM CHARITY TO COMMUNITY

Rather than attempt a history of charity, it will be useful to select both historical and contemporary sketches which help to illuminate the themes which have already been engaged. There are many books written on the subject of charity, including a number of important legal texts,[3] though most of these are written in a broadly black-letter or technical fashion. For present purposes, much of the historical material is drawn from David Owen's leading work.[4] However, it is worth remembering that in England charity has been heavily associated with the courts of equity and attendant Christian notions of duty, decency and concern, though the history of charity and its motives show it to be much more ambiguous than the flowering of an other-regarding nature.

A good point to begin is to ask why people make charitable overtures in the first place. There are conflicting views on motives as may be expected since motives are often mixed. In researching contemporary issues of neighbourhood care, for example, some

2 Cp Confederation of British Industry, 'Initiatives Beyond Charity', Report of the CBI Task Force on Business and Urban Regeneration (London, 1988).

3 See eg Michael Chesterman *Charities, Trusts and Social Welfare* (Wiedenfeld and Nicolson, London 1979).

4 *English Philanthropy 1660–1960* (Harvard University Press, 1965).

scholars have been convinced that 'reciprocity' rather than altruism is the driving force. This sees care, if not charity, as an exchange rather than a gift; that is to say a social exchange. Donors may not anticipate the same measure of mutuality or even expect assistance in times of need from the same people. Rather donors, for example, might experience a deep sense of the debts of care they had incurred to quite different people in different contexts; often in the quite remote past. Nevertheless, four distinct bases of active informal helping can be discerned.

Now charitable giving is not the same thing as helping, and certainly not the same thing as neighbourliness, but they all appear to be impelled by equally complex motives with one form of giving shading into another at different periods of social evolution. Be that as it may, their taxonomy is roughly as follows: altruism – the acceptance of a norm of beneficence as an absolute guideline for personal life; tradition – a practice of taken-for-granted helpfulness strongly implanted in early experience and carried over as an unconsidered principle of present activity;[5] status – the culling of self-esteem from the patronage aspect of the relationship, and reciprocity itself.[6] Some see altruism as more properly a special, masked form of reciprocity, which might represent necessary (as in survival of the species) co-operation tinged with love. This is interesting in itself since it suggests that the acceptance of mutual inter-dependence soon encourages people to see their own vulnerability in others. Caring for oneself then frequently translates into a caring for others who touch on particular nerves through personality, circumstance or proximity. This is the point at which the philosopher's absorption with the nature of being and the social work fascination with motivating individuals and groups become linked.[7]

Others have attempted to trace the ethical roots of reciprocal caring, not least in terms of the bond between mother and child. This is supremely a bonding incapable of being understood in terms of contractual relationships. And given how dominant the contractual theme for organising social relations has been in the recent pronouncements of the New Right (NR), it will be helpful to observe that human beings must dig deeper than lawbooks in order to understand themselves.

5 Barry Knight *Voluntary Action* (Centris, London 1993) p 13. Indeed by the middle of the nineteenth century volunteering was becoming one of the traditional values of the 'respectable' working-class family, though its relationship to self-help and self-determination should not be overlooked.

6 Martin Bulmer Neighbours *The Work of Philip Abrams* (Cambridge University Press, 1986) p 10.

7 For the research which gives rise to this speculation see *Bulmer passim.*

'The important point for the present discussion is that caring is not a one-way process but one in which the person receiving the care actively responds, and stores up basic experiences and ethical obligations which may emerge later as apparently purely "other-regarding" behaviour.'[8]

Whether altruism be disguised or undisguised, 'unilateral transfers' represent 'the distinguishing mark of the social, just as exchange or bilateral transfer is the mark of the economic'.[9] The failure of the recent past is the failure to combine respect for individual choice with the need for an active sense of community. Yet some forms of charity, of philanthropy and of giving, do not fit in easily with either conviction; they may undermine self-help and the self-esteem which makes real choice possible while doing little to advance the sharing nature of our needs. Charity as paternalism may well be usefully examined in such a light.

In the eighteenth century, for example, many charitable efforts were seen to have distinctly mercantile overtones, and putting the poor to work reflected for many the simple intention to get the most out of the labouring force of the nation. Again, the requirements of Britain's maritime interests were never far in the background as witness the retention even today of what may be seen as a surprisingly disproportionate number of maritime charities. Even where 'Christian charity'enjoined a personal interest in the lower orders, in extreme cases even visiting them in their labourers' cottages, the activity was accompanied by a conviction that truly familiar intercourse would be degrading. The exercise was constructed to a considerable degree in order to nurture in the poor a sense of gratitude to their superiors.[10]

This is not light-years away from the attitude of many 'donors', including progressives and liberal reformers, that 'childishness' was all that could be expected from the 'dependent', who could lose their rights through a process of social reciprocation best expressed in the formula: need = dependency = non-competence.

'Sociologists of caring institutions and agencies have identified category upon category of caring agents as little more than a sort of moral secret police.'[11]

---

8 *Bulmer* p 117.
9 Richard Titmuss *Commitment to Welfare* (Allen and Unwin, London 1968) p 22.
10 *Owen* pp 15, 99.
11 *Bulmer* p 224.

Dependency is a concept which has recurred constantly in the literature of the NR, usually in the context of hostility to state-provided social welfare, though occasionally as a conviction that dependency undermines individual choice. What can be added is that the carer or donor who is the 'subject' is in danger of treating the recipient as an object who is, no doubt subconsciously, rejecting the meeting of 'other minds' and failing to participate in genuine community life. NR nostrums have not always identified ways of proceeding which notably improve on the old. Thus, a body of contemporary research indicates that many of the inherited forms of charity remain paternalistic, top-down and feudal in nature. This is bound to be counter-productive if current thinking favours self-direction. Much of the newer contract culture too seems to reproduce the old top-down models where the main lines of accountability are upwards to funders rather than downwards to 'customers' or recipients. A more democratic and less deferential culture would be more in keeping with the claims made for the new structures.[12]

THE VIRTUOUS TRIANGLE[13] REVISITED

For one reason or another, poverty has normally been regarded as intolerable by the ruling classes, yet their responses to this feeling have varied and are still difficult to unravel even now. Historically, there has been a shift from individual giving to the formation of charitable associations, to various forms of self-help, to involvement by the state, to partnerships between state and third parties through to attempts to impose market-type solutions of one sort or another. Just as the instrumentalities have altered through time so have the goals. Periodically the aim of government has seemed to favour freeing up the 'consumptive' atomic individual to indulge their own market instincts as an end in itself. There have also been welfare statist approaches to the art of government which stake out a shopping list of needs to be provided for individuals partly through their own efforts and partly by a caring state. This has involved a belief in collective responsibility, although actions taken have frequently been bureaucratic and have often involved minimising the

---

12 Charles Landry and Geoff Mulgan *The Future of the Charities and the Voluntary Sector: Themes and Issues* Working Paper 1 (Demos, London 1994) p 3.
13 Ie individual, state and community.

very freedoms espoused. However blunt an instrument the welfare state may be, part of its *raison d'être* has been to encourage a view of humankind which is other-regarding as well as self-regarding. To borrow a phrase, welfarism has portrayed solidarity as the social face of love. This has involved free-willing citizens sinking their caring sovereignty into the general collective. At other times intermediary associations, loose or formal, have been seen as a natural expression of the individual's need to act in social settings. The state, on this formulation, is little more than a necessary evil.

The distinctive technique of Tudor/Stuart philanthropy was the charitable trust which owed much of its existence to a Christian-ethic based system of equity. Its ethical base was still evident during the course of the eighteenth century when modern humanitarianism emerged and propelled charitable effort to an unexpected degree. As Owen has commented, for all the mixed motives it was:

> '... impossible to miss the compassion with which certain members of the middle and upper classes could view the misfortunes of the lower ... Nowhere was the characteristic eighteenth-century hopefulness about mankind and the improvability of society more splendidly embodied than in such transparently sincere philanthropists.'[14]

By the mid-nineteenth century a number of changes had occurred: one was a distrust of the 'professional mendicant' which gave rise to judgements about the deserving and the undeserving poor; another was the impact made by industrialisation which was creating poverty and inequity on a scale previously unknown. The effect of these developments was to filter out direct almsgiving in favour of charitable societies which could serve as intermediaries between the individual philanthropist and the beneficiary. The charitable, semi-professional organisation had arrived whose function was to bring a more cultured judgement to the disbursement of monies. Cultured or not, prioritisation for disbursement became a salient feature of the period, both in terms of the worth of the beneficiaries and the nature of services provided: hospitals and schools, institutions for the deaf and so on. In any event, priorities were imposed by effective cash limits for the poor, for charity was assumed inevitably to be the main vehicle for providing working-class welfare in so far as this was not performed by workers' associations or friendly societies.

14 *Owen* p 14.

Widespread destitution characterised much of the nineteenth century, leaving available charitable resources, however accurately targeted, woefully inadequate to meet palpable need, even allowing for extensive self-help campaigns and the encouragement of the voluntary societies. Although Victorian philanthropists 'attained notable triumphs ... they gravely misconceived the nature of the problem and underestimated its dimensions'.[15] Only a more fully developed industrial system could provide the necessary resources needed to banish poverty, not to mention need. Only the state, as will be seen, could prove equal to orchestrating the programme. When it began to do so, it did so reluctantly; probably with good reason.

One thing is clear: the voluntary sector could not meet the needs of the poor in an industrialised society.

> 'Charitable agencies, with their improved techniques of case-work, could do much for individuals – and here their contributions continued to be indispensable. They could give vital service in particular situations. But when the problem was seen as one that, in essentials had little to do with the actions of individuals, their adequacies and their failures, then the shortcomings of private charity lay exposed. To help individuals handle the unavoidable and grinding poverty of their lives with what success they could, even to assist them in meeting their special crises, was one thing; to ask why and whether destitution and the evils associated with it were necessary in a modern society raised a different order of issue. As men's views of what constituted a tolerable minimum became less restricted, it grew obvious that the major social tasks lay well beyond the resources of private charity, however ambitious its aspirations and devoted its performance.'[16]

What emerges is that whereas private charity pioneered action by the state, its ultimate inadequacy in the face of industrial society was manifest. Yet practically every contemporary public social service had its roots in some sort of charitable provision and it seems clear that even now charity retains a flexibility and flair for innovation which the state can rarely muster.[17] Similarly, although the state is ineluctably involved in ensuring the adequacy of basic provision, there is room for considerable debate as to whether the

15   *Owen* p 96.
16   *Owen* p 6.
17   See eg PEP *Report on the British Social Services* (London 1937) p 49.

state should itself be the provider or whether it should more properly enable. The state should retain responsibility for ensuring that whatever programmes are devised do not contribute to dependency but instead foster a spirit of dignity which allows some level of common citizenship.

Partnership arrangements between the state and other bodies are not, as might be thought, a modern development. From the 1830s, for example, education was becoming a public–private enterprise while the institutions for juvenile delinquents operating in the 1840s and 1850s were all based on the voluntary principle, yet formed an auxiliary, if not integral, part of the penal system of the nation. Earlier this century, different forms of loose linkages emerge, from the Citizens' Advice Bureaux to 'quasi-political' behaviour by voluntary bodies. Such bodies gathered data on pressing social evils, set in motion the machinery of democratic agitation and generally disturbed the complacency of the state's 'benevolent bureaucracies'.[18]

In more recent times, especially from the 1960s, there emerges an interlinking of voluntary organisations undertaking work which the statutory agencies could not or would not do. Increasingly the voluntary sector received monies and support from the statutory sector at the expense of a certain degree of independence heralding the emergence of a form of social welfare corporatism; here the funder tends to co-opt the voluntary sector for its own purposes. During the 1970s the Manpower Services Commission and the Housing Corporation in the UK were clear and outstanding examples of this. Interestingly the Housing Corporation has since been even more closely sucked in to government's strategic housing plans and, although the MSC has gone the way of all flesh, the TECs have simply taken its place.[19] One other issue may be considered. The partnerships in which Victorian philanthropy became entangled with collective action and social unity in the early years of this century seem also to be reflecting an older political theory of the need for checks and balances in the institutions of society to contain the exercise of power by those who held it. This constant historical theme should serve notice on the modern centralists who see the the market as the only countervailing force.

At this point it is worth dwelling on one particular virtue of

18 *Owen* pp 501, 537.
19 *Knight* pp 29–30; Alan Cawson (ed) *Organized Interests and the State: Studies in Meso-Corporatism* (Sage, London 1985) and Patrick Birkinshaw, Ian Harden and Norman Lewis *Government by Moonlight* (Unwin Hyman, London 1990) especially ch 4.

voluntary organisations which the statutory services seem largely incapable of matching: the innovative character of their activities. Beveridge had pointed out, for example, that the state had, for the most part, provided a uniform service for all citizens while the scope for personal help, for individual care and the provision for those who need something different remained the province of what is now usually referred to as the third force or sector.[20] Furthermore, this sector tended to encourage self-discipline by making a choice among possible objects of its benevolence. The opportunity for experimentation remains a strength of the voluntary sector while larger organisations can accumulate experience which is then made available to government for the purposes of influencing social policy. Without wishing to undermine the enormous contribution of the state sector, voluntary agencies continue to carry out diverse and productive experiments of a kind from which statutory agencies are largely excluded. Public bodies are constrained by financial and managerial regimes which tend to close off experimentation, fail to deal with the unexpected and ignore the cases which fall outside the rules. In a social setting, this is the equivalent of the justification for privatisation; it is certainly an argument for the state as enabler rather than an all-purpose provider.

THE INDIVIDUAL, COMMUNITY AND POLITICS

Bodies intermediate to the individual and the state not only contribute to pluralism but also help to counter the dissipation of neighbourhoods by successive waves of industrialisation.

> 'Where the state is the only environment in which men can live communal lives, they inevitably lose contact, become detached, and thus society disintegrates. A nation can be maintained only if, between the state and the individual, there is intercalated a whole series of secondary groups near enough to the individuals to attract them strongly in their sphere of action and drag them in the way, into the general torrent of social life.'[21]

20 Quoted *Owen* p 246.
21 Emile Durkheim *The Division of Labour in Society* (Free Press, New York 1933) p 28.

This can be seen as both a rejection of the centralising state and also of the atomising of individuals into pure market-appetites. Durkheim's insight is confirmed by contemporary social work research which indicates a link between caring and belonging to informal common membership groups.[1] It is also clear that, rather than the state and the market representing alternative mechanisms for solving social problems, history suggests that both states and markets operate more efficiently in civic settings. Social capital, and trust, common standards and networks can improve the efficiency of society by facilitating co-ordinated action and fostering partnerships of various sorts, whether workers' organisations, tenants' associations or other community groups.[2]

Friendly societies are a leading example. These were set up in the UK under an Act of 1793. The idea was that people who knew each other would pay money into a common fund in order to be able to draw on that fund when in need. Primarily they were used for sickness or funeral expenses. The nineteenth century was the heyday of these bodies though they have declined this century with the advent of the welfare state. The Royal Commission of 1874 revealed a fascinating picture: thousands of different sorts of societies including the better known such as the Oddfellows, the Ancient Order of Foresters, the Order of Druids and so on. What is of interest is that the members of these organisations paid enormous respect to the institution as such, with little evidence of individual ego (as was not the case with many of the great philanthropers), high *gemeinschaft*[3] standards were imposed, and mutual respect was assumed. In addition to the staple benefits, some societies provided old age pensions, and lump sum endowments at varying stages of life.

With the advent of the Registrar of Friendly Societies in 1829, new and emerging areas of need were brought under the rules of friendly society registration. These included cattle insurance societies, working men's clubs, co-operative stores, farmers' trading societies, housing societies, building societies, trades unions, trustee savings banks and the like. These were largely the result of working-class voluntary action to improve its basic condition, although one commentator has wryly observed that 'the list

---

1 *Bulmer* p 114.
2 *Landry and Mulgan* p 6.
3 *Gemeinshaft* is an expression which denotes a society or legal order whose subjects are respected according to whether or not they advance the interests of the institutions as a whole rather than according to whether they have infringed particular, detailed, rules.

includes a large slice of the financial institutions that we take for granted today ... and whom young people may consider form part of the rubric of capitalist society'.[4] What is to be found here is a mixture of motives and perceptions. These societies were clearly about material provision through self-help, but self-help in communion with others. That communion was often expressed in terms of institutions which not only had broad aims and outcomes but which were normative associations expressing canons of decency and duty. They represented opportunities to play out otherwise denied civic roles and taught large numbers of people the arts of accounting, management, leadership and responsibility which were absent from the anomic industrial context in which they found themselves. This has led a well-known market supporter to observe that:

> '... as the historic record amply demonstrates, voluntarism not only offered superior quality services but also provided opportunities for developing the personal skills necessary for liberty. It is only if such opportunities are widely available that freedom can be made safe from tyranny.'[5]

Some of the lessons to be drawn from this discussion will be drawn in a moment. However, it is apparent that not only is the centralised state inadequate as a holistic solution, but so is the market. The third angle of the virtuous triangle is a necessity. In recent times the primacy of the market over other forms of social expression has been widely proclaimed, not least because it has been rightly realised that a perfectible society with the state as architect is a chimera. But marketism is clearly not enough when the identification of a set of irreducible human needs moves to the top of the agenda.

> 'This new philosophy [that of the NR] undermined the traditional ethical and political assumptions underpinning voluntary action that had held sway up to the time of Wolfenden. Ethics were central because there was the idea of an individual doing something or giving something that would provide a benefit for another. This ethical element motivated most people who promoted the role of voluntary action in society.'[6]

---

4 *Knight* p 15.
5 David Green *Reinventing Civil Society* (Institute of Economic Affairs, 1993) p 130.
6 *Knight* p 41.

One of the advantages of spending a little time on the development of philanthropy and community is to see how much overlap exists between complex political ideas and the most innocent sally into apparently discrete pockets of national biography. Yet social living is a seamless web and once a little is unpicked it rapidly courses through the remainder of the material. So the myriad charitable trusts which characterised Victorian England were not only directed to estimable objects but 'also imparted a special flavour to English society'. By taking responsibility for their citizenry in a way that some regard as unique in Western society at least, the English were determined to conduct their affairs without the interference of a centralised state. This not only rings a current ideological bell but is part of something more enduring: viz the determination to maintain in Britain 'a conspicuously pluralistic commonwealth'.[7]

The case for the autonomous individual is clear and undeniable; the role of the state in the liberation of the individual equally so. Some form of community third force is not only a historically continuous fact but an innate expression of how human beings relate to each other. These remarks may be obvious but for the practitioner of statecraft they have not always been self-evident truths, and accordingly the public and institutional apparatus has not accurately reflected a concern to keep all three in mind, let alone in balance. Thus the partnerships between the state and its accomplices have rarely been finely drawn in institutional terms and have never been addressed at the deeper level of constitutional politics. What institution has the main role? What are the bargaining arrangements, how much transparency? What should be the arrangements for 'corporate planning', the competences of the state and third force forms?[8]

There is abundant literature on the corporatisation of the voluntary sector and on its occasional colonisation by the state. There have been accusations by government that voluntary bodies have inappropriately involved themselves in politics while in recent years concern has been expressed that the management committees of voluntary associations have shifted from being mere reference points for both members and government to taking on, more and more, the manner and style of local authority committees or other governmental organisations.[9] The third force is in fact seemingly used for the purposes which governments have in hand, and so by

---

7 *Owen* p 596.
8 Many of these issues have been addressed by the author and others: see Patrick Birkinshaw, Ian Harden and Norman Lewis *Government by Moonlight* (Unwin Hyman, London 1990) *passim.*
9 *Knight* p 31.

undermining local and regional government, using that force as a cheaper form of service delivery than the statutory sector, though this may follow from a genuine conviction that voluntary bodies are more sensitive and effective than any available alternatives. In recent times tax rebellions have certainly played their part. As one commentator has remarked:

> 'The 1980s saw a resurgence of materialism. But, unlike that in the nineteenth century, the new materialism was unheroic in the sense that it relied on few radical transformations of matter and relied almost entirely on radical transformations of money.'[10]

The mid-1970s had witnessed a tax-welfare backlash, the logic of which pointed to reduced social expenditure, especially in the field of welfare. The third force, heavily dependent on volunteers, was a tool conveniently to hand. However, it does not do to be reductionist; other factors can be seen to be pointing in the same direction. There is a loss of faith in government and public administration and there is a degree of searching for alternative ways of alleviating needs and managing services. There is also ample evidence to indicate that, other things being equal, people prefer neighbourhood altruism to public provision as a means of coping with dependency and personal misfortune.[11]

What is lacking is an attempt to provide a clear philosophy for identifying the optimum balance between individual self-help and autonomy, the need for the state to steer or pilot the perceived needs of its citizens into agreed channels and intermediate forms of social life which satisfy the urge for communion, for self-expression, for self-development and for experiment in individual and group settings. Intermediate associations are a prerequisite of an enquiring, pluralistic and democratic state. The UK has not paid them adequate attention recently and this is as true in the field of interactive local social formations as it is true in the field of experimental politics. Not that the two are unconnected.

CHOICE, CARE AND COMMUNITY

Even though existential vulnerability mandates co-operation, the British community tradition is an honourable one. Even now, for

10 *Knight* p 33.
11 *Bulmer* p 9.

example, only one in 20 old people live in institutions, which says something about the support networks in which friends, families and neighbours play a significant role. It was ever thus: 'an Englishman rarely stands aside from public business . . . He does not live withdrawn . . .'. This has been expressed historically not just at the individual but also at the civic level. This is evidenced by the traditional philanthropy of the City of London and also in the newer centres of population. 'Perhaps it is enough to say that associated philanthropy was a valid expression of the social temper of the nineteenth century.'[12] Moreover, whatever aspersions can be cast on the motives for caring, it is crucial to bear in mind that although certain attitudes to caring may degrade people, such people can certainly be degraded by the absence of caring.[13] Degrading as a word says much about common humanity and reminds people what it is to be fallen; to be not themselves; not to be autonomous. Happily the latter part of the twentieth century has seen a widespread search for alternative means of belonging.[14] Nor is this restricted to any particular class for, as Owen has shown in his epic treatment of English philanthropy, even the poorest may assist in the good work. Indeed the poor may often be the best placed to do so since they may have more experience of the spirit in which the beset are treated.

Two major themes have been brought together here – the necessity of living active lives in social settings and the ability to act autonomously. Even the poor may be assisted in ways that maximise the opportunity for making their own choices. There is enormous scope for using resources in more empowering ways to give end users of services choice as to how they should operate. There is, after all, strong historical evidence to indicate just how far people will go to uphold their own dignity and autonomy. The lengths to which people went to avoid the stigma of pauperism is perhaps the clearest illustration while even in the late nineteenth century there were some relatively enlightened political efforts to raise people's self esteem and offer them encouragement to help themselves. Joseph Chamberlain, for instance, proposed encouraging voluntary provision for old age by granting state aid to those who through saving had taken steps to provide for themselves.[15] Although he was not always able to carry the servants of the state

---

12 Owen p 164.
13 See W Gaylin (ed) *Doing Good: the Limits of Benevolence* (New York, Pantheon 1978) *passim.*
14 Eg Maurice Roche *Rethinking Citizenship, Welfare, Ideology and Change in Modern Society* (Polity Press, Cambridge 1992).
15 *Owen* p 506.

with him, Beveridge too was an advocate of choice in the area of social welfare, believing that it both encouraged self-development and also acted as an introduction to political awareness. The turn of the century clearly coincided with a sea-change in social welfare in a number of respects, some of which have already been noted. But one such change was the detectable movement away from a concentration on avoiding total destitution towards encouraging autonomy through diverse programmes of voluntary action.

There is a necessity not only for government to readdress its relationship with intermediate bodies of all sorts, though especially voluntary organisations, but also to consider the institutional restructuring of the state. In concluding this section two quotations are apposite:

> 'It is now recognised that the consumer is not a passive recipient but is someone who has an important part to play in assessing the relevance and utility of the services provided. Moreover, the consumer is not alone. He or she is located in an informal network of family, friends, and community. The strengths or weaknesses of these informal networks, or communities, will thus have a direct bearing on the effectiveness of services. Public and voluntary services must now take this into account and that will involve a very different way of operating.'

> 'Wherever possible consumers should be encouraged and helped to form their own associations and, even if that should prove impossible, the presentation of their interests should be arranged so as to create opportunities for hearing their authentic voices. Consumers of public services are not the purchasers so this power is not available to them ... But it is important for the effectiveness of public supply systems that the consumer should be given the equivalent of some purchase on the system. This is not necessarily an idea which will come easily to some voluntary organisations, which have in the past encouraged and maintained a cosy relationship with their clients.'[16]

ALL TOGETHER NOW: THE ROLE OF THE STATE

Individual autonomy requires a level material playing field; this in turn requires that the state orchestrates the delivery of certain

16 *Bulmer* p 55.

welfare goods which in turn involves the 'third'or voluntary force at particular points. But autonomy is about more than material goods – it is about self-discovery and forms of communion with others. One consequence of recognising this is that forms of welfare delivery must be directed at encouraging autonomy and must be shaped in such a way as best benefits the recipient. Given that recipients live and communicate in their social settings, family as well a broader community, the welfare system, both state and third force, needs to be shaped to satisfy local and individual requirements. This means not only a limited, empowering, role for the state, however conceived, but the encouragement of local and community structures which will do more than just deliver services. These structures will need to bargain and trade with the state – even to compete and contest with it. This is the logic of a state comprising pluralistic forces and associations; it is also the logic of allowing charity, generosity, compassion and fellowship effective outlets. Since these matters are central to the human condition, and certainly central to the moral heritage of the nation, they need to be given institutional encouragement and expression. This has repercussions for both political and legal institutions which are currently not elaborated with these ends in mind.

From the 'state's' point of view, there must be an attempt to target welfare and social services within community settings; the state must inquire as to what is needed, what will most effectively work and how local groupings will wish to respond. What is probable is that for this consultation to be satisfactory there should be encouragement at the local level of associations of various kinds: the 'purely' voluntary, the mixed social enterprise embracing both welfare services, lobbying and community action and hybrid forms of a more overtly political nature. All this is closely allied to the movement for citizens' self-management of a range of public services.

Dominant forms of local association in the post-war UK have included the Citizens' Advice Bureaux which have mediated the concerns of the state and others; they have explained to authorities the needs of the citizen and to the citizen the intentions of the authorities. Other voluntary bodies have been able to stimulate, restrain and criticise the proceedings of statutory authorities as well as to collect data on particular evils and social needs in addition to the pioneering work already noted.[17] It is also important to understand that the statutory services established under the first

---

17 See eg *Owen* pp 536–537.

Attlee administration were not intended to create a state monopoly of welfare. There was recognition of the tireless, autonomous and original work conducted by endless committee members up and down the country; hardly surprising given that leading members of that administration had cut their civic teeth on intermediate associations.

Even so, the relative autonomy of these bodies has shifted and been trimmed. Charitable bodies have periodically been berated for what were seen as their 'political' activities, many of them have been more and more locked in to delivery mechanisms for pre-determined state programmes, and they have occasionally been criticised for over-emphasis on the 'professionalisation' of charities and voluntary associations. Needless to say, the post-Thatcher emphasis on accountancy regimes and Financial Management Initiative (FMI) have also had marked effects on the third force. Even the role of the National Council for Voluntary Organisations has not avoided controversy, for just as it has played an increasingly active role in representing the views of voluntary bodies to government, so other bodies have stood outside these arrangements which have been seen to be too cosy and corporatist.[18] This is perhaps unsurprising when the 1980s could be characterised as a period when many voluntary organisations were seen simply to be tracking the behaviour of government in a reactive form. Innovation, change and radicalism were seen to be the province either of the state or the private sector.[19] Not only was the third force increasingly seen as the sub-contractor, but its identity was in danger of being defined in terms of the other, more dominant, 'partners'.

Here are the horns of a dilemma. Because Britain lacks a clearly defined constitution with qualified powers, limited territories and fundamental, enforceable rights, central government can play fast and loose with all other groupings. Since there is still dispute at the political/constitutional level as to whether citizens have social/material/welfare rights at all, it is scarcely surprising that no sophisticated political jurisprudence exists as to the rights of heterogeneous, even if ranked, groups intermediate between the central state and the individual. While there is clearly nothing wrong in central government delivering services through third parties in a dominant/servient mould, there is clearly something wrong in restricting recognised third parties to such a role. If experiment

18 *Knight* p 293.
19 *Knight* p 53.

and choice are to be the watchwords, then different categories of intermediate organisation should be empowered and afforded rights and protections. This might well require that attention be paid to new legal forms, perhaps as the twenty-first century's equivalent of the friendly societies.

In a short essay brimming with ideas, the think-tank 'Demos' has posed important questions about revised legal structures for the voluntary sector which would reflect their different natures. In recognising the likelihood that the voluntary sector can become an ersatz political platform for its leading actors, Demos queries the dividing line between traditional politics and the third force. This by now should be recognised as history repeating itself but, in any event, they are right to raise questions about the restrictions on freedom of campaigning policy and to ask whether consideration should be given to the desirability of providing a privileged position for bodies which are explicitly designed to develop and promote arguments.

> 'In addition to the question of free speech there is a parallel question of how advocacy should be organised. As donors and public sector funders switch away from funding campaigning towards funding service provision, and as incumbent voluntary agencies become non-profit service providers a new generation of consumer groups has developed. These have begun to challenge the old generation agencies, which began as consumer organisations and now have become producers. Where will the funding for individual advocacy and policy campaigning by these new groups come from?'[20]

All of which leads from traditional voluntary activity into community action. Community development involves the formation of ordinary people in their localities to give collective expression to their concerns. This was recognised in the UK in the 1960s and 1970s following the US War on Poverty programme but community development was discredited by Marxist entryism so that its liberating potential was never realised. However, local authority outreach programmes and the NR's commitment to self-management schemes are part of the same logic. In fact, the language of the NR is rationally congenial to new associationism, even though it is not always expressed in the language of love once espoused by a currently discredited member of the NR tendency.[1] On the other

20 *Landry and Mulgan* p 15.
 1 *Knight* p 39.

hand, the empowerment of communities chimes perfectly well with the mood of the times even if the rhetoric is politically stronger than the actualité.[2] The secret is to encourage association-ism in harness with self-development and awareness which would necessitate central government recasting the welfare system to offer concrete advantage to those who committed themselves to their community. It would, however, need to be somewhat subtler than workfare, which reeks of punishment more than honour.

CONCLUSION

It may well be that the informal system of social care, except within families, is waning and that any substitute will take new forms. The newer networks may be considerably more political in the sense of making demands on government and the statutory agencies may have to deal with community organisations as equals rather than patronising them. It has been powerfully argued, for example, that 'some serious surrender of powers is unavoidable if one really wants any significant measure of social care to be provided within neighbourhood social networks'. Parallels may be sought in the USA where neighbourhood associations have become formal members of urban partnerships with legal recognition being given to neighbourhood councils which exercise varying degrees of autonomy over planning and service delivery for their respective areas. Neighbourhood associations believe that they can deliver services to local residents more efficiently than bureaucracies.

> 'Neighbourhood care is a real possibility in our sort of society. But not on the basis of reinforcing or renewing the traditional informal networks as the Seebohm and Wolfenden Committees seem to have imagined. Those networks are dying and should be allowed to die. Today, neighbourhood care means working out a constructive relationship between the state, nationally and locally, and neighbourhoodism, the politicised voice of local attachment.'[3]

As Bulmer has pointed out, local mobilisation is a broad topic which touches on issues of decentralisation and community politics.

2 *Landry and Mulgan* p 6.
3 P Abrams, 'Social Change, Social Networks and Neighbourhood Care' (1980) 22 Social Work Service 18–19.

Abrams cut through much of the rhetoric of community care but failed to establish precisely how neighbourhood mobilisation would promote neighbourhood care. It is important that the potential for partnerships be tapped, but many voluntary bodies will not be able to relate to new associationism without becoming more aggressive; the passive, used, partner of the recent past will not be readily embraced by neighbourhood politics while government will need to accept that, as well as voluntary bodies vocalising the felt needs of the neighbourhood, the ancient concern with ethics and reciprocity will need to remain at the forefront of activity.

> 'The switch to the market economy is partly occasioned by a realisation which we have only very slowly and painfully come to recognise. This is that the major social needs which we have cannot be met by any single agency or system. Needs are vast, complex and constantly changing requiring a myriad of pragmatic responses and cannot be met in a systematic way on a planned or dirigiste basis. In many cases there are no such things as "solutions"; that is to say a definable remedy that will once and for all dispose of a problem. . . . If there is progress it can only be achieved by recognising that it depends upon the interaction of all the parties involved in a particular issue. There are separate and distinct roles to be performed of course but the key to improvement, or resolution, lies in the proper working out of the relationships between them on the basis of a shared responsibility.'[4]

The philosophy for the virtuous triangle needs to be developed. In the process the state must find its own level; must respond with an adequate concern for subsidiarity; must find a level at which its constituency can relate but at the same time make it possible for dialogue to occur between it and a wide range of forms of community expression so that the basic goods of the constitution – the floor of rights to which all are committed – can be most appropriately delivered.

This new triangular relationship should ultimately produce a more mature form of politics since the present is dominated by a handful of political activists and a mass of the politically inert who have lost their faith in active politics. Community self-awareness should serve, as it has always done in minority faiths, as an introduction to political awareness. Given that a pluralistic society is the only truly democratic society, then the reconstruction of the state

4 *Knight* p 42.

from a dozen different points of entry represents an opportunity to revise and reaffirm the political compact in a modern setting.

The rediscovery and the reshaping of community resonates with felt need. The gains of recent years in rejecting bureaucracy and paternalism and the rediscovery of markets must not be thrown away, but the individualism which markets at their best celebrate must operate in the context of other minds and other souls. The legal order must be reshaped to seek out the virtuous triangle.

Chapter 6
Associations, choice and labour

The case for intermediate associations as a necessary component of choice was put some time ago by Lord Beveridge:

> 'In a totalitarian State or in a field made into a State monopoly, those dissatisfied with the institutions that they find can seek a remedy only by seeking to change the Government of the country. In a free society . . . they have a different remedy; discontented individuals with new ideas can make a new institution to meet their needs. The field is open to experiment and success or failure.'[1]

What are or should be the limits on the right to form associations? At first blush the answer would seem to be that there should be no limit other than that such rights must be balanced by the duty not to harm others or to prevent them from exercising their own human rights choices. This poses something of a conundrum which is not easily resolved, and yet while there are no simple or clear-cut solutions, it should at least prove possible to identify some of the inconsistencies of the politics of the recent past.

One item will be apparent straight away. The common law has long recognised what sociology explained later: viz that groups may possess coercive powers denied to most individuals. Thus the laws relating to unlawful assembly, riot, affray and, even to some extent, laws relating to combinations, especially civil and criminal conspiracies. On the other hand, the potential of associations and voluntary bodies for personal liberation and for fighting injustice is considerable. Friendly societies and provident associations are a case in point. Their history indicates that membership in them allowed the industrial worker a status his working life failed to

1 *Voluntary Action* (Allen and Unwin, London 1948) p 60.

offer. Although having to sell his labour to make a living, in the lodge he was a member of a fraternity committed to ideals. In that environment 'there were no bosses'.[2]

The legitimacy of these bodies was increasingly recognised by the state, especially in the second half of the nineteenth century when facilitative legislation was introduced. This, as has been mentioned, had two aims: first to provide information which would be useful to societies in framing proper rules and setting contribution and benefit levels; and, secondly to provide information to members of the public to enable them to judge for themselves the position of each society. The actual management of the societies was left to the members and their officers.[3] Consequently, the members marginalised the state bureaucracy and manifestly helped their nearest neighbours as themselves. Green charts the eventual demise of mutual aid after the end of the Second World War and shows how Beveridge's wish for the societies to be incorporated into the welfare state was overturned by government and civil service advice. This period 'in particular shows how the intellectual leaders of the day failed to understand the value of diversity in allowing for social progress'.[4] It represented the antithesis of encouraging self-help and social citizenship and on this account must be regretted.

There is clearly a great deal in common between voluntary associations and the labour or trades unions which most commentators, including Green, fail to address adequately. The degree of militancy exhibited by these latter bodies may well be the crucial determinant in judging them to be good or bad, liberating or constraining, but the forces against which they railed need to be taken into account in forming a balanced judgement about their present place in the scheme of things. A balanced assessment is what has been patently lacking in recent years.

Now the creation of 'surplus value', so to speak, through the cooperative and provident societies, is something that many, including the New Right (NR), would wish to commend. They encourage entrepreneurial welfare and pose no involuntary restraint on others. Their revival in welfare terms could have important repercussions for rates of taxation. However, if choice and human rights lie at the heart of the social enterprise, it seems difficult to object to defensive alliances or associations whose object is to ensure, for

---

2 David Green *Reinventing Civil Society* (Institute of Economic Affairs, London 1993) p 49.
3 *Green* ch 8.
4 *Green* ch 10.

example, safety conditions. Since physical security and well-being is crucial to any concept of human choice, the industrial environment, though not only the industrial environment, must be protected. What should be addressed is the balance between state regulation of the health and safety regime and the role of voluntary and/or labour associations in securing such a regime. This has been given scant attention by British governments in recent times but some role for labour associations in contributing to the improvement of the industrial environment can scarcely be denied. In fact, it is doubtful if much advance in this area has occurred since the Robens Report in 1972.[5] Of course, basic guarantees must be laid down by the state, just as it lays down basic standards for the national curriculum in education, but the implementation of those standards and their regular, especially local, adjustment would seem to demand some sort of partnership between worker and employer. And just as most employers operate through some collective identity, it is natural that the same should apply to workers.

In Beveridge's free society, institutions established to meet needs clearly included the trades or labour unions. Unions have traditionally played an important role in most Western societies at least since the Second World War, as witness, eg the texts approved by the International Labour Organisation, the Council of Europe, the Economic and Social Council of the UN, the International Covenants on Civil and Political Rights, on Economic Social and Cultural Rights and the like. Now it may well be that the traditional trades union model will no longer serve its purpose and that it must undergo change or give way to other models that do. These are matters of signal difficulty which cannot be resolved here. What is more important is that the primary conditions for the exercise of choice in the workplace are repatriated or rediscovered. The language of mutual exclusion has, unfortunately, tended to drown out rational debate over these matters.

THE SHORT AND THE LONG TERM

It is as well to begin by refashioning certain statements from the 1960s and 1970s. It is perhaps no accident that the subtitle of the text which has been chosen to rekindle this discussion is 'Essays in

5 *Health and Safety at Work* Cmnd 5034 (HMSO, 1972).

Retrieval'. Its author observes that the capitalist economy is distinguished from the simple exchange economy by the separation of capital and labour; that is to say, the existence of a labour force without its own sufficient capital and without a choice as to whether to put its labour into the market or not. Regardless of wider share ownership, pension fund investment and the like, the analysis is sound, although arguments can be lodged at the margin. Macpherson argues that this lack of choice is a form of coercion which can in principle be reduced through the regulatory and welfare state, thereby increasing the amount of effective individual liberty.[6]

Whereas all governments accept the need both for regulation and for welfare,[7] the philosophy underpinning intervention is usually somewhat amorphous. In recent years there has been a great emphasis on the labour 'market', which has largely meant atomising individuals and exposing them to unequal power. While it is arguable that greater choice can be created through increased shareholding, and that works councils or other expedients would mitigate the inequality, there is a lack of fit between present circumstances and the larger claims of the NR concerning freedom and choice. The total set of social and economic arrangements needs to be addressed alongside the civil and political if citizen choice is to be maximised. Present ideology is confused, underdeveloped and frequently partisan.

It would be fair to say, for example, that most of the NR is opposed both to minimum wage regulation and the 'Social Chapter' of Maastricht, while being somewhat ambiguous about the UK's commitment to the European Social Charter of the Council of Europe. Thus, even some of those who do not wish to renege on Treaty obligations are content to acquiesce in the status quo since the enforcement arrangements of the European Social Charter are notoriously deficient. It has to be asked whether such opposition is consistent with a commitment to choice as the ruling human sentiment and to a floor of basic material entitlements necessary for human beings to find their own identities.

It is sometimes argued that particular regulatory interventions aimed at assisting the generality of citizens would in fact have the opposite effect. If those who entertain such positions genuinely believe that avoiding counter-productive interventions is their duty to their fellows, then their warnings need to be carefully heeded.

6 CB Macpherson *Democratic Theory: Essays in Retrieval* (Oxford University Press, 1973) pp 146–147.
7 See eg *Competitiveness: Helping Business to Win* Cm 2563 (HMSO, 1994) ch 5.

But it has to be said that the normal language of the NR would have to be strained to accommodate such an interpretation. Furthermore, it will not do to argue that the NR's prescriptions over the long term will best encourage the necessary level playing field of material opportunity to thrive, since in the long run we are all dead. There is an obvious objection to the long-termism claim: viz that planning, on the definition of the NR, is not possible in the absence of sufficient information. This is sauce for goose and for gander time. The total politico-economic platform on which any member of the NR may choose to stand represents a plan; no more no less. Some regulations are removed; others retained. The balance between regulation and devil-take-the-hindmost (a particular version of marketism being adopted in the absence of any 'perfect' market) is a commitment to a particular form of politics. In other words, a plan by any other name can go awry.

The matter can be approached by another path. It can be persuasively argued that some aspects of choice cannot be effectively legislated for and in some senses choice is genuinely anti-statist. But to follow that logic, then a 'market' give and take between capital and labour, so to speak, would have to be opened. Choice between available options could be bargained or negotiated by free agents, or their freely chosen representatives. But this is not what has been happening recently. For good or for ill, the regulatory apparatus of the state has been wheeled on to the platform at extremely regular intervals to weaken the negotiating position of organised labour. Up to 1994, there had been nine Acts in 15 years which have progressively weakened the trades unions. Not only has collective bargaining outside the public sector effectively ceased, but the balance of legal and economic power has decisively swung away from organised labour. Recently, for example, the ILO invited the UK government to reconsider aspects of the Trades Union Reform Act 1993 which allowed employers to discriminate against trade union members in pay and conditions of work. This was said to be incompatible with freedom of association.[8] Such regulatory intervention might be legitimate if it could be shown that *overall* community choice would thereby be enhanced. Significantly, no such defence was mustered. It will not do to equate a free market in labour with the preferred position of capital without respect to labour's own view of what constitutes a free market in labour. If the very concept of markets is contestable, the concept of the labour market is especially so.

8 *The Guardian*, 25 June 1994.

SOME UNDEBATED QUESTIONS

High unemployment *as a policy* is quite clearly anti-choice on any reading. High unemployment as an uninvited guest is another matter and clearly poses enormous problems. But the general approach to it can be mapped out if there is to be consistency about the level material playing field in the here and now. First, all energies must be directed towards putting people back to work as the first economic priority; secondly, losers must be cushioned by some form of material adjustment. This is quite consistent with the duty of all to provide for themselves as far as possible and not to be cosseted or feather-bedded. However, the point to be taken is that publicly pursued policies which inhibit the power of labour to express its voice must be justified according to the atomic make-up of choice.

On what grounds can such inhibition be defended? Because such associative order might interfere with markets? The problem here is that the particular market which is to be preferred to a 'free' labour market is in fact value-laden. Preference is given to some markets over others. The language which is normally employed is the 'freeing up of labour markets'; 'flexible labour markets [sic] play a key part in a competitive economy. They allow employers to deploy their workforce in *the most efficient way*' (emphasis added). Since 1979 the government has followed a wide-ranging strategy aimed at improving the working of the labour market, the main objectives being:

> '– to encourage good employment practices. Successful firms encourage genuine dialogue between managers and workers, offer good training and working conditions and rewards which fairly reflect individual performance. It has also introduced tax reliefs to encourage financial participation by employees;
>
> – to improve industrial relations. This has been through imposing restraints on trades unions and unofficial action;
>
> – to maintain a fair framework of individual employment rights while minimising costs to employers. In doing so the Government has sought to strike "the right balance".'[9]

A number of fascinating points and contradictions are to be found here. First, 'flexible labour markets' are not defined; simply

9 *Competitiveness: Helping Business to Win* Cm 2563 (HMSO, 1994) pp 50–51.

assumed. Labour markets are those which allow employers to be competitive with other products, not to bargain, signal to signal, with labour itself. Secondly, such markets encourage 'efficiency'. Again, there is no definition; only mere assumption. Efficiency in doing what to whom? Perhaps efficiency can be equated with profit maximisation, but that need have nothing to do with markets, nothing to do with human rights and nothing to do with 'choice'. 'Freeing up' labour markets ought, in strict logic, to mean offering some measure of human rights choice to labour and that must *prima facie* include organised labour since to associate with others is a basic human entitlement. The logic chopping of the White Paper is simply to 'strike the right balance', which leads nowhere in terms of rights or choice analysis.

What is interesting is that the document speaks of good employment practices as including 'genuine dialogue' and worker 'participation'. Now there can be little quarrel with that – dialogue is a major way of expressing the choices people wish to see adopted and participation in any aspect of social life leads back to basics; back to the social-ness of human interaction. Furthermore, the commitment to 'minimum standards' rekindles the commitment to some version of positive rights; to the level material playing field. All that is missing is a genuine analysis of the primary rights of labour, organised or otherwise. What is offered instead is a form of intuitive realism which pays lip-service to the workplace decencies without re-treading the ground of basic individual entitlement.

Without pretending that the exercise is anything but challenging in the extreme, what is needed is an attempt at constructing a rights-based scheme of entitlement between labour and capital. For most of living memory this issue has been contested as a war of all against all or it has not been contested at all, either out of collective frailty or in the belief that the state will regulate tolerable accommodations. What has not been much in evidence is an agenda characterised by a respect for mutual choice in capitalist relations. The industrial order has careered from one primitive response to another; from internecine strife to the near-total suppression of the aspirations of labour.

The 'original position' of capitalist exploitation, whether intentional or not, was to deny human rights and choice to vast swathes of workers who lived in intolerable conditions, died before their time and sold themselves to the nearest devils. This state of un-nature was, of course, superseded both by regulation and voluntary associations in order to alleviate conditions and assuage the raw inequalities inherent in the relationships. However, the primary issue of what basic conditions needed to be established for genuine choice to be restored across the divide was scarcely ever addressed.

Until the necessary conditions for choice to operate in the workplace, and indeed in the wider social sphere affected by capitalist relations, are identified, it will not be possible to allocate the optimum role for welfare associations and trade unions in their dealings with the power of capital. However, there is no doubt that they have an important part to play and that they have, in recent memory, been unfairly proscribed. It may be that 'old labour' is decaying but ways must be found of putting people back in touch with themselves as choosers and not beggars at work. It is almost certainly the case that the theoretical categories which apply to analysing markets more generally are inadequate to confront some of the central issues of the dignity of man posed by the workplace. Fairness, morale and the human motivation which fires human action all require more detailed investigation than they normally receive. As has been remarked elsewhere, it is likely that work may not be the 'disutility' often proclaimed by economists and that it may well be rational, for example, for workers to demand rewards from work which are not entirely economic. What if, after all, work and people are not mere commodities and that work 'offers a sense of place in a hierarchy of social relations'?[10]

One thing is certain: the facts of industrial life in the UK are at odds with a genuine commitment to choice. The most detailed survey of the evolution of worker–management relations in recent times indicates that modern companies have not replaced trade union influence with other devices. On the contrary, modern practices such as 'human resource management' are actually rarer in non-union than in union workplaces. Non-managerial employees are increasingly being treated as mere factors of production so that few employees have any mechanism through which they can contribute to the operation of their workplace in a broader context than that of their job. Recent growth in the inequality of wages and earnings is being matched by a widening in the inequalities of influence and access to key decisions about work and employment.[11]

One influential commentator, Handy, has argued that companies exist increasingly for 'themselves', without regard to their workforce, or indeed the wider community. In such circumstances he questions whether companies ought in law to be capable of

10 Will Hutton *The State We're In* (Jonathan Cape, London 1995) p 99.
11 Neil Millward *The New Industrial Relations* (Policy Studies Institute, London 1994).

being bought and sold like material objects by shareholders driven by the need for short-term dividends. If they wish to behave in such a fashion, they should, he insists, be treated as investors and not owners. The implication is that by operating as both they are denying the genuine choices of workers, consumers and others.[12] This is not the view expressed publicly by government, which refers to 'some form of employee involvement in over 90 per cent of all workplaces',[13] though no analytical evidence is provided to disturb the Policy Studies Institute thesis; rather there are sporadic references to self-managed teams and the occasional buy-out of a bus company. The White Paper on *Competitiveness* (Cm 2563) pledges itself to effective employee involvement while continuing to reject the European Commission's directive on information and consultation. The major government initiative in this area has been to produce a booklet on best practice.[14] The document is, however, short on philosophy and long on paternalism.

The UK's approach differs from that of the rest of the European Union under the Maastricht social protocol. In June 1994, the other members legislated to increase the rights of workers in multinational companies by establishing works councils in transnational companies with at least 1,000 employees in the community, excluding the UK. The law is designed to ensure that workers are consulted about strategic corporate decisions which could affect their livelihoods, such as changing technology, shifts in production from one country to another, or large-scale redundancies. What is important for present purposes is that the Social Affairs Commissioner has claimed that the law could improve the competitiveness of business by strengthening its most important asset: viz good relations between management and staff. It might be added that if, in the maelstrom of 'competing capitalisms', the Anglo-American model, especially the British, is ill-equipped to succeed in world markets, then some more co-operative form of capitalism might be needed. If so, the relations between labour and capital may need a root-and-branch reinstitutionalisation. It may well be that, in the longer term, the insistence on 'freeing-up' labour markets is inimical to the larger enterprise.

If labour is to be denied rights and if organised labour is to be restrained, then the social morality of such restraint, the inhibitions

12 Charles Handy *The Empty Raincoat* (Hutchinson, 1994) and for similar sentiments see Royal Society of Arts, 'Tomorrow's Company: The Role of Business in a Changing World', Interim Report 1994.
13 *Competitiveness: Helping Business to Win* Cm 2563 (HMSO, 1994) p 53.
14 *The Competitive Edge* (Employment Department, 1994).

on choice, need to be publicly defended. If choosing is to be extended to labour in its several forms, then the time is ripe for a wider political settlement in which the rights of labour are instituted as a basic constitutional entitlement. It has been said that the future of trades unions is not as a key governing interest in the state or as the vanguard of the working class. Rather, they are the vital social partners in managing a capitalist system so that the gains are spread more equitably. Otherwise, modern governments will have forfeited their claim to protect society's 'small platoons'.[15]

The rights of labour are intimately connected with the equally critical question of the nature of the modern corporation in aiding and abetting or inhibiting choice and human rights more generally. There are numerous models on offer and little would be gained by listing them here. However, Part III addresses the issue of the minimal constitutional and institutional responses to these dilemmas.

15 Will Hutton, *The Guardian*, 8 July 1994.

Chapter 7
Markets, competition, privatisation and regulation

MARKETS AND CHOICE

If choice at the generic level is part of life in the traditional democracies under rule of law constitutions, it is difficult to see how it can be limited to the realm of high politics and not inform, for example, economic life. *A fortiori* the same is true of social choice, or the right to choose how to live providing one is other-regarding. This must extend to the right to choose one's leisure pursuits, entertainment, privacy, to participate in the community, to be in company or to be left alone, to avail oneself of comradeship and so on.

The Council of Europe is expressly committed not only to a democratic society but also one which is pluralistic,[1] which suggests that market systems and politico-social systems are intimately connected. JK Galbraith speaks of the moral sanction of the market system stemming from the individual who is placed by the economic system in ultimate command of himself. This economic theory is associated with a political theory which places the citizen, as voter, in ultimate authority over the production of public goods:

> 'These economic and political theories are basic to a larger image of a democratic ... society which is comprehensively subordinate to the ultimate power of the individual. The individual being in charge, he cannot be in conflict with the economic or political system. He cannot be in conflict with what he commands.'[2]

---

1 *Declaration Regarding Intolerance: A Threat to Democracy,* adopted by the Committee of Ministers, 68th Session 1981 and para 6 of the 1982 Declaration on the Freedom of Expression and Information.
2 *Economics and the Public Purpose* (Penguin, London 1975) pp 29–30.

Not that things always turn out this way, as Galbraith himself makes clear; but this is the ruling theory. Others, in their several ways, take it for granted that a description of economic freedom must embody participation in the democratic process, even if they tend to the view that concentrations of wealth sustained over lengthy periods can endanger not only economic but political freedom too.[3] Gray, in particular, stresses that the defence of the market is best conducted not in terms of its contribution to an imaginary general or collective welfare, but instead by reference to the well-being of the individual. For him, the constituent ingredients of 'autonomy' are the capacity for rational deliberation and choice, the absence of coercion *and the possession of resources needed for a life that is at least partly self-directed.* There is also a wide measure of agreement, especially among those on the political right, that the kind of economic organisation that produces economic freedom also promotes political freedom because it separates economic power from political power and enables the one to offset the other.[4]

The market is also a powerful incentive system. The lure of profits encourages individuals to seek out better ways of satisfying the demands of customers. Markets, at their best, can be a highly efficient discovery process, and not only about existing circumstances. They generate new information by searching for unused opportunities that, when discovered, can be used by others. Furthermore, competition encourages and fosters innovation, risk-taking and entrepreneurship which is incapable of being centrally planned.

The most powerful aspect of competition, the supposed concomitant of markets, is how it challenges and threatens those established in any industry or institution. Competition through the development of a new commodity, new technology, new supply and new organisation is the most powerful form of innovation.[5] Several of these assumptions seem to be reinforcing, a point underscored by the Council of Europe.

3 Alan Peacock, 'Economic Freedom and Libertarian Thinking' in Christopher Johnson (ed) *The Market on Trial* Lloyds Bank Review vol 2 (Pinter Publishers, London/New York 1989). Amarta Sen, 'The Profit Motive' in Christopher Johnson (ed) *The Market on Trial* Lloyds Bank Review vol 2 (Pinter Publishers, London/New York 1989); John Gray *The Moral Foundations of Market Institutions* (Institute of Economic Affairs, 1992) and Norman Lewis, 'Markets, Regulation and Citizenship' in Roger Brownsword (ed) *Law and the Public Interest* (Franz Steiner, Stuttgart 1993).
4 See eg Milton Friedman *Capitalism and Freedom* (Chicago, 1962) pp 9–12.
5 Cento Veljanovski, 'Market Driven Broadcasting: Not Myth but Reality' (1990) 18 Intermedia (No 6) 18.

The 1982 Declaration on the Freedom of Expression and Information, to which reference has already been made, says:

'that the freedom of expression and information is necessary for the social, *economic,* cultural and political development of every human being, and constitutes a condition for the harmonious progress of social and cultural groups ...' (emphasis supplied)

This belief is directed to the individual's ability to discuss freely *political, social, economic and cultural matters.* The Committee on Security and Co-operation in Europe Final Accord in Moscow in 1991 also spoke of the development of societies 'based on pluralistic democracy'.

A number of matters now come together. First, the nature of these basic rights has to be reflected in clear constitutional terms. The sum total of choosing frameworks needs to be addressed, including the economic calculus. However, more specifically, if markets are to be about many-faceted transactions whereby signals are picked up and responded to in conditions of equality, then there are important repercussions for commercial and competition law. The classical market requires freely available information about product, price, quality, servicing and a range of other features, otherwise it is not a classical market. The duty of government then, becomes one of moving existing 'markets' as far as possible in the direction of classical markets lest free choice is impeded since what will exist is a set of second- or third-best options which may restrict political and social freedoms. David Green again:

'We have come through a long period during which the battle of ideas has been fought between two rival economic systems. The market economic system won the argument because it facilitated economic growth. But if communism had been capable of generating still greater growth, would that have been a decisive argument in its favour? Few think it would, yet much political debate occurs within a framework of economic rationalism. The battle against collectivist economics has led us to over-estimate the importance of markets in maintaining liberty and to neglect both the moral dimension of a free society and the corruption of law making by politics.'[6]

6 David Green *Reinventing Civil Society* (Institute of Economic Affairs, 1993) p 152.

Green believes that re-constitutionalising the UK and relocating the spirit of community are necessary preconditions for the moral universe to be affirmed in a setting which allows free individuals the maximum choice of lifestyle.

It has been shown that markets cannot emerge without the support of the state. The role of facilitative law is, then, crucial.

> 'Without law, markets will not even come into existence, at least in any efficient sense. Law is antecedent to market co-ordination, to the economic activity of agents, to the working of Adam Smith's invisible hand.'[7]

Others are more confident still in proclaiming that 'states create markets and the possibility of markets'. Indeed, a recent study has argued that even markets in international trade are not spontaneously organised but constructed and shaped by governments. The following is an even more powerfully presented view that markets, like human beings, can only operate within social settings. Their impersonality, therefore, is confined.

> 'What a man buys does not tell us what he wants from life; what he is able to sell is only to a small extent the fruit of his unaided efforts. There is in the background the society in which his wants and his efforts take shape, the facilities and opportunities, the social capital and the social pressures that condition his behaviour. We are more conscious perhaps than Adam Smith of the need to see the market within a social framework and of the ways in which the state can usefully rig the market without destroying its thrust.'[8]

The market order is thus a system of free exchange governed by rules which governments enforce, but it should not be subject to arbitrary and coercive intervention by government in relation to the details of exchanges between individuals. Freedom and compulsion are largely antithetic and it is clearly preferable that individuals should choose their own life-styles.

7 *Seriatim:* James M Buchanan, 'Public Goods and Natural Liberty' in T Wilson and A Skinner (eds) *The Market and the State: Essays in Honour of Adam Smith* (Clarendon Press, Oxford 1978).
8 Buchanan pp 272–277. Peter Evans, Dietrich Rushmeyer and Evelyne Stephens *States versus Markets in the World System* (Sage, 1985); Alexander Cairncross, 'The Market and the State' in T Wilson and A Skinner (eds) *The Market and the State: Essays in Honour of Adam Smith* (Clarendon Press, Oxford 1978) p 134.

Support for these sentiments can be found in the German Basic Law and its attendant jurisprudence, which is predicated on the compatibility of a free market with a socially conscious state. This Law seeks to promote a unified political economy based on the principles of personal freedom and social responsibility. But the freedom of the individual and the responsibility of the state are constrained by the constitutional framework within which the economy operates. This framework includes the rights of property and inheritance, freedom of choice in the exercise of a trade and profession, freedom to form and join economic or trade associations, freedom of commerce and industry flowing from the general right to personality and the principle of the social welfare state.[9]

THE SOCIAL MARKET

For some, the social market simply represents capitalism plus a substantial welfare state. This may be unacceptable to those who are opposed to the crowding out of civil society by the state. Green wishes to return to the view of the 'Ordo' group of liberals who belong in the liberal-classical tradition but who do not believe that markets are self-correcting. In particular this group saw industrial monopoly as a constant danger. They were critical of *laissez-faire* economics and believed that freedom rested not on markets alone, but on a well-constructed system of law and morals. Nevertheless, while expecting the state to assist the casualties of a market economy, they were concerned that the redistributive welfare state would destroy the fabric and richness of civil society by 'cramping the space for personal idealism'.[10] This is consistent with a return to obligation and to community, to self-help and to caring and sharing, and to an acceptance that the burdens of late-twentieth-century capitalism are too heavy to be borne by voluntary groups unaided.

Many of the former Iron Curtain countries are now constitutionally committed to a free market economy, to democracy and to some version of social fairness. Thus the Constitution of the Russian Federation, prepared with the active assistance of the European Commission for Democracy through Law, speaks of the social

9 Donald P Kommers *The Constitutional Jurisprudence of the Federal Republic of Germany* (Duke University Press, 1989).
10 *Green* pp137–138.

market economy, freedom of economic activity, diversity of ownership, and fair competition. It also proclaims the right of the state to
regulate economic life in the interests of the individual and society.
Economic relations are built on 'a social partnership between the
individual and the state, employee and employer and producer and
consumer'. The document goes on to stake out a claim both for
rights of ownership, free enterprise, the 'right to free labour' and a
raft of social rights similar to those adopted by the Council of
Europe. The right of the establishment of voluntary associations is
also guaranteed.

Documents such as these recognise real autonomous choice in a
coherent and patterned fashion. The economies of the region will
no doubt play havoc with the balancing act which the constitutions
appear to require, but the fact that such documents are drawn up
with the assistance and support of the Council of Europe shows
that the free world is moving in the direction of the full panoply of
human rights and an acceptance that genuine choice should have
constitutional foundations.

MARKETS AND EFFICIENCY

Most writing on markets relates to consumer markets or markets
for goods as opposed to investment goods,[11] yet the relevance of
some primary goods for the state is implicit in the demand for a
material level playing field of opportunities.[12] The market for corporate control, financial markets and the nature of international
markets are all too complex for treatment in a work such as this;
suffice it to say that there is currently considerable uncertainty
within and between governments on how far 'unbridled' competition should be permitted, how far protecting native industry is
justified and when regulation should be introduced to iron out dys-
functions, whether of a competitive or social variety. Legal and constitutional considerations have played only a minor part in what
have, up until now, been regarded as primarily political matters. It
is doubtful if this state of mind will be helpful in the future.

---

11 Nove, however, seems to argue that many of the same considerations must apply:
A Nove *The Economics of Feasible Socialism* (Allen and Unwin, London 1983).
12 And see Norman Lewis, 'Markets, Regulation and Citizenship' in Roger
Brownsword (ed) *Law and the Public Interest* (Franz Steiner, Stuttgart 1993) especially at pp 117–120.

It is clear that, constitutional entitlements apart, efficiency is a contested concept. A short excursus will help the argument. There are at least three aspects to economic efficiency: allocative, internal and dynamic. Allocative efficiency needs no further rehearsal. Internal refers to the provision of any given level of output at the minimum attainable cost. Dynamic efficiency can best be grasped as the reproduction of allocative and internal efficiency over time in the face of technological and taste changes by an appropriate investment path. The fundamental mechanism for achieving this is a structure of sanctions and incentives to evaluate static efficiency in present value terms. The relationship between these different concepts, and their bearing on competition is complex and controversial.

'However it is certainly the case that internal efficiency is a necessary but not a sufficient condition for allocative efficiency.'[13]

Even leaving social considerations out of account, there may well be good reason for the state to intervene or regulate in order to secure longer-term 'dynamic efficiency'. Added to this dilemma for the policy-maker is a problem which the accountancy profession has recognised, that of identifying the efficiency of market and quasi-market operations. Thus it has been argued that many accountants' criteria for assessment are social constructions or deliberate choices to express matters in preferred ways. According to this view, accountancy is not a neutral art but a series of techniques for presenting a particular version of reality. The most obvious illustration of a highly selective form of receptivity to outside disturbances is regarding the effects of activity on the natural environment as non-facts.[14] Even governments admit that current accounting practices 'may favour companies which grow by acquisition rather than organically'.[15]

MARKETS AND COMPETITION

Competition seems a simple concept and yet its nature is often the subject of fierce dispute. An influential and independent report says

13 Michael Williams, 'The Political Economy of Privatization' in Martin Holland and Jonathan Boston (eds) *The Fourth Labour Government: Politics and Policy in New Zealand* (2nd edn, Oxford University Press, 1992) p 149.
14 Michael Power, 'The Politics of Financial Accounting' (1993) 64 Political Quarterly 272 *et seq*.
15 *Competitiveness: Helping Business to Win* Cm 2563 (HMSO, 1994) p 103.

that to be internationally competitive today a company needs a supportive operative environment. Businesses are increasingly having to compete for the attention and approval of individuals, be they customers, suppliers, workers, investors or members of the community in which they operate. Much influenced by Germany, where companies are often seen as social enterprises, and Japan, where they are regarded more as communities, the report predicts that tomorrow's company will identify its key relationships, define its measures of success in each case, set itself appropriate targets, evaluate its performance against those targets and ultimately report on all its stakeholder relationships.[16] A business, it is claimed, is no longer just an economic instrument and it should not be forgotten that the original meaning of a company was a group of companions, members one of another.[17]

Over and above these complications there is the concept of 'destructive competition'; for example, where the most efficient production techniques require heavy fixed asset costs so that short and long-term marginal costs differ, where demand is variable and entry by competitors is attractive at periods of high demand. Here competition may lead to pricing below the level necessary to ensure capital replacement at the optimal level. Left alone, the market would not allow the most efficient techniques to prevail. Furthermore, it is accepted that dominance of the market by a single supplier may be desirable since natural monopoly has the lowest costs and therefore makes optimal use of the resources of the economy.[18]

A recent United Nations study found that trans-national corporations account for one-third of global output and that one-third of all world trade is already intra-firm.[19] Because of this, questions regarding the social responsibilities of these corporations demand increasing attention, as do the critical issues of redefining policies and confronting national governments. Nor is there clear agreement on what contribution classical markets and competition have made to the recently thriving economies. To take the case of the Asian economies, the World Bank believes that the 'Tigers' have established global competitive advantage through the rigours of competition, although it admits that market-friendly government

16 Royal Society of Arts, 'Tomorrow's Company: The Role of Business in a Changing World' Interim Report 1994.
17 And see Charles Handy *The Empty Raincoat* (Hutchinson, 1994).
18 See Cecil Rajana *Liberalisation, Deregulation and their Impact on Enterprise Performance: Exploratory Issues in Public Policy* (Indian Institute of Public Administration, New Delhi, July 1994).
19 *The Guardian*, 31 August 1994.

intervention has been important.[20] However, this view has been contested by others who claim that vigorous interventionist policies have been pursued which greatly assisted structural change. Markets were only opened up to free trade later and when it suited them.[1] One point emerges clearly: both markets and competition need redefinition so that a clear-headed view of what is happening in world trade is developed by governments who should intervene according to their economic and social priorities. They ought not to seek to plan except in a broad-brush fashion, but they must have the best information possible upon which to take decisions and should have a clear view of national priorities.

Governments understandably wish, through trade policy, export promotion and the like, to help 'compete more effectively in international markets'. Sometimes government has sat by and watched British businesses disappear on the grounds that the market knows best, while at other times it has sought to help British business to win. Nonetheless, it continues to assert the need for strong competition at home to enhance international competitiveness.[2] Empirically such competition is infrequent; the world is not like that. However, even imperfect markets are more likely to guarantee choice than any alternative model on offer while government needs to be sure that it understands the logistics of intervention. All-knowing governments are a danger of the most severe kind, but they have a duty to attempt to understand what they can by the best methods available if they are not to fail to aspire to their citizens' conception of the good life.

Consideration will have to be given to some constitutional or sub-constitutional set of principles such as a commitment to market economics, economic growth and social justice. The theme will not be developed yet but deliberative standing machinery, once established, would help to ensure that research and deliberations were centrally informed by these principles.

THE RECENT PAST

In recent years governments have sought to extend choice and some version of competition into public services. Sometimes they

---

20 WBD Report 1991.
1 Ajit Singh (1993) 7 International Review of Applied Economics 109.
2 See *Competitiveness: Helping Business to Win* Cm 2563 (HMSO, 1994) especially at pp 81 and 137–138.

have been privatised, at others contracted out after competitive tender and, more recently, 'market-tested'.[3] All these experiments chime with the logic of choice, diversity and experiment and many of them are to be welcomed at face value. The major reservations must concern the machinery adopted to arrive at these decisions.

Contracting out of public services on the present scale is a recent phenomenon and yet contract has always been associated with choice and markets. How far choice is actually secured by contracting out is an open issue,[4] yet in principle there ought to be many occasions when it is actually enhanced. However, there are other advantages of contracting out, not least in the potential for promoting constitutional values through an institutional separation of functions. The parties to contracts have separate interests and it is important to make that clear just as it is valuable to reduce unnecessary administrative discretion. Experimentation in choice of providers also promises many advantages, while removing delivery functions from government provides the opportunity for policies to be more carefully and intelligently crafted.[5]

The reforms which have taken place are in their early stages but current research indicates a very mixed picture given the stated objectives. In particular, as has been mentioned, there is some evidence that the reforms are more cost-driven than choice-driven and that such choice as there is is more likely to be made by the purchaser than the consumer.

There is no doubt that recent British governments have been bold and radical in introducing new experiments across the face of British public life. The fact that the record is so mixed and many of the successes questionable reinforces the argument that the British state and its institutions are too centralised and insufficiently informed to deliver on policies which might well command broad agreement.

PRIVATISATION, EFFICIENCY AND COMPETITION

It is worth stating at the outset that 'Privatisation is not a rigid ideological policy of marketisation, but shorthand for a group of

3 See eg *Next Steps Review 1993* Cm 2430 (HMSO, 1993).
4 See Osborne and Gaebler *Reinventing Government* (Addison Wesley, New York 1992).
5 See eg Norman Lewis *How to Reinvent British Government* (European Policy Forum, London 1993) and Ian Harden *The Contracting State* (Open University Press, Milton Keynes 1992).

policies able to assist in the transition of the inefficient into the productive.'[6] It has been pursued for a number of reasons, some ideological, some simply political and some economic.[7] In the Foreword to the 1991 White Paper *Competing for Quality*[8] the following statement is to be found:

> 'Services may be bought either from the private sector or within the public sector: we have no dogmatic preference for either ... we believe that public sector managers and staff will welcome the opportunity to compare the services they provide *in fair and open competition with the best of the private sector'*. (emphasis added)

Yet the White Paper *Continuity and Change*[9] heralded a move from market-testing to straight privatisation. This is because market-testing is expensive and private sector bidders are reluctant to bid when most contracts are won in-house. This would indicate a preference for privatisation and hostility to the public sector regardless of quality. This would not only represent unaccountable politics but a diminution of choice.[10]

Even so, the advantages of privatisation have been stoutly argued:

> 'Whereas reform of the public sector through cost cutting and restructuring merely delays the reassertion of monopolistic and inefficient practices, a direct break with the public sector through privatisation frees the entity to identify and then to engage in what should be its primary function, the efficient delivery of a given service or product.
>
> The most important aspect of this process is in reacquainting the unit, be it the airline, a trucking firm or a steel plant, with its commercial objectives. No longer under political control it will be able to build plant where it is most cost effective to do so, raise capital on the open market without the need to consider the budgetary constraints of government, and set

---

6 Graham Ward, 'Reforming the Public Sector: Privatisation and the Role of Advisers' (1993) 64 Political Quarterly 301.
7 Cosmo Graham and Tony Prosser *Privatizing Public Enterprises* (Clarendon Press, Oxford 1991) especially the Introduction.
8 Cm 1730 (HMSO, 1991).
9 Cm 2627 (HMSO, 1994).
10 And see John Sheldon *The Financial Times*, 8 June 1994, but see *Taking Forward Continuity and Change* Cm 2748 (HMSO, 1995).

prices at a market level rather than as a result of political sensitivities to consumer response.'[11]

Yet none of this is unchallenged. There is no reason to suppose
that merely transferring a natural monopoly from public into private hands will produce an output more valued by consumers or
that gains in allocative efficiency will only come about via gains in
internal efficiency. Support for privatisation therefore should rest
on the increased internal and dynamic efficiency imposed by capital market competition. Williams concludes, on the available evidence, that the effects of ownership on allocative efficiency are
indeterminate, and that it is increased competition rather than
changes of ownership *per se* which generates gains in internal efficiency.

The lessons for political science are straightforward. They are
that it is not possible to assess efficiency in abstraction from the
social ends of economic activity which cannot simply be reduced to
market-enforced commercial objectives. Again, although the separation of the state and the economy is generally desirable, it is
equally true that the mixed economy has evolved as a means of
managing the social inadequacies of unrestrained market mechanisms, so that any significant shift in the mix 'can be expected to
ameliorate one set of problems only by exacerbating others'.[12]

Privatisation has been one of the key players on the recent political stage and is part of a huge constitutional shift which, regardless
of the merits of the changes worked, has been such as to merit the
kind of constitutional debate which current political institutions
do not allow.[13] New Zealand, on the other hand, has been more
open and principled. Thus, Annex 4 to the 1988 Budget statement
lays down the government's objectives, principles, criteria and
guidelines for asset sales. They include reducing public debt, subjecting state-owned enterprises to professional business management, avoiding future demands for government cash and

---

11 Graham Ward, 'Reforming the Public Sector: Privatisation and the Role of the
Advisers' (1993) 64 Political Quarterly 299.
12 Michael Williams, 'The Political Economy of Privatization' in Martin Holland
and Jonathan Boston (eds) *The Fourth Labour Government: Politics and Policy in
New Zealand* (2nd edn, Oxford University Press, 1992) p 149. The treatment of
efficiency at pp 149–160 is the best yet observed by this present non-economist
author. If half-true it lays waste much of the political programmes of the past
15–20 years.
13 Norman Lewis, 'Regulating Non-Governmental Bodies: Privatization,
Accountability and the Public–Private Divide' in Jeffrey Jowell and Dawn Oliver
(eds) *The Changing Constitution* (2nd edn, 1989) pp 219–246.

minimising commercial risk and enabling ministers to concentrate on economic and social policy. Each sale is assessed on a case-by-case basis with the overriding objective the maximising of both economic welfare and revenue to the Exchequer.

It has been made quite clear that the case for privatisation is separate from the case made for efficiency. There are publicly owned enterprises in New Zealand that are efficient by any standards. Of course both corporatisation and privatisation seek to improve efficiency, not only in the affected markets but also in the markets in which the industries become actors. Furthermore, privatisation must not to impede the government's broader macroeconomic or social policy. This implies that the cost of any particular asset sale must include those of making good any degradation of objectives, including social objectives – eg employment considerations.[14]

Nevertheless, there remains something in the argument that private enterprise may be generally preferred. In a private enterprise both internal control by the shareholders and external control by the capital market provide incentives to avoid inefficiency. Shareholders monitor managers to ensure that they maximise income and failure to do so will lead to the sale of shares with other managerial groups bidding for control of the company in the belief that they will be able to obtain a better return for the company's resources. In a public enterprise, capital market monitoring does not work, while internal monitoring will be performed by politicians who are not necessarily interested in how efficiently managers allocate resources. This is the bottom-line justification for private market enterprise, and to modify it requires careful justification.

The justification for privatisations in Britain has never been made clear and empirically would seem to have shifted over time. No grand theological debate has taken place; nor is there an obvious theatre for such an event.

REGULATION

Regulation is almost always a second-best enterprise and many studies have indicated that it is in itself an inherently 'inefficient' process. Even so there are notorious externalities which need to be addressed. It is worth summarising some of the conclusions of the

14 *Williams* p 146.

Royal Society of Arts Report on 'Tomorrow's Company' (Interim Report 1994). UK trade in manufactured goods moved into deficit in 1983 for the first time since the industrial revolution. Only 6% of UK companies proved to be in the 'best performer' section in a survey comparing them with six of the leading industrial nations. Short-termism, lack of investment and over-concern with shareholders, partly encouraged by the structure of company law, were all identified. Some classic blunders have been committed as a result of a *laissez-faire* approach.

At the turn of the last century, the potential of electricity was becoming clear and many believed that the British government should pressurise industry into constructing a national grid. The City of London, however, would only provide the money for the super-profitable parts of the country to receive electricity. Commitment to free markets prevented Britain from following the German example where government had given a strong lead. As a result, Britain entered the century without a national grid or a strong power generating industry. Some consider that the same mistake may be about to be made with the fibre optic network, not least because of government's reluctance to interfere with markets.[15] At the global level, two of Britain's biggest overseas aid charities, Christian Aid and Oxfam, have accused the World Bank of impoverishing the third world by relying on market-oriented policies involving spending cuts.[16] And so on.

Recent observations on the nature of capitalism by UK observers have international counterparts. So, for instance, in the USA it has been said that developments in the twentieth century have undermined the 'privateness' of major business corporations, with the result that the traditional bases for distinguishing them from public corporations have largely disappeared. Indeed there have been US experiments in adding so-called 'public' members to corporate boards of directors, while more recently the fact of public interest in 'market' economic activity has been recognised by the open creation of corporations as mixed public–private entities.[17]

There are many reasons for regulating desired goals into existence.[18]

---

15 Will Hutton, *The Guardian*, 28 June 1994.
16 *The Guardian*, 20 June 1994.
17 Gerald E Frug, 'The City as a Legal Concept' (1980), 93 Harv LR 1129–1139; however on similar themes see the much earlier influential work of A Berle and G Means *The Modern Corporation and Private Property* (1932) and the heavy footnoting of Frug.
18 But see Norman Lewis, 'Markets, Regulation and Citizenship' in Roger Brownswood (ed) *Law and the Public Interest* (Franz Steiner, Stuttgart 1993) especially at pp 126–130.

Even New Right (NR) governments will intervene when they see fit, whether to encourage public–private partnerships or to encourage industry to open state schools in conjunction with parent groups. The recent debate on how Britain's man-made environment can be improved is instructive. Government officials have stressed the need to pay attention to the design of buildings, the layout of communities, creation of successful town centres, the preservation of heritage and much else besides.[19] There is no denying the pace of continued regulation. What is more evasive is a clear unifying philosophy.

There are avant-garde methods of service delivery and budget-stretching through seed-corn experiments, equity investments, the sale or leasing of property, joint ventures etc. The logic of markets, the logic of choice, extends to politics too. Local communities can, to paraphrase, represent the mother of all invention. This is one way to attempt to achieve what Vibert refers to as the need to produce a constant response to changing customer needs, to examine alternative means of provision, to review what the market will provide and where the gaps are; to look at how the public and private can best relate and to promote competition between public and private providers.[20] There are other ways to provide public services and funding short of the traditional ones if government is imaginative enough. However, there is a need to think these matters through institutionally.

What requires attention is the untheoretic, pragmatic approach to regulation in the UK.[1]

'There is no tradition that utilities, as natural monopolies, are somehow held in common. Regulation was designed to be "light" and "flexible", mimicking what private competition would have achieved had the industries not been monopolies. As a regulatory concept this is woeful, allowing a wide range of views as to how the beast might be shadowed. One regulator may interpret the competitive model as an excuse for breaking up the industry into smaller competing parts; another for setting maximum rates of return; another for regarding pressure from the capital markets as a surrogate for competition and allowing the monopoly to remain intact. None of them have any clear idea of the national or common interest; some may

19 *Financial Times*, 14 June 1994.
20 Frank Vibert, 'Contract and Accountability, the Social Market and the Fourth Term', speech to the Annual Conference of the Tory Reform Group 1992.
 1 And see Tony Prosser, 'Privatisation, Regulation and Public Services' (1994) Judicial Review 3–17.

feel that it is naturally achieved by competition, others that it has to be asserted.'[2]

There is a recognition that primary public interests are involved and yet regulation is characteristically conducted by bargaining with 'partners' responsible to their shareholders and to no other stakeholders. An open regulatory framework operating within a context of citizen rights and due process has not so far recommended itself to those responsible for the repair of the machinery of government.

With such an attitude towards pragmatic adjustment, with a mind-set not dominated by the concept of rights, the market has become a dominating theme in itself rather than being an instrument for the delivery of choice. If people must be treated as ends rather than means then it follows that the market must be treated as a means and not an end. Current regulatory institutions do not operate on this basis. It is hardly surprising therefore that regulation of the larger economy in the interests of the long-term needs of the country is largely absent, thus denying the likelihood of predictable and stable growth over time.

CONCLUSIONS

Although respectful disagreement with Sir Isaiah Berlin has been widely expressed, there is also common ground. He makes it clear that he cannot accept full market freedom as the value to be prized above all others. He is unsparing in his criticism of *laissez-faire* as having been destructive of the conditions for liberty and regarded the case for state intervention to secure these conditions as overwhelmingly strong.[3] What has been missing is a clear and public philosophical programme grounded in a contemporary catalogue of human rights operating alongside a set of congruent social and economic objectives interpreted through processes of institutional fact-finding and dialogue.

There is something wrong when City institutions can overturn the wishes of a large majority of individual shareholders who wish to appoint a consumer watchdog to the board of directors of a recently-privatised water company. Increased customer complaints

2 Will Hutton *The State We're In* (Jonathan Cape, London 1995) p 291.
3 Isaiah Berlin *Four Essays on Liberty* (Oxford, 1959).

and concern with the natural environment appeared unimportant to a board concerned only to pressure institutional shareholders into proxy compliance.[4] This is evidence of a more general failure to recognise the essential nature of the public corporation, its changing role and the fact that public participation in the economic activity so generated is largely involuntary. There is a failure to recognise that efficiency has different facets and is interpreted differently by different constituencies; there is a failure to confront raw economic power in its relationships with individual citizens, groups of citizens and their needs. The present system of company law is unbalanced and unresponsive.

Frug argued that the defence of the business corporation as a means of decentralising power, equivalent in many ways to the desirability of federal politics, does not in itself justify the preference of corporate power to what he called 'city' power:

'Indeed, it is ironic to defend the currently hierarchical, massively centralized corporate structure on the basis of decentralization of power. If by corporate independence we seek economic independence from a centralized state . . . cities could perform these tasks as well as corporations now do. For the vast majority of people who deal with corporations only as consumers, workers or neighbors, corporations serve no purpose that any other form of centralization could not also serve.'[5]

This statement has to be seen in the context of seeing city powerlessness preventing the realisation of public freedom; the ability of persons to participate actively in the basic social decisions that structure their lives. The public/private distinction no longer justifies protecting corporate power against the wishes of those who live in affected communities. Current structures appear, ironically, to value hierarchical organisation over more democratic forms.

It is easy to resist Professor's Frug's conclusions and yet many of the notes he strikes chime with contemporary views about choice and delegation. Market models are generally to be preferred over state models; central planning is discredited; the market is an arena with huge potential for citizen choice. Yet contemporary markets are extraordinarily mixed; competition is both contested and distorted; efficiency can be measured in numbers of different ways and the interests of large corporations often conflict with the interests both of elected governments and citizen needs. This

4 *Financial Times*, 30 September 1994.
5 Gerald E Frug, 'The City as a Legal Concept' (1980) 93 Harv LR 1142–1143.

morass of economic activity takes place within social and political constructs which help create and/or define them. The souls of individuals are the elective concern of politicians and the architectural concern of statesmen at the constitutional level.

Not everyone will wish to go the way of the Constitution of the new Republic of Albania where art 10 reads:

> 'The country's economy is based on the diversity of ownership, the free initiative of all economic subjects and the regulatory role of the state.
>
> Economic initiative of juridical and physical persons cannot develop contrary to the social interest and should not impair the security, freedom and dignity of man.'

But some may think the sentiments aptly expressed.

Part III
A jurisprudence for modern politics

Chapter 8
The legal order

RISING ABOVE POLITICS

The preceding chapters go to the heart of current political dilemmas and try to make sense of them. The discussion has attempted to show where apparently disparate arguments are related and the position has been adopted that social, economic and political fabrics through time exist to satisfy the needs of human beings. This is not a claim that it is possible to understand the total environment or to avoid mistakes committed with the best of intentions. It is merely to argue that it is crucial to attempt to identify overarching principles and to use them to usher in improvements. That is the basic proposition.

There is a degree of common ground, almost amounting to unanimity, that man is a choosing animal and that social systems ought to reflect that. However, it is rare in discussions of politics to go beyond these simple but rich propositions and to analyse their inner natures so that what is almost universally believed becomes what is almost universally desired. A jurisprudence for modern politics should reflect that state of affairs.

A word needs to be said at this point about 'the legal order' in which so much faith is being invested. Although the constitution is paramount and pre-eminent, and although it allows elected politicians under appropriate conditions to make 'laws', there is now beginning to appear a middle range of legal order which is 'almost constitutional', a range composed of not quite 'ordinary' laws but laws which are capable of reflecting uncertainty about how people get from some places to others. Some beliefs are very strongly held without knowing how they can be expressed with sufficient clarity as to define their precise shape or to know precisely how they might find practical expression in the years ahead. Even so, it is becoming increasingly clear that to liberate the human spirit more is needed than periodic elections which enable fashionable nostrums to dictate the passage of laws which appear to have legitimacy and yet which do enormous damage to the life chances of countless individuals.

What is needed is a constitution which encourages politics and political institutions, to say nothing of social and civic arrangements, to maximise the potential for choice across the national landscape. This is not the constitution which exists in the UK but is the one which the logic of claims about choice suggests that it should have. Such a constitution will have a lot of work to do and as such it needs to be crafted with considerable skill.

The constitutional structure is the framework on which hangs the state. And given that the state is not just a set of institutional arrangements but a set of purposes too, the irreducible legal order needs some vision of what the state is for. It is no good providing a mere framework in which any old argument can be disputed between combatants. Institutions are important and it is vital that the right ones are chosen, but they are there to advance human beings' natures and their needs. Legal scholars have traditionally taken their assumptions from the nature of the legal order of shared but unspoken understandings, an approach which avoids all the difficult and important questions.[1] Constitutional lawyers above all should know that their labours cannot be theory-free and that advocating choice is to assume a view of human nature. A legal order which does not recognise this state of affairs is bogus and illegitimate. It is time that constitutional scholarship broadened its horizons to proclaim its commitments to social action as well as to endorse the proposition that a free-willing society is hostile to central direction and that the institutions of society, both political and social, must be mutually interactive through a system of checks and balances. As Green has put it: 'liberty was always that combination of institutions which saw life as a struggle against human imperfection'.[2] A part of this understanding necessitates a constitutional appreciation that legal autonomy is a precious metal reflecting the necessary separation of the processes of law from the implementation of political programmes.

Although the state is forbidden to be intrusive, it must still be the ringmaster orchestrating the performance and, from time to time, the institutional restructuring of the state to fulfil its primary purposes will need to be considered. This is such a time. In recent years there has been a welcome acceptance of the fact that the consumer

1 RG Collingwood *An Essay in Metaphysics* (Clarendon, 1940).
2 David Green *Reinventing Civil Society* (Institute of Economic Affairs, 1993) p 134.

of public no less than private services should not be regarded as a passive recipient. However, the further imaginative leap has not taken place. The position has not yet been reached where the role of the citizen in assessing the utility and relevance of the services provided is systemically recognised. To some extent 'politics' has been replaced by a kind of market but it is a centralist market, the logic of which is contradictory since it assumes that the terms of the 'contract' under which the public service consumer consumes is set by the monolithic public service itself. Virtue, on the other hand, necessitates the citizen's active role in politics as well as his role as consumer. Furthermore, none of these consumers is in fact alone but is located in informal networks. Wherever possible, the presentation of community interests should be arranged so as to create opportunities for hearing the voices of those affected.

The state which bonds with free-willing citizens is a state comprised of pluralistic forces and associations. Not only does this necessitate a strong commitment to federalism for political institutions, but it implies support for intermediary organisations between citizen and state. Where people group together to express common interests it is important that those groupings have standing and are recognised as legitimate partners in the conduct of state business both at the national and local level. The sentiments of recent administrations in the UK have, after all, been to endorse the enfranchisement of local people in the government of their affairs, albeit that this has taken the form of enfeebling representative politics. The impulse is correct even if the form it has taken has been less than heroic. It is, of course, crucial that the voice of the people be heard at regular and not merely spasmodic intervals. This means that not only must local politics be resuscitated but that such politics should interact with a wide range of forms of community expression.

THE FAILURE OF THE PRESENT

There have been genuine advances in recent years. The Next Steps (NS) initiative has produced gains but it has done so at the same time as revealing the hollowness of ministerial responsibility. It cannot be stated forcefully enough that the relatively low profile of constitutional and administrative law in the UK is directly linked to the claim that ministerial responsibility to Parliament provides the core democratic protection lacking in non-Westminster systems.

Once that claim can be shown to be unsubstantiated, then it becomes apparent that there is a hole in the heart of the nation's accountability mechanisms. Parliament can and should be reformed; it is a vital artery in the network of nationhood, but it requires reinforcement in a number of respects.

The report of the Treasury and Civil Service Select Committee of the House on the Role of the Civil Service in 1994 is an important document. Its recommendations do not always coincide with the views expressed to it by government spokesmen, even if they are not exceptionally radical; yet the lacunae in the system are plain for all to see. Secrecy has always characterised the practice of British politics. Where the truly important decisions are shielded from public gaze by a culture of secrecy, then it is extraordinarily difficult to contest the official viewpoint and to mount effective counter-challenges.

In a country such as Britain, it hardly needs to be said that there is an in-built hostility to arbitrary power. Unfortunately, the ruling assumption is that a democratically elected Parliament able to call ministers to account is a sufficient condition to preclude the accumulation of such power. Formally, the judiciary constitutes the other part of the guarantee and its record in building up a commitment to the rule of law should never be underestimated. However, in spite of the recent advances made in the jurisprudence of judicial review, the law, to use Dyson's telling phrase, has never been 'the great interpreter of the pattern of politics'.[3] As executive dominance has become the reality and the sovereign Parliament the shadow, a constitutional and administrative legal order has not emerged to reinforce the sentiments underlying the rule of law which represented a commitment to oppose arbitrary power. Perhaps the rule of law never claimed to be the facilitator for a citizenry which could engage in the full range of self-discovery, but it undoubtedly set out its stall to oppose arbitrary and capricious conduct by the governors. Even that crucial rule has not been refurbished to cope with the changing times.

Few of the changes of a 'constitutional' nature introduced in recent years have been legislated for. Legislation and legal processes are still not central to the landscape of political change and conduct. This is a disturbing feature since it suggests a lack of conviction. Moreover, unfolding patterns of accountability and institutional maturity often accompany judicial analysis and legal exegesis. A government bent on citizen empowerment should pay

3 Kenneth Dyson *The State Tradition in Western Europe* (Martin Robertson, Oxford 1980).

respect to the separation of powers rather than letting an unaccountable centre determine what role the market should play, what imperfections to its operation should be allowed, how much regulation there should be, what level and quality of public service should be provided et al. Privatisation is but one issue and yet it will serve as well as any to illustrate the problem. The underlying dilemmas have been discussed; yet not all legal systems treat them in the same way. As leading commentators have said:

> 'In France the constitutional provision can be seen not as a straightforward prohibition on such privatization, but as the requirement of a particularly demanding form of democratic scrutiny for such fundamental change.'[4]

Some other legal systems seek to guarantee more than a level of rational policy debate, critical though that is. The Indian Constitution is particularly interesting in proclaiming both human rights and self-development. It was a product of a very particular set of circumstances but dealt with them 'not as a neutral parchment' but as a document containing within itself a policy with a distinctive sub-set of philosophical commitments. Its crucial features for present purposes are arts 12–35 which guarantee specific enforceable fundamental rights and the more unusual (in constitutional terms) arts 36–51 which set out 'non-justiciable' directive principles of state policy and governance aimed at the furtherance of social justice. The Preamble also contains a commitment to secure for all citizens 'Justice, social, economic and political'.

This powerful constellation of juridical materials has been given impetus since the late 1970s by a remarkable degree of judicial activism usually summarised as either 'Public Interest Litigation' or 'Social Action Litigation', which has seen the constitution interpreted expansively to enforce the rights to life, livelihood, dignity, freedom and cultural and educational rights as well as to be free from pollution. In the establishment of these particular facets of justice, the non-justiciable directive principles can be identified as having played the most creative role. Among the most significant achievements have been the widening of the doctrine of standing, allowing the courts to shift from traditional individualism to a broader community orientation, the simplification of proceedings even to the point of developing an 'epistolary jurisdiction', the appointment of public fact-finding commissions of enquiry to

4 Cosmo Graham and Tony Prosser *Regulating the Privatized Industries* (Oxford University Press, 1991).

relieve a petitioner from difficult burdens of proof, the monitoring of orders made by the court, and new remedies initiating affirmative action.

The Indian courts have also shown that broadly-stated human rights can contain the seeds of an elaborate set of expectations both political and social. The landmark decision of *Maneka Gandhi v Union of India*[5] interpreted a fundamental right of the constitution as a positive right for the first time, so breaking with the European liberal tradition. This decision has resulted in the state having to create the necessary conditions for the enjoyment of those rights in appropriate cases. The significance of this approach for the juristic enterprise is considerable, timely and worthy of the closest study by lawyers in the rest of the common law world. Other decisions are equally striking to the common lawyer versed in the British system. For example, the right to human dignity has been held to be implicit in the fundamental right to life and liberty.[6] The right to life, pregnant with atomic crystals in the view of the Indian judiciary, has been held to be 'more than mere animal existence' and embraces the 'right to livelihood' and perhaps even more significantly the 'quality of life'. In this latter instance for the residents of hilly areas access to roads was held to be life itself, and the state government was ordered to take ameliorative steps.[7]

Bolder still have been the attempts of the courts to grapple with the right to a clean environment and they have ordered the government to evolve a national policy for the location of toxic or hazardous industries. Articles 21 and 32 have been the pegs upon which most of these arguments have been hung. The former deals with the protection of life and personal liberty; the latter with the right to constitutional remedies.[8] Now constitution-makers in Europe may wish to shy away from creating a rights-based version of the social compact ultimately enforceable through the courts, but, at the end of the day, it is dishonourable to speak of citizens having rights and then to let governments play fast and loose with them on the basis that they have been elected to carry out sensitive programmes which require a delicate balancing of interests.

The Indian example is a reminder that real constitutions do not

5 AIR 1978 SC 597.
6 *Doctor Upendra Baxi v The State of Uttar Pradesh* (1983) 2 SCC 308.
7 *Olga Tellis v Bombay Municipal Corporation* AIR 1986 SC 180 and *State of Himachil Pradesh v Umedram* (1985) 3 SCC 545.
8 For a summary of these developments and a more general treatment of Indian judicial activism see Yasmin Shehnaz Meer, 'Litigating with Fundamental Right: Rights Litigation and Social Action Litigation in India' (1993) 15 Delhi Law Review 38–57.

permit the derogation of human rights or arrogating the nature of the right to choose to a paternalistic central authority. On the contrary, the language of choice, of the New Right and of the demure state insists on the opposite. But the logic of the positions adopted has not been followed through. If there is something bigger than governments – the right of individuals to express themselves, the opportunity to live in communities and groupings of one's own choosing – it requires institutional expression. At this point the legal order and legal autonomy is the only player in the field, so much so that appeals to it have attracted some unlikely bedfellows. Consider the position adopted by the New Republicans in the USA, characterised by the speaker of the Congress, Mr Gingrich. In 1995 he sought to introduce a balanced budget amendment to the US Constitution which would restrict the ability of politicians to tax and spend as they please. In other words, he was prepared to allow a court to instruct elected parliamentarians to cut social security programmes.

> 'They think that they cannot be trusted to put away the old pork barrel. Ideally they want judges and lawyers to keep them in their place.'[9]

None of this suggests that law should replace politics. However, the conventional law/politics dichotomy is misleading and needs to be substituted with a law/politics spectrum where the middle is perhaps a bit of each. Political institutions need to be reformed and expanded; the procedures of Parliament need to be altered to reinstate some semblance of information and debate in the political process. If the political machinery reflects national needs and understandings, the formal legal system will necessarily be low-key. However, there is not such a clear divide between law and politics as is usually claimed. The ombudsman, for example, may be seen to be an ancillary political device yet equally it may be thought to be part of the informal legal order. It matters not as long as the total set of institutions and values reflects basic needs.

The legal order is also more diffuse than is commonly accepted. The great issues of state, including human rights, must ultimately rest with the courts. But courts are long-stops and quality-control devices and not carts pulling horses. On the other hand, the legal order can make a contribution different in kind from its traditional role. If, for example, something approximating to the

9 *The Guardian*, 6 March 1995.

Indian directives of state policy were to be adopted, this would afford the legal system a more normative role than is traditional. Such principles could play an exhortatory and/or directive role in the large spaces left between clear constitutional rights and duties and factionalised politics. However, institutions intermediate to the courts and the political machine can also play a crucial constitutional role if they are crafted intelligently.

New Public Management, public choice theory, and an enabling state can live harmoniously with a revised legal order which is committed to open debate. Contract, for example, has become a fashionable political creed with considerable potential in the public sphere providing it operates in a conducive atmosphere.

> 'The use of contract has a valuable role to play, but within a broader constitutional and legal framework which encourages a more considered and open set of consultative practices throughout policy and management processes. Structured competition cannot be regarded as a substitute for reasoned policy and planning. To ensure resources and objectives are properly matched, further consideration needs to be given to financial, management and information schemes. All the objectives espoused here can be significantly affected by the quality of developments in law as well as the exigencies of economics and politics.'[10]

THE GOLDEN METWAND

Law is best understood as an institutional expression of legitimate order. Thus, 'the rule of law' captures its ethos while collections of instructions and directives tend to lose the flavour. Yet it is the latter which has fixed itself in the public mind as the hallmark of the legal; it is usually termed *gesellschaft*; the simple right/duty loaded instruction which emanates from an accepted source of authority. As others have shown with great eloquence, such a model is partial, ahistorical and lacking in theoretical sophistication.[11] Sadly, because it enjoys such demotic currency, it stands in the way of a

---

10 Norman Lewis *How to Reinvent British Government* (European Policy Forum, London 1993) p 31.
11 Ehrlich, Llewellyn, Kamenka and Tay and Unger all immediately come to mind. For these treatments see eg Ian Harden *The Contracting State* (Open University Press, Milton Keynes 1992) and *Lewis passim*.

clearer understanding of the nature of constitutions. This is not inevitable and in India, for example, law has been ascribed 'a social auditor' capable of monitoring the systemic influence of principles of belief.[12] It has been pointed out that even the doctrines of the common law make no sense except in terms of underlying and explanatory principles which transcend the immediate context and form part of a philosophical tradition.[13]

The purposive role of law is too often overlooked. Most lay-persons and an uncomfortably large proportion of trained lawyers view the study of law in an exceedingly narrow way. They conceive of it only as what Habermas has called 'bourgeois formal law',[14] what others have called 'rule of law' law[15] and what is in reality a highly localised (historically speaking) form of the genus law. See, for example, Eugen Ehrlich:

> 'Though we know very little of the law of the early times of the peoples from whom the civilised nations of Europe have sprung, there can be no doubt that of what today is mostly, and sometimes even exclusively, called law, i.e. of the fixed rule of law, formulated in words, which issues from a power superior to the individual, and which is imposed upon the latter from without, only a few negligible traces can be found among them.'[16]

The potential for law and lawyering is in fact considerably broader than the traditional perspective and holds out the possibilities of consumer control, of constraining the administrative exercise of governmental power, which is typically beyond the reach of existing legal principles which merely control the results, with the furtherance of policy goals and of the use of law as a political resource. Indeed, once *gesellschaft* notions of law are rejected as inadequate, it is clear that things legal have considerable potential for influencing political change. Responsiveness, it has been argued, in a range of agencies, municipal government, health, welfare and the generally expanded state, is possible only if citizens

---

12 The huge difference in culture and political practice between India and the UK in no way undermines the argument for an expanded concept of law.

13 Roberto Unger *The Critical Legal Studies Movement* (Harvard University Press, 1986) *passim.*

14 *Legitimation Crisis* (trans McCarthy, 1976) p 86.

15 See eg Roberto Unger *Law in Modern Society* (1976).

16 *Fundamental Principles of the Sociology of Law* (trans Moll, 1936) p 28.

themselves are enfranchised and given effective representation in the processes which determine modes of official behaviour.[17]

Trenchant attacks on narrow concepts of law have been made in recent years in the field of company law and accountancy. For example it has been said that it is the task of the legislature to set out the basic framework for corporate governance and to place the auditor within that framework. Only once a model has been established which is workable and which has general support can further progress be made on the next level of issues. However, by dealing with corporate law piecemeal over many years, reacting to EC initiatives rather than leading them, and gratefully handing over consideration of major accounting problems to professional bodies, the government has abdicated its basic responsibility to formulate coherent companies legislation based on a consensus amongst those affected. Freeman speaks of:

'a disturbing concept of the role of law. Again we see law depicted as a negative influence summoned up to do the unpleasant duty of enforcing detailed requirements: a device which might actually become an obstacle to enterprise, so that it is better avoided. The notion that law might have a positive and profound role in formulating guidelines for corporate society is not even contemplated.'[18]

Law can and often should be facilitative. So, for example, it can be used to encourage markets, not necessarily by merely punishing aberrant behaviour. This is possible through standards and quality assurance machinery, measuring promises through performance indicators and the like. It can also help to energise institutions. Encouraging the voluntary movement is an illustration. It follows that government in its duty to improve the quality of life, encourage comradeship and community, should lend assistance to community group mechanisms which, after all, fits naturally with the obligation to let society flourish. The UK is already committed to such a role through its membership of the Council of Europe and being party to many of its recommendations. So, for example, Recommendation R (81) 18[19] not only reaffirms commitment to

17 See eg EA and JC Cahn, 'The War on Poverty; the Civilian Perspective' (1964) 73 Yale LJ 1317 and Norman Lewis, 'Towards a Sociology of Lawyering in Public Administration' (1981) 32 Northern Ireland Law Quarterly 89 *et seq.*

18 Judith Freeman, 'Accountants and Corporate Governance: Filling a Legal Vacuum' (1993) 64 Political Quarterly 287–288 and 294–295; see also George Goyder *The Just Enterprise* (Andre Deutsch, London 1987).

19 Concerning Participation at Municipal Level.

democracy at all levels of the state and to bringing decision-making as close as possible to citizens, but it also advocates strengthening the working conditions of voluntary organisations and setting up local services and administrative offices to facilitate contacts between local authorities and citizens.

As it is, legal institutions tend to be as conservative as the political. So, for instance, the difficulties experienced with 'standing' in the common law world should not be seen as a merely technical matter; allowing groups to litigate opens up a new world whereby the enfranchisement of pluralistic interests begins to transcend traditional politics, a politics which, after all, is tightly reined in by the party system. If the right to associate and to contest entrenched positions through freely accessible information is taken seriously, then the liberating forces of the 'golden metwand'[20] must be unleashed. This would indeed represent the institutional expression of legitimate order. It is not just traditional law that is hemmed in by a particular view of politics; even more recent, ancillary, institutions reflect such thinking. The ombudsman is an example, being restricted to individual complaints of maladministration rather than being able to assert community rights or indeed human rights as do some of the world's ombudsmen.[1]

Let us return to the Indian experience of Social Interest Litigation for a moment. It is easy to argue that India and the West are poles apart but that is an irrelevance. What the Indian judiciary has done is to put into operation an expanded concept of law which both Ehrlich in Germany before the First World War and the American realists during the 1920s and 1930s had theorised and re-located in its historical context. The flexible virtues of the law should not be wished away – they are bridgehead concepts inherent in social organisation and a nation which does not take advantage of them is simply the poorer for it.

Social Action Litigation indicates some of the possibilities. The Indian courts have taken to establishing fact-finding commissions. Acknowledging the difficulties of some classes of litigants in identifying and adducing evidence to support their claims, the courts have, from time to time, appointed commissions to undertake fact-finding missions, submit reports and make recommendations. These powers are not the same as but are closer to the powers of the traditional ombudsman systems. A few examples will illustrate the point.

20 The rule of law has often been described as the golden metwand.
1 Norman Lewis, 'The World Ombudsman Community: Aspects and Prospects' (1993) 39 Indian Journal of Public Administration 663–676.

In *R L & E Kendra Dehradun v State of Uttar Pradesh*[2] following a petition concerning the detrimental effects of the mining of certain limestone quarries, an interim order was granted on the basis of an expert recommending the closure of the quarries. In *Bandhua Mukti Morcha v Union of India*,[3] in responding to a letter complaint about the bonded labour system in Haryana State, the court appointed experts to study the social and legal aspects of the problem and two advocates to inquire into factual allegations. In *Wangla v Union of India*,[4] the fact-finding commission appointed by the court was mandated to examine the quality of butter which had been imported into the country soon after the Chernobyl nuclear incident; and so on.

Moreover, in Social Action Litigation judicial involvement does not end with the granting of the order. In a bid to ensure corrective action, courts monitor the implementation of their directions at periodic intervals. This appears to have the effect not only of helping to improve administrative standards but of imposing an additional level of legal accountability on the executive to live with the law which they have created.

It is only a matter of time before the British courts become accustomed to interpreting human rights provisions of various sorts. One of the younger generation of judges has said that in the community of developed democracies, the stage has been reached where it can be said that human rights have become axiomatic. Only the judiciary can ultimately determine their meaning in disputed cases.[5] When this occurs, the whole approach to law and the legal process will alter since human rights are incapable of being analysed in a brute or empiricist fashion or eked out from a corpus of doctrinal experience. They will have to take their flavour from a philosophical view of the nature of man which, in a rational polity, would involve examining the larger constitutional framework. In these circumstances the practice of law and politics would never be quite the same again.

Current concepts of the legal in the UK are unworkably narrow and disguise choices which are being made elsewhere. The best work of the Critical Legal Studies Movement has shown that even 'mechanistic' approaches to law, the British tradition over a number of centuries, are crypto-philosophical; they either know not

---

2 AIR 1985 SC 1368.
3 AIR 1985 SC 652.
4 (1984) 3 SCC 161.
5 Sir John Laws, 'Is the High Court the Guardian of Fundamental Constitutional Rights?' [1993] PL 60.

what they do or what version of law and politics they uphold, or avoid trying to resolve the philosophical dilemmas lying dormant in the principles of the common law which they apply. Law as the expression of a nation's beliefs and institutions is dramatically richer than the common-or-garden version found in popular imagination and overmuch professional practice. Thinking the constitution through from first principles would change this for the better. Ultimately the judiciary would have to decide the hard cases in a purposeful way. They would necessarily do so in ways which are unfamiliar to the present generation of British public lawyers. But this is only part of the new balance to be struck. A constitution wedded to augmenting choice will insist on the reform of political institutions too; on the processes of Parliament no doubt and on the ancillary processes of politics as well; contemplating advisory committees, non-departmental public bodies, something resembling a Standing Administrative Conference and a reformed ombudsman system. The total institutional apparatus of the constitution needs to strike a balance between the legal as judicial, the legal as other instrumentalities and a reformed and devolved politics.

FREEDOM OF INFORMATION

Freedom of Information (FOI) ought by now not to be in dispute. As in dealings between individuals so in dealings between them and the state and between intra-state organisations. Disputes can only revolve around the *how*, and the exceptions to FOI.

This is not the place to expand greatly on FOI since there is so much sophisticated writing available in the area. A few propositions however need to be addressed. First, it is impossible to overestimate the importance of FOI in a democracy; without it all pretence to an open society is a sham. Secondly, it should never be forgotten that official information belongs to the people; it is public information and does not exist for the advancement of individual politicians or members of the executive. This is not to deny the necessity for exemptions which are genuinely in the public interest but these should be allowed only after the fullest debate. However, the onus is on those who claim the exemptions and the requisite burden of proof should be demanding. Even then, there must be a public interest override and it goes without saying that neither the scope of the exemptions nor the determination of what constitutes the larger public interest can reside in the executive.

At the time of writing, the British government has placed its faith in an ombudsman-backed Code of Access to Information which distances itself to some considerable degree from the preceding propositions. There is little point in analysing the weaknesses of the present arrangements, especially in the light of their novelty, but the regime contains many disappointing features.

Access to personal files, information on the environment and on health and safety nowadays cause little argument. Nor indeed does its enforcement. It is access to information held by government about the policies adopted, to be adopted and their implementation where the arguments take place. The point scarcely needs developing but one illustration afforded by David Green will serve. Speaking of the demise of the Medical Institutes on the establishment of the National Health Service in 1948, he shows that they were never properly understood or taken seriously by the civil service who offered a constant stream of advice in favour of their abandonment. The advice, says Green, was 'invariably misleading' and of a very low calibre. 'It was of the kind that flourishes because it is given in secret and cannot therefore be challenged publicly.'[6]

Advice tendered by civil servants is often regarded as the most controversial area. The arguments for exclusion are too well-known to need rehearsing though it is important to note that some countries, for example Sweden, appear to work perfectly smoothly without this form of protection.[7] However, the whole matter feeds into the policy process which is of the most critical importance. At the very least, if policy choices are to be properly evaluated by people outside the government, the factual information passing between the civil service and the minister needs to be disclosed. It is also quite intolerable that policy options rejected should be shielded from the public gaze when they constitute perhaps the only yardstick by which the general public can gauge the wisdom of the action taken and can participate in a genuine evaluation of the policies adopted. Policy evaluation is a pretty inexact science at the best of times but when it is conducted by those who are responsible for both the policy itself and its implementation, it is scarcely a recipe for perceived objectivity. The maxim that 'justice should manifestly be seen to be done' is one of the glibbest uttered by politicians and it should engender scepticism when it is not applied

---

6 David Green *Reinventing Civil Society* (Institute of Economic Affairs, 1993) p 112.
7 See eg Lennart Lundquist, 'Freedom of Information and the Swedish Bureaucrat' in RC Chapman (ed) *Ethics in Public Service* (Edinburgh University Press, 1993) pp 76–91.

to the executive. Furthermore, if the broadest possible input into the policy-making process is to be encouraged, it is difficult to see how interested publics can make the most useful contributions when the basis for policy preferences is not disclosed and when reasons for rejected alternatives are held back.

Enforcement of FOI around the world is variable; some combination of courts, FOI commissioners and/or ombudsmen will be found. Almost all, quite sensibly, require as the first stage a formal response from the government authority itself, usually within a stipulated time-scale. Thereafter the enforcement mechanisms vary, but it is extremely unusual for the courts to be excluded altogether; though of course in the ultimate sense they never can be. This is to say that *ad rem* FOI legislation will provide for court involvement at some stage in the proceedings, even if, for example, it is when an ombudsman or commissioner no longer wishes to engage in negotiation or mediation with government but determines that a formal ruling of entitlement is desirable. On the other hand, the courts should not represent the normal mechanism for the enforcement of FOI legislation and this is so even in the USA where no intermediary is specifically appointed. As has been pointed out in relation to the UK Data Protection Registrar, he works by conciliation and persuasion most of the time and usually gets results.

> 'But everybody knows that the reason they have to be reasonable when he makes a request is that if they are not he will go to court. And occasionally he does. And that is the context in which the legal right applies.'[8]

It may well be that an ombudsman figure is the preferred mechanism for enforcing what has, ultimately, to be legislatively based, but only the courts can give meaning to rights in cases of institutionalised dispute.

One more thing needs to be added. Where public services are contracted out it is important that 'public' information passing into the private sector does not become automatically protected. The New Zealand Ombudsman, as Information Commissioner, has something to offer since not only is he able to invoke a public interest override even in cases of 'commercial-in-confidence' but he publishes the names and prices of tenderers, though not 'make-up' or 'item' heads which can be extremely sensitive. He also

8 Maurice Frankel, contribution to *Open Government Seminar* proceedings, Campaign for Freedom of Information and the Association of First Division Civil Servants (London, 1993) p 25.

publishes *Tenderers Notes* as guidance to those involved in the tendering process. Furthermore, he has persuaded the government to publish details of consultancies where there is no public tender and, in his role as ombudsman, can investigate the fairness of the tendering process. Concerns with commercial confidentiality are well understood but the ombudsman takes the view that such claims are not of themselves sufficient ground for withholding information under the legislation. A realistic assessment is made of the likely consequences of disclosure and of whether those consequences come within the ambit of the specific interests protected by the statutory withholding provisions.[9]

The suppression of consultancy appointments and their reports in the UK is rapidly becoming one of the developments most poisonous of the well of democracy. It is intimately connected with government reliance on 'task forces' deliberating in private. A crucial example is the decision of one Cabinet minister to side-step the government's commitment to market-testing and to move into wholesale privatisation of departmental activities. In November 1993, Mr Michael Heseltine was reported to have drawn up plans based on consultants' reports to sell off all Whitehall's industrial laboratories.[10] Elsewhere, reports have suggested that Home Office research projects are being systematically withheld on the grounds that their findings did not coincide with ministers' views on law and order.[11] The list of examples is an exceedingly lengthy one which does no credit to a free society.

Whatever dangers the government sees in citizens' resort to law are as nothing compared to the systematic suppression of information which is the stock-in-trade of contemporary British political practice. It is also worth noting that the government's own Efficiency Unit has recently expressed concern about the utility of consultants' advice. In the year 1993–94, government expenditure on consultants amounted to some £865 million with little effect on supposed efficiency savings. For its part, the government has refused to identify the savings which it had previously claimed the use of consultants would produce, a matter which had earlier been questioned by the Efficiency Unit when it identified shortcomings in the award of contracts.[12]

9 See eg 10th Compendium of *Case Notes of the Ombudsman* vol 2 (Wellington, 1993) and the High Court decision in *Wyatt Co v Queenstown Lakes District Council* [1991] 2 NZLR 180.
10 *The Guardian*, 29 November 1993.
11 *The Guardian*, 4 July 1994.
12 *The Guardian*, 1 March 1995 and Efficiency Unit, Cabinet Office *The Government's Use of External Consultants* (HMSO, August 1994).

ACCOUNTABILITY, POLICY-MAKING AND CONSULTATION

For the political enterprise to fulfil national purposes, the machinery of government must provide opportunities and structures for debating policy. Parliament ought to be a powerful instrument in this process although the British Parliament is generally accepted to be in an enfeebled condition compared to a number of its counterparts around the world. Reform of its procedures is clearly necessary if the claims of the Glorious Revolution are to have contemporary meaning. However, a reformed Parliament is a necessary but not a sufficient condition for genuine policy debate to take place. The requirement for informed national discussion of the major issues addressing the nation is so fundamental that meaningful consultation needs some form of constitutional entrenchment. Whether this should take the form of a subsidiary directive of state policy within the constitution itself or whether it should form part of an Administrative Procedure Act which enjoys special status probably scarcely matters.

Government retains the duty to insist on certain universal standards but it also has a duty to listen before it imposes obligations and it is imperative that policy inputs be pluralistic. Policy needs to be enriched from a wide variety of sources if available expertise is to be tapped. This requires paying attention to two important matters. The one concerns the relationship between central and local politics and the other the need to adopt broader consultation practices, ultimately enforceable by law if need be.

In this respect, there is a great deal to be learnt from the administrative law of the USA although it is important to guard against the excesses of an overly-litigious culture. After a deal of expensive and protracted administrative law suits in the USA in the late 1960s and 1970s, a *modus vivendi* now appears to have emerged. The Administrative Procedure Act (APA), particularly s 553, lays down minimum 'notice and comment' rule-making provisions whereby a proposed rule must be advertised in the daily *Federal Register* for the purpose of receiving public observations on the proposed rule or policy. Individual statutes may impose more exacting standards depending on the subject matter, but the APA represents minimum-floor requirements for consultation.

The area is complex and has shifted, doctrinally speaking, over the years but the central disputes have revolved around the extent of consultation and the nature of the opportunity to rebut presumptions. Trial-type proceedings on the one hand and mere tokenism on the other represent the ends of the spectrum of debate, but for the most part a practical compromise has been reached. The policy-making body or 'agency' determines the nature of the consultative process but in doing so keeps a 'record' of comments received and the reaction made to them. This record is reviewable by the courts who are primarily concerned to ensure the rationality of the process.

Within this general requirement, consultative practices will vary from agency to agency but the courts have sought to promote some version of rational discourse.[13] Close examination of agency conduct reveals the relative rarity of protracted litigation these days and yet the spectre of the court as the trustee for 'due process writ large' has clearly affected the way the agencies go about their business. Furthermore, the occasionally protracted nature of the rule-making process owes more to the internal control systems of the agencies and their relationship with the executive than to the provisions of the APA.

In one form or another, these requirements of the APA date back some 60 years although the Act is now almost a consolidated treatise on major themes of American administrative law, including FOI and the 'Sunshine' legislation to which later reference will be made. In other words, without constituting subordinate directives of state policy, the APA and its requirements are *de facto* a supplement to the American Constitution. It is something resembling this status to which the apex principles of UK administrative law should aspire.

What is needed is a revitalised law and politics which seeks an optimum balance between the two. This is as apparent away from Westminster and Whitehall as within them. It applies equally, or perhaps even more forcefully, to local politics, to Non-Departmental Public Bodies (NDPBs), Extra-Governmental Organisations (EGOs) or whatever the nomenclature and to the balance of 'market versus ballot box'.[14] The offensive against local government has been defended primarily in the name of the market but also 'through encouraging participation and taking an active part in the way things are run locally, with the active citizen rather than the municipal citizen in charge . . .'.[15] Although there is

13 See Administrative Conference of the United States (ACUS) *A Guide to Federal Agency Rulemaking* (2nd edn, Office of the Chairman, Washington DC 1991) and ACUS *Federal Administrative Procedure Sourcebook* (2nd edn, Office of the Chairman, Washington DC 1992).

14 Kevin Morgan and Ellis Roberts *The Democratic State: A Guide to Quangoland* (Dept of City and Regional Planning, University of Wales College of Cardiff 1993) pp 13–14.

15 John Patten MP *Rolling Constitutional Change: The Conservative Approach to the Constitution and Constitutional Reform* (European Policy Forum, 1993).

some merit in this argument, it suffers from a number of defects, not least that *local politics* is vindicated by the concepts of choice and opportunity. Furthermore, the enormous power of patronage exerted by central government over those who are supposed to represent community interests is quite impossible to justify.

> '... it is not citizens who have been empowered so much as self-governing trusts in the health service and governing boards in the case of grant-maintained schools, boards on which there is no parental majority.'[16]

One respected political journalist has labelled this 'a mandarins' confidence trick'.[17] Many will agree, but the point is that, whether or not local politics are revived, the extended or para-state organisations need to be subjected to strong (legal) requirements that they should consult the people. If the emasculation of local government is to be tolerated, even partially, there is even stronger reason for third force bodies to be subject to the more advanced techniques of administrative law.

In fact the language of consultation is common currency. In 1994, for example, the President of the Board of Trade stated that industry and consumer organisations should have more opportunity to comment on monopoly inquiry findings before the government decides whether to accept recommendations of the Monopolies and Mergers Commission (MMC). This statement was made in response to pressure, in recent years, for the Commission's broader findings to be opened to wider scrutiny. Such consultation is to be welcomed but once the argument is conceded it becomes immediately clear that it has wider implications. Thus, genuine tensions in competition policy have recently appeared which have manifested themselves in the different approaches of the MMC and the Office of Fair Trading (OFT). The former seems to have moved to a 'pro-industry' policy which seeks to assist the creation of strong UK champions in the global market while the latter appears to favour markets free of any anti-competitive restraints unless they can be shown to benefit the consumer. Some commentators feel that this is an indication that the Department of Trade and Industry has lost interest in competition policy. Leaving aside obligations under European Union law, there may well be sound arguments for such a shift in policy given that

16 *Morgan and Roberts* p 14 and more generally the detailed research provided in *EGO Trip* (Democratic Audit of the UK, London 1994) *passim.*
17 Joe Rogaly, *Financial Times*, 7 May 1993.

markets, competition et al can present extraordinarily sensitive issues for governments to address. Yet again, what is sauce for the MMC must be sauce for the OFT and the DTI and the absence of a widespread debate in such a crucial area is to be lamented.[18]

There are those who have argued seemingly since time immemorial that the British practice of consultation is in reality quite as effective as in other countries where distinct legal requirements exist. This is unpersuasive for a number of reasons. First, a mere practice of consultation allows government to decide when and if to consult. Secondly, it allows government to determine the quality of consultation without there being any check on the openness of the process, its inherent rationality or the level of information made available to allow an informed assessment.

THE REMAINS OF THE STATE

The defects in the present constitutional and legal order may be disputed across political divides even though the argument presented here is that there ought to be very little that should separate persons of good will. This is an opportune time to reassess fundamentals since systems of governance are being recast. The task forces to which reference has already been made are challenging both the shape and extent of the UK system of governance in a way which rivals Runnymede, the Glorious Revolution and the Tamworth Manifesto. But the level of national debate accompanying this restructuring is risible in one of the world's oldest democracies and that it seems hardly to have registered in the national consciousness says an enormous amount about the gradual erosion of decision-making to an unaccountable executive. What is being determined is the remains of the state.

The process perhaps begins with the 'Next Steps' (NS) exercise which can be dated roughly from 1988, although its origins may be traced from the introduction of the FMI in 1982. The complex aims of that initiative included devolving power downwards and identifying levels of responsibility which formally challenged the purity of the doctrine of ministerial responsibility. It strengthened financial monitoring and control but did little to promote managerial initiative. From 1988 onwards, instead of being seen in Whitehall as a secondary level of activity, subordinated to the real

18 See eg *Financial Times*, 2 February and 17 May 1994.

business of policy-making, management was elevated into a respectable part of the civil service's activities.[19] Since these developments are now well-known, one brief explanatory quotation will
suffice:

> 'The aim should be to establish a quite different way of con-
> ducting the business of government. The central civil service
> should consist of a relatively small core engaged in the func-
> tion of servicing Ministers and managing departments, who
> will be the "sponsors" of particular government policies and
> services. Responding to these departments will be a range of
> agencies employing their own staff, who may or may not have
> the status of Crown servants, and concentrating on the deliv-
> ery of their particular service, with clearly defined responsibil-
> ities between the Secretary of State on the one hand and the
> Chairmen or Chief Executives on the other.'[20]

The rest is, to some extent, history but there are two points worth
making. The first is that being an internal Efficiency Unit[1] report it
did not receive all-party let alone more pluralistic input. This is
important if choosing requires maximum information and dialogue as it must. This is, characteristically, not particularly
remarked upon in a British setting, since that is how government
normally does business: with insiders and with considerable circumspection. The second point is that the original 'Ibbs' Report
was not even made public since it apparently attacked head on the
ignoble pretences surrounding the greatest myth of the constitution – ministerial responsibility. That report recommended, 'a
change in the British constitution, by law if necessary, to quash the
fiction that ministers can be genuinely responsible for everything
done by officials in their name'. This would have allowed a real
devolution in the responsibilities to executive agencies and would
have involved 95% of the civil service involved in the delivery of services.

However, 'The salesmanship failed. The Ibbs report was sat on
for months and then diluted liberally ... the revolution that never

19 These developments are now well-documented but see especially Kate Jenkins
    Improving Management in Government: The Next Steps (HMSO, 1988); Diana
    Goldsworthy *Setting Up Next Steps* (HMSO, 1991) and Philip Giddings (ed)
    Parliamentary Accountability: A Study of Parliament and Executive Agencies
    (Macmillan, London 1995).
20 *Jenkins* para 44.
 1 The Efficiency Unit is based in the Cabinet Office or Office of Public Service and
    Science (OPSS).

was.'[2] Back in 1968, the Fulton Committee had made similar representations and although many bodies were 'hived off' in the 1970s as recommended, the review of the constitutional implications, which was also recommended, never took place. In its 1977 Report, the Expenditure Committee recommended developing 'proper control mechanisms for hived-off bodies'. It is now clear that Fulton, Ibbs mark 1 and the Committee were correct. Events since 1988 have amply confirmed the absence of clear lines of responsibility or truly effective devolution. A new constitutional settlement has been called for and is not yet in place.

It is worth stressing that the major upheaval which was NS, in many ways an admirable development, has occurred almost entirely without legislation and relatively little Parliamentary oversight. The major exception is the 1994 Treasury and Civil Service Select Committee (TCSC) Report on the Future of the Civil Service,[3] a crucial document, but one which commented, inevitably, not only *ex post facto*, but without displaying an adequate understanding of the nature of the changes currently being undertaken and without seeming to mind that Parliament itself was riding pillion, if indeed it had not already fallen off the machine altogether.

DICTATING CHANGE

Separating the policy and the delivery process can have considerable advantage and should serve to concentrate the mind wonderfully.

'The logic is that it should encourage government at both central and local level to take their budgets to pieces and challenge inbuilt assumptions. Priority search techniques should be adopted as soon as responsibility for policy outcomes is established. Within such an exercise decision-takers need to rank in priority order a number of influences to be considered in determining resource priorities. Markets aside, this is the stuff of politics and what we have said about new forms of enfranchising citizens through the consultation process needs to be slotted in to the policy formulation process. Whether we

2 Peter Hennessy *Whitehall* (Secker and Warburg, London 1989).
3 The Role of the Civil Service, Fifth Report (HMSO, 1994).

are talking about market research surveys, monitoring
processes, quality control of complaints-handling systems or a
judicially-backed "hard look" standard of rational discourse in
public life, the expansion of the democratic mandate must be
asserted.'[4]

The newer systems of government require institutions that are
responsive to their customers, offering choices of non-standardised
services that lead by persuasion rather than by instruction. This is
not to say that the bureaucratic environment is never relevant;
merely that it should be seriously and constantly questioned. But in
general there is increasing support for the view that government,
central or local, should be concentrating on defining problems
and then assembling resources for others to use in addressing
them.

A non-centralised approach is called for. If governments decen-
tralise authority they are forced to articulate their 'missions' and to
monitor results. In terms of both national and local politics managers cannot control decisions. What they can do is to concentrate
on the mission, especially through structuring the market-place,
creating incentives that move people in the direction the community wants to go while letting them take most of the decisions themselves. In today's global economy, the power to tax and spend
cannot conceivably produce all the jobs, all the health care, all the
constant training needs, the child care that a modern society
demands. The solution is simply stated. Concentrate on the outcomes after taking the best advice, relate the chosen outputs to the
outcomes and then conduct an evaluation technique which can be
applied to each service need. The question to ask is where government gets the best deal? The minds of policy-makers should be
open and they must be prepared to innovate. What is to be
expected is a flourishing private and voluntary sector operating
alongside good-quality public services.

In order to provide the kind of government that is most relevant
there will have to be a comprehensive assessment of need, a specification of standards of service, the development of monitoring
and inspection facilities and readily accessible complaints procedures. Progress is already being made on these fronts but there is
some way to go and there remains a need to assess both the effectiveness and the accountability of the procedures adopted to
secure best results.

4 Norman Lewis *How to Reinvent British Government* (European Policy Forum,
London 1993) p 20.

There is no point in pleading for the retention of failed, especially bureaucratic structures. But what is needed is a genuinely national debate about the direction in which the nation wishes to move. Both Hayek and Green argue that present public-sector services should be subjected to tests of their necessity. This might be achieved by subjecting each government activity to a 'necessity audit' to establish whether it belongs in the public sector or not. But, as Green maintains, the reasons for questioning public-sector provision must be clear. It is not enough to proffer a general inclination for non-intervention, or *laissez-faire* or small government. The fundamental question is whether the government is using its power to direct the energies of the people to a given end. That is to say, is the government using people as a means or is it providing them with means? Green then proposes a series of questions about the appropriate location of service delivery which asks about efficiency, self-help, experiment and innovation, the absence of monopoly and the preference for local over central services.[5] These propositions logically inhere in the arguments which have already been presented, but they are out of kilter with the secrecy which is accompanying changes presently being fashioned in the UK.

Since Next Steps was accepted as a generally desirable aim, there has been a quickening of the pace of privatisation, the strong emergence of the Citizen's Charter and more recently the extension of market-testing. These developments forcefully underline the commitment to choice for customers, the preference for markets and the private sector, the use of regulation as a second-best strategy and a reorganisation and re-examination of what is seen to be the 'core' public sector. These constitute part of what the Prime Minister has called his 'Big Idea'.

If fully implemented this idea would constitute a real revolution in the way the UK is to be governed and there is a danger that such a revolution is occurring without reshaping national institutions to meet the challenges. Much of the change is desirable but it requires the replacement of fading conventions with real constitutional guarantees, not least in the field of contracting out where the legal implications have not been adequately considered. This may be contrasted again with the position in New Zealand where similar change has been accompanied by legislation, by increased deliberative powers for Parliament and by an effective ombudsman

5 David Green *Reinventing Civil Society* (Institute of Economic Affairs, 1993) pp 128–129.

who has extensive powers as Information Commissioner. This is also but one of a number of arguments in favour of a Standing Administrative Conference.[6]

THE PRIOR OPTIONS

When options for change are being considered within current governmental practice, executive dominance largely uninformed by public discourse is the order of the day. Given that the machinery of government is at stake, it is even more fanciful than normal for the government to plead a recent electoral mandate. But compared with other democracies, the UK is relatively unencumbered by legal niceties when the need is for a felt change of direction or the override of previously announced policies.

Before a Next Steps agency is established (or indeed when it is ripe for review), a series of tests known as 'prior options' are applied. Is the activity necessary? If it is, does it need to be in the public sector or can it be privatised? Can the function, either in whole or in part, be contractorised? The agencies themselves, where they are already established, are expected to participate actively in reviewing these issues. It is quite extraordinary that such momentous changes can be envisaged under the present exiguous Parliamentary arrangements. Parliament, after all, will lose considerable control over privatised and contractorised activities and yet, under present arrangements, it has little or nothing to say about the processes by which such decisions are taken. The most active role it will play is where legislation is necessary for, say, privatisation of British Rail. This is after-the-event and subject to the usual constraints.

What is important for the public lawyer is the process for review. There does exist a short unpublished Cabinet Office document – *Review of Agency Framework Documents* – which is interesting without casting a great deal of light on the detail of the operating procedures. The *Next Steps Review* 1993 announced that each review will set out a list of agencies under review or due for review in the following year. 'This new policy of openness in respect of agency candidates ... will provide opportunities for those in outside organisations with innovative ideas about how functions can best

6 This and related matters are discussed *in extenso* in the author's evidence to the Treasury and Civil Service Select Committee, vol 11 (1994).

be discharged to put them forward in a timely way.' One small step for both man and mankind. The 1994 *Review* at Annex B does indeed contain a table showing progress in undertaking reviews. However, there is no mention of the process itself nor indeed of any comments or observations made to the reviewing department. Certainly, there is nothing in the nature of a 'record' such as is normal under American administrative law.[7] The monthly document 'Government Opportunities' does now, however, publish both review intentions and a brief summary of review outcomes.

It is formally the sponsoring department's responsibility to conduct the review. Even so, the report will be sent to the Treasury for comment. Then a collective decision is taken involving, it is thought, a handful of Cabinet ministers, though sometimes the Prime Minister's views will be taken in advance. The Cabinet Office and Treasury will, naturally, be heavily involved and some of the larger reviews have involved outside consultants. Since many of these may be expected to have a predilection for privatisation, this might be expected to raise a few constitutional eyebrows.

It is not clear what criteria are adopted for selecting among the 'prior options'. There are, apparently, some rather loose criteria employed such as Value for Money (VFM) and competition but such documents as do exist are not in the public domain save in so far as they repeat the observations made in *Competing for Quality* and the *First Report on the Citizen's Charter*. Whether other internal documents are different in tone is impossible to say in the absence of a Freedom of Information Act. It is believed that the criteria are 'broad brush' and that no open social and economic cost–benefit analysis is employed. Furthermore, the coherence of the exercise was somewhat undermined by the Trosa Report which suggested that the implementation of market-testing had been too centralist and had not always taken account of the management coherence of the agency.[8]

Privatisation also illustrates some of these concerns. Bald assumptions have been made in official literature about the desirability of particular privatisations without any close scrutiny or justification presented. In particular no attempt has been made to explain why a New Zealand approach to such matters is inappropriate, an approach which some think desirable for both the Royal Mail and British Rail. New Zealand established State Owned Enterprises (SOEs) in 1987 in circumstances where the country

7 See Norman Lewis, 'Reviewing Change in Government' [1975] PL 105–113.
8 Sylvie Trosa, *Next Steps: Moving On* (Office of Public Service and Science, February 1994) paras 6.25–6.27.

faced a 'highly sheltered public sector' which did not face the true costs or benefits of the resources employed. The SOEs were set up as limited liability companies with the Crown owning all the shares. If the government wanted to maintain for social reasons the supply of any goods or services which the SOE regarded as unprofitable it must contract with the SOE on a commercial basis. The Public Sector Borrowing Requirement (PSBR) is not used in New Zealand in relation to those bodies who seek resources from the financial institutions according to commercial criteria. There is no constraint on SOE activity to ensure that the size of the state declines; the objectives are commercial while non-commercial transfers became apparent, which assists the policy choosing exercise.

The commercial success of most of the SOEs is a matter of record yet this is not the point at issue here. What is, is how the decision to privatise or retain within the public sector was made. The characterising feature has been a case-by-case evaluation so that where privatisation is preferable, the argument is presented after an appropriate institutional examination in a way that ensures the best terms for the public. Not only has this not been done in Britain, but party-political and ideological forces have frequently impeded both efficiency and choice. Furthermore, it is worth repeating that there are examples in the UK where the public sector is prevented by government from competing effectively with the private sector. This is a matter commented upon adversely by the Treasury and Civil Service Select Committee in 1994. They expressed themselves to be surprised at the proportion of the 1992–93 Competing for Quality programme in which in-house bids were not permitted, especially in view of the government's own statement that 'for a genuine value for money test to be applied, in-house teams should have the same opportunity to put forward a firm bid on the same basis and timescale as the private sector'. They therefore recommended that in future all government departments should inform Parliament at once of any decision to exclude an in-house bid from a competition together with the reasons for each decision. What is also worth noting is that in 1994 the all-party Transport Select Committee of the House took the opportunity of examining the government's case for privatising the Transport Research Laboratory and was not convinced by it.[9]

'We welcome the broad thrust of Government guidance on public access to contract information, but public access need

9 Quoted in TCSC (1994) para 178.

not be the same as public availability. We recommend that
Parliament should be informed at the earliest available opportunity of all contracts and service levels reached under the
Competing for Quality programme, together with the identity
of the successful tenderer, the nature of the job, service or
goods to be supplied, the performance standards set and the
criteria for the award of the contract.'[10]

The situation has now entered a new and more dramatic phase.
Some of the task forces set up in recent years have impinged upon
the future of the functions of government. Three working groups
or parties are of particular importance. One, under the chairman-
ship of Sir Colin Southgate, submitted a plan for the down-sizing
and restructuring of the Treasury in late 1994.[11] This may or may
not be a good idea but if implemented would have major repercussions for the kinds of macroeconomic tasks to which the
Treasury would, in the future, be suited. It cannot be acceptable
that matters of such moment are planned in a sectarian fashion
without the widest variety of inputs.

There is also the Private Sector Forum. Originally established to
make recommendations on deregulation, thus taking unnecessary
bureaucratic pressure off industry, it appears to have become the
major adviser to government on what activities need to remain
within government and those that do not. Officially the Forum was
established to provide a channel of communication on Competing
for Quality issues between the private sector, government departments and agencies at which individual market-tests are not discussed. The Council of Civil Service Unions has expressed concern
about possible commercial advantages arising from the Forum and
called for guidelines on its operation, a call rejected by the government.[12] The major public manifestation of these deliberations so
far has been the highly controversial Deregulation and Contracting Out Act 1994.

A third body which is preparing evidence on the shape of government is the Home Office's 'review of policy core and ancillary
tasks'. This is aimed at making the police more efficient by identifying 'ancillary' jobs that could be divested, possibly to private
firms. This has been done by asking chief constables to complete
questionnaires categorising police tasks as mainstream or ancillary.

10 Para 26.
11 *Fundamental Review of HM Treasury's Running Costs* (HM Treasury, October
    1994).
12 TCSC, 'The Role of the Civil Service', Fifth Report (HMSO, 1994) para 190.

A number of the apparently identifiable ancillary tasks include many jobs which bring the police into peaceful contact with the public, playing a vital role in community relations and police intelligence gathering. Senior police officers have expressed alarm that the exercise is a prelude to widespread privatisation. Newspaper reports say that the review is sitting in secret without a co-opted police expert and is already committed to implementation of the policy of hiving off ancillary functions. Although the review has set up a discussion group with police, this merely considered its findings after they had been made, rather than helping to set the agenda. Senior officers have urged the establishment of a Royal Commission which would ensure an adequate debate.[13] It is clearly unacceptable if the general public first becomes aware of the issues when it is too late to affect the outcomes.

There are alternative systems on offer. The USA Federal Advisory Committee Act 1974 (FACA) is one of four statutes passed since the Second World War intended to stimulate public participation in government affairs, the others being Freedom of Information Act (FOIA), 'Sunshine' and Administrative Procedure Act (APA). Together they represent the four pillars of open government and are generically referred to as 'Access Laws'. They have assumed the mantle of sub-constitutional principles in that they inform the very nature of the way government has operated in the USA and, although they date from different periods, their origins can be traced back as far as the Roosevelt Administration. Although not constitutionally entrenched, they undoubtedly enjoy a special affection, status and rank.

Although FACA is fired by a concern for open government, it was also intended to prevent the waste of public expenditure and to that end it specifies that advisory committees (ACs) be terminated no later than two years after they are established unless specifically exempted – so-called 'sunset' legislation. The legislative history indicates several concerns but among them was the fear that ACs can be a convenient nesting place for special interests seeking to change or preserve a policy for their own ends. Such committees, stacked with giants in their respective fields, can overwhelm a decision-maker or at least make them wary of upsetting the status quo. Even after the Act, clear instances of abuse have been identified which confirm the Congressional fears about industry-controlled committees. The main issues addressed are balanced membership, openness of meetings and availability of

13 *Observer*, 10 June 1994.

documents, the avoidance of conflicts of interest and more general canons of accountability.

Under FACA the term 'advisory committee' is defined to include committees, boards, task forces 'or other similar group or . . . subcommittee' established by statute or established or utilised by the President for the purposes of obtaining advice or recommendations for the President or one or more agencies of the Federal Government. The main exclusion relates to committees comprised wholly of full-time officers or employees of the government. Thus, although FACA encompasses many contacts between officials and others which would not be regulated in the UK, it does not extend to all contacts. In particular, it excludes meetings with pre-existing groups, individuals, and with groups of individuals where the purpose is to obtain individual opinions rather than advice or recommendations as a group.

Establishing a committee requires the publication of a formal notice in the Federal Register and such a committee cannot lawfully meet until its charter has been filed. This requires a statement of aims, mission etc while there exist vital procedural requirements such as notice of intention to hold (open) meetings and the availability of documents for inspection. In practice, some three-quarters of all AC meetings are open to the public. FACA also requires that all ACs must be fairly balanced in terms of the points of view represented and the functions to be performed. This is not party political balance but the result will often be much the same as if it were. Without an enforceable balanced representation requirement, it would not be possible to prevent ACs being used to rubber-stamp the views of the appointing authority or to prevent it from being manipulated by the regulated interests. This means that not only will there almost invariably be consumer representatives but that groups or persons directly affected will normally have some representation.

The procedural provisions of FACA are not contested and the Clinton Administration is particularly keen on public participation. ACs are seen in the US as being 'a bridge to the people' and it will by now be quite clear how such legislation could have a major impact in a UK setting given the dramatic changes which are now being recommended behind the lace curtains. This might still leave aside the question of consultants' reports which are also playing an increasingly important part in the governance of the UK but it needs to be added that FOIA requirements will often require publication of consultants' papers. This is also true in New Zealand where, although commercial-in-confidence requirements apply to the FOI laws, there is an overwhelming public interest override.

GOVERNMENT AT THE CORE

As the Treasury and Civil Service Select Committee (TCSC) makes clear, at the time of the deliberations of the Fulton Committee in 1968 there appeared to be a wide measure of consensus about the role of government. Such consensus 'has subsequently disappeared'.[14] However, this does not mean that constitution-building has become impossible but rather that there is a need to think more clearly about the irreducible core of nationhood. The Contracting Out and Deregulation Act 1994 made a very crude gesture in this direction without involving the body of the nation.

The Act is interesting in part because of its use of Henry VIII clauses allowing the Secretary of State to override primary legislation by statutory instrument, albeit with consultation arrangements considerably more enhanced than is usual under the British system. What is more important is s 71 of the Act which imposes restrictions on the contracting out of functions. To some this is an official attempt to indicate what is regarded as 'core' government. For the most part, the exclusions relate to the powers of courts and tribunals, the liberty of the individual, the protection of property and the ability to make subordinate legislation. Now whereas these areas would be regarded by many as 'core', they may not be ineluctably so while for many people the list would be considerably longer.

The more structured and open practices adopted in the US have already been noted.[15] However, they have no appeal for the present UK government which regards such decisions as being the province of the government of the day and essentially 'political'. This in spite of the fact that some spokespersons had agreed that there was 'a certain spinal cord of State which cannot be under the private sector': judicial functions, regulatory functions, the exercise of high-level discretion, the liberty of the subject and the direct application of armed force.[16] One might be forgiven for detecting a certain inconsistency here. Furthermore, there is also an implicit rejection of general government philosophy in the recommendation that Next Steps reviews be from time to time accompanied by statements of the virtue of particular agencies remaining in the civil service.[17] There is a further recognition that some issues should rise above politics in the recommendation that the government issues guidance to ministers on circumstances in which it

14 TCSC, 'The Role of the Civil Service', Fifth Report (HMSO, 1994) para 172.
15 57 Federal Register No 190, 30 September 1992, Washington DC.
16 TCSC, 'The Role of the Civil Service', Fifth Report (HMSO, 1994) para 175.
17 *Ibid* para 179.

would be appropriate to offer briefings to Opposition politicians on matters which relate to the machinery of government or which are not of current party political controversy.[18] Although this is a welcome addition to establishment thinking, it goes nothing like far enough in terms of engendering a genuine national debate.

Another issue of importance is the government's professed attitude towards 'strategic' contracting out. It has expressed the view that there are circumstances in which it might take a strategic decision not to continue as a direct provider, for example because in-house provision might detract from a department's ability to concentrate on core functions or because the private sector might be better equipped to provide a particular activity due to a better understanding of market needs or special expertise. In addition, in 1991 it was said that there should be a general presumption in favour of contracting out new services. When questioned by the TCSC however, the minister responsible became coy of talking about the criteria involved.[19] Although the general sentiment is one with which it is easy to feel comfortable, it is not enough in matters of such importance to make bald statements without supporting argument tested against contrary opinion.

Contracting out is facilitated by the Deregulation and Contracting Out Act 1994. Sections 69 and 70 provide for the contracting out of both ministerial, 'office-holder' and local authority functions though in all instances it provides for some measure of consultation, the details of which are not specified in the Act. Furthermore, some public protection is given by s 72 which provides that contracted out functions shall be treated for all purposes as if done by the minister, etc, himself. Although the remainder of the section is somewhat ambiguous, it does seem that attempts to ensure that contractees' action can be investigated for maladministration have been made. What has not been attempted, however, is a readdress of the general position on 'public' contracts contracted out to the private sector, a matter which many think is long overdue if the special nature of a public contract is to be recognised.

MAKING POLICY

This is an appropriate moment to lock together a number of earlier themes and to relate them to the legal order. Next Steps has

18 *Ibid* para 218.
19 *Ibid* para 191.

sought, to some degree at least, to separate out high policy-making and the management of public services. However, most of the effort has gone into the latter with some critical dissatisfaction being expressed concerning progress on refining the policy process and making it more accountable and effective. This is a complex area with no simple solutions yet the problems are relatively easy to state. The New Zealand experience of the late 1980s summarises the dilemmas faced by policy-makers.

The financial management reforms of that period are now reasonably well-known to those versed in New Public Management but one of the achievements was identifying the relationship between outputs demanded from departments and the outcomes to be achieved; crudely put between the delivery of targets and the relationship between them and what is being aimed at. It becomes more difficult for ministers to hide the quality of their advice when compelled to provide a link between outputs and outcomes when they have sole responsibility for the latter. To take a perhaps over-simple illustration: if the inputs in the police service are more resources, the outputs more arrests and the outcomes less crime then the fact of more arrests having no impact on levels of crime suggests the abandonment or at least the serious questioning of existing policies. If the minister disagrees, then (s)he is going to have to come up with some better defence of his or her budget than is normally presented. This should mean that the civil service would not have to defend the outcomes; merely the outputs. The minister and his or her policy advisers would then be in the firing line and accountability ought thereby to be enhanced.

One suggestion for redefining lines of responsibility and accountability is the establishment of agencies within Whitehall for the creation of policy rather than simply implementing it, such as a Monetary Policy Agency in the Treasury, an Energy Policy Board, a Crime Reduction Bureau, a Family Poverty Watch, a Training Policy Agency and so on. These would have to be identifiable, accountable and to a large degree transparent. The degree of public information available would necessarily increase even in the absence of a Freedom of Information Act. The composition of such policy agencies would be all-important. They would clearly represent no real advance if their membership were restricted to those who already form policy communities.

There is backing for such ideas. For example, the Australian Industry Commission scrutinises all forms of assistance to industry. It holds public hearings and publishes consultative documents. It also regularly reviews aid cases after they are approved to assess costs and see whether assistance has had its intended effect. The result of this vigorous and open process has been to cut Australian industry's dependence on state aid by about two-thirds in the last twenty years.

Similarly, the Trade and Industry Select Committee has recommended the establishment of an Energy Commission on the grounds that energy can never be left entirely to the market. It was fired by the belief that greater openness is needed in energy policy, not least since the public is entitled to know the costs of any intervention in the market. The Commission's remit would be to advise, monitor and engage in broad-ranging consultation. Interestingly, the Select Committee recommended that where the Commission's advice was rejected, the government would have a duty to give reasons. What follows is that such a duty would be ultimately court-enforceable if necessary. This would not give the court any substantive voice in determining matters of policy; it would simply require it to implement the duty to ensure open discourse.[1]

There are obvious difficulties in confronting the reform of the policy-making process; electoral short-termism, the average shelf-life of ministers, their reluctance to set clear policy objectives lest they bind themselves too closely or risk offending interest groups. Next Steps was supposed to improve this situation in forcing ministers to set out in public documents the objectives for which they would be accountable. In fact, however much clarity may recommend itself to business-minded executives, it might be expected to have little appeal to ministers. And so, thus far, it seems to have proved. Yet, the whole argument for leaner, more empowering, government is that it should concentrate its energies on those areas of national policy for which it retains responsibility once the 'core' functions of the state have been determined. To recap: government, according to the new gospel, should concentrate on sound policy-making with service delivery being delegated to competitive centres capable of greater efficiency and which allow the consumer to occupy a central position. Freed from the details of service delivery, government as client should be able to concentrate on new ideas for service provision and quality.

There is a related issue which ties in with 'the remains of the state' question discussed earlier in this chapter. Hitherto there has been a tendency for government, and in particular the civil service, to keep adding new jobs to the old without any global strategy.

1   *British Energy Policy and the Market for Coal* HC 326 (HMSO, 1993) and Graham Mather, *Responsibility, Accountability and Standards in Government* Memorandum to the Treasury and Civil Service Sub-Committee on the Role of the Civil Service (European Policy Forum, 1993).

Newer trends are away from this style of operating. Instead, there is a move to reviewing existing work and to redeploying resources wherever possible. This is a major advance but is one change amongst many. Privatisation, contracting out, the Citizen's Charter, the purchaser–provider split are all important ingredients of reinvented government. But they have been developed almost independently without any real game plan being disclosed. It is not clear what vision of government, what vision of the state is at work here. However, people across continents with little direct contact with each other commonly find that they are moving in the same direction. There will usually be a common logic in their actions if it is sought out. The present British experiences reflect patterns emerging elsewhere in the democratic world community. Yet it is not clear whether leaders of opinion have a firm defence for the changes occurring, or what kind of state they are creating and precisely where they want to go. A constitutional concordat would represent the beginning. But there is also a need to redefine the nature of the political system.

A satisfactory constitutional resettlement would be shot through with statements of principle about the rights of citizens to be defended which would, of itself, prevent the executive diminishing larger expectations. Furthermore, any substantial alteration in the processes or institutions of government or the role and nature of the civil service would have to be the subject of legislation which would be tempered by the revised procedures of Parliament which would be a necessary accompaniment. There is much to be said for requiring such changes to be put before a Standing Administrative Conference. This ought to ensure that 'dictating change' in the way which has been witnessed in recent years would be *ultra vires*.

The institutional changes required to bring the policy process closer to the philosophy of choice would have to involve important changes. As far as most legislation was concerned, pre-hearings would be required. Thus, to take the Swedish model as the one coming closest to a model of consultative discourse, after a Bill's first hearing, a standing committee with full powers of inquiry would be established. This would hear evidence from the general public in much the same way as does a Select Committee of the House, and to resolve doubt, it ought to be able to commission research, which would not only take some of the present unfair advantages away from the executive, but cause it to be more circumspect in its proposals in the first place.

Of course, whenever important legislation is presented, a White Paper normally precedes it. This is one of the potentially beneficial features of current arrangements which could be usefully built upon to underwrite the principles of choice and debate. In particular, responses to White Papers ought to form part of a 'record' in much the same way as is the case in the USA. Even if the courts were not involved in this process, the fact of a public record to which the executive would have to respond would present both Parliament and the public greatly enhanced powers of informed criticism.

Delegated legislation or significant non-legislative rules or policies ought to be subject to something resembling APA rule-making procedures. A British APA equivalent ought to become a conventional or custom and practice supplement to constitutional arrangements. This legislation and its rule-making requirements, to say nothing of 'Sunshine', should also apply to a broad range of bodies such as Non-Departmental Public Bodies (NDPBs)[2] which could be specified in a Schedule to the Act and added to from time to time as the occasion demanded. Local government should be subject to similar requirements.

How would this affect changes in public management styles such as are presently occurring under New Public Management? The first point is that certain institutions would enjoy a special status under the constitution and could not be altered except in conformity with constitutional requirements. However, beyond this, whenever it was felt that the nature of public institutions was being altered by stealth and the executive chose not to use rule-making procedures to accompany the changes, the Standing Administrative Conference would come into its own. Given that the SAC would have the power and the resources to conduct its own investigative agenda, it could open up a full national debate on any issue which it regarded as sufficiently important to merit its attention. The empowering legislation would require the government of the day to take a 'hard look' at its recommendations or be subject to the supervision of the High Court so that it would not be possible for a 'remains of the state' exercise to be conducted in an atmosphere of cloistered secrecy.

SUBSIDIARITY, FEDERALISM AND COMMUNITY

Support for the positions adopted has been expressed, ironically enough, by a Westminster politician. The argument is so clearly and forcefully stated that it deserves extensive quotation:

2 The official description of what the public ordinarily calls 'quangos'.

'Somewhere between the musty lavender of the mayor's parlour and the red braces of the recession-beached technocrat there is a better vision for local government; it is about independence, democracy and accountability. A wider agenda of pluralism must break and devolve the centralist state in the UK, [and] an essential part of that is that local authorities must be set free from the constraints imposed by central government. This requires both a leap of imagination and the political will to make them *constitutionally independent* of the executive. This task goes even further than "re-inventing government": the challenge is to re-invent democracy in our country. Within that context, local government now needs to state its vision and to reclaim the powers accrued by the Executive.'

'It is time to ensure that duly elected local authorities are guaranteed their independence. They should be free to carry out their local mandate safe from political interference and insured against financial manipulation by central government. Of course central government must still be able to lay down standards of acceptable service levels and minimum provisions, and to publicise those standards to ensure that they are understood by the citizens at large. That is the point at which the role of the centre ends and it must be for local government to deliver those standards to at least the level required or to be held accountable by the citizens through the ballot box. The petty interference in local decision-making which has typified recent years must be denied any legal basis.'[3]

Two points of clarification need to be added. The first is that the (relative) autonomy of local government must pay regard to the right of the centre to macro-manage the economy; the second is that such constitutional reform is a logical and necessary step in a free and choosing society quite apart from the arguments in favour of rekindling a spirit of community. Whatever the model of 'politics' in the loosest sense which is adopted, the state angle of the virtuous triangle should wherever possible be located nearest the people affected. As Allen has remarked, the UK is a diverse and complex society where needs and preferences differ widely by area,

3 Graham Allen MP *Independent Local Government* (European Policy Forum, November 1993).

race, age etc. Responding to this diversity with appropriate flexibility and sensitivity requires a highly decentralised system, which
after all is part of the justification for markets; what is needed
therefore is a system of 'political' markets – not a 'Brezhnev-like
command politics'.[4]

Allen is one of many who counsel the ratification of the
European Charter on Local Self-Government as a beginning,
although he regards it as important that local government should
both have a right to undertake locally whatever is not prohibited by
statute and to receive a set percentage of national taxation taken
from income tax. It follows ineluctably that such powers be laid
down either in a detailed written constitution or a specially protected Parliament or Local Government Act.[5]

The pattern of world politics seems to be moving in two seemingly contradictory directions, although the contradictions
become resolvable on closer analysis. The first direction is towards
larger regional groupings of (loosely) federated sovereign states, at
the outset for the purposes of trading but gradually becoming inte-
grated in other settings too. The second, quite marked across continents, is the preference for local and community action,
revolving around common cultures and experience. These developments are perfectly consonant with the celebration of choice as
a guiding sentiment for political arrangements. Turning to the
larger picture, it is clear that for choice to be real it must be possible. That in turn requires giving a local dimension to the pulses of
power which increasingly must beat in extended settings if they are
to be effective in regulating global players in the world's markets.
This is explicable both from the point of the need to belong and to
act in manageable and meaningful social settings and to ensure
that the larger principles which are being set at the regional group-
ing level can find outlets tailored to smaller-group choice.

It may be recalled that Green favours local self-financing units of
government. He develops his argument along lines which are four-
square with the preceding analysis in identifying the opportunities
for experiment and variety. Having taken the view that there can be
no absolutely right answer about the necessity for a service to be
public or private, or publicly financed yet privately provided, he
welcomes the opportunity for different localities to experiment,
some with more or less public services, others with direct provision

4 *Ibid.*
5 And see also Kevin Morgan and Ellis Roberts *The Democratic State: A Guide to
Quangoland* (Dept of City and Regional Planning, University of Wales College of
Cardiff 1993) p 15.

and still others with local finance combined with competitive tendering by private agencies. 'But units of local government should experiment at their own cost.' It is fundamental to liberty, he believes, that people should be free to say yes or no to taxation, and without full information about the services they are receiving in return for their taxes it is impossible to form a rational judgement.[6]

It can be added that individual units of local government would have a great deal to learn from their counterparts elsewhere in this process of trial and experimentation and be in a position to put before their electorates a series of tested alternatives from which they could express their own preference. Central government could play a useful role in bringing together in an accessible form different experiences in both types of and systems for service delivery. This would represent a government partnership which would usefully serve the people in place of a monolithic, all-knowing central apparatus which, alone in the Free World, has chosen to impose a system of compulsory competitive tendering across the face of what is left of local government. The removal of local government altogether would represent an authoritarian response which should shame any government which has rightly railed against the brutalities of democratic centralism in the former Communist bloc.

Whether local/regional government should be totally self-financed or whether it should continue to receive subventions from the centre can be debated, although clearly the greater the financial dependence on the centre, the greater the likelihood of interference and the less chance of local autonomy. In any event, constitutional clarity would have to be established by legislation protected from easy repeal. Whatever concordats were struck at the political level between the centre and the localities should be clearly public as should the preliminaries to such a settlement. These arrangements would not only encourage innovation but would be accompanied by the appropriate degree of protection by the legal order. There would be discretion as to the delivery of goals, subject naturally to legally enforceable provisions concerning consultation, but precision in relation to citizen/customer rights once the particular mode of service delivery was chosen. It would also be important to devise a method for mediating disputes between local and central government, a matter to which little attention has been paid if the work of the Audit Commission is discounted. Genuine differences of opinion can be expected to occur

6 *Green* p 129.

between central and local government in circumstances where the fullest consultation is sometimes absent. The courts have been slow to infer duties of consultation in this area, even when they are prepared to do so elsewhere.[7]

One particular proposal for revenue raising deserves mention. It is that something like half of local government income presently raised should continue to be disbursed from the centre though in a dramatically different fashion. This proposal envisages one total lump local government sum being given to an independent Local Government Commission legally separate from central government and charged with formally distributing resources to each local authority. Membership might be primarily comprised of elected local government representatives themselves. The rest would be raised locally according to local preference.

In addition to this ring-fenced resource, central government would continue to offer specific help for particular problems just as the Federal Government in the USA can assist individual States of the Union on time-limited projects. Bids might be appropriate for such items as economic hardship caused by major company closures or a profound inner-city housing crisis.[8] These latter suggestions would fit well with the responsibility of government to take positive or affirmative action in relation to the material floor of well-being already discussed. If combined with the European tradition of consultation between industry, labour and community over planned company closures, this would go some way to institutionalising the level of social concern and respect owed to all. Furthermore, additional value would be added to the local social and industrial stock if local governments were sufficiently free as agents to engage in partnerships with the private sector free of the constraints which so often mystify the private sector and inhibit worthwhile developments in urban regeneration.

One important constitutional limitation is also suggested by Allen: viz for a balanced budget provision to guard against profligacy and tighten control and accountability by the electorate. Borrowing for capital programmes need be in no wise inhibited if interest payments are accurately reflected in the annual expenditure columns. As to regional government, Allen again provides a valuable suggestion. There is no reason, he argues, why regions should not be demand-led by local representatives not only deciding what powers and form the region should have, but also being

7 Eg see *R v Secretary of State for Transport, ex parte the GLC* [1985] 3 All ER 300.
8 Graham Allen MP *Independent Local Government* (European Policy Forum, November 1993) p 4.

prepared to pay for their operation. He interestingly describes this
as 'menu versus blueprint'.[9]

This is resonant of the innovative local initiatives described by
Osborne and Gaebler in the USA, where they found that local communities afforded the resources and the opportunity to influence
their own lifestyles were often able to produce remarkable
improvements in literacy and education, law-enforcement and general community safety. Having a purchase on their own futures frequently worked as an incentive to alter their environments for the
better. The argument, then, is for the legal order to facilitate
experiment and choice within local communities. Diversity is
almost bound to be the result – perhaps to the dismay of the political centre, but so be it:

> '. . . we must be mature enough to accept that the price of one
> Council's job creation initiative, service delivery programme,
> or innovative community care scheme may be another
> Council's Grammar School, or contracted out cleaning con-
> tract.'[10]

This is not the place to elaborate on the arguments for devolved
Scottish and Welsh Assemblies since they have been so well made
elsewhere. The gains would be greater democratic control, more
effective scrutiny, the promotion of social and economic regeneration, greater collaboration with the regions of the European Union
and a more accurate reflection of political culture in the exercise
of political power.[11]

All this reflects the spirit and the movement of the times where
central agencies are increasingly exhorted to limit their role to
policy transmission and evaluation. Particularly against a background of shrinking resources, it is sometimes felt that the responsibility for crisis management of public services should be moved
away from the centre to the periphery. Sweden in the 1980s is a
good example of the state of affairs recommended by Green,
where greater freedom of management at regional and local level
was accompanied by reduced contributions towards the support of
public services from the centre but without the constraints on local
government spending through capping expenditure or altering
the means of raising taxation. Further downwards devolution of

9 *Ibid.*
10 *Allen* p 7.
11 See *Morgan and Roberts*, especially at pp 30–35.

responsibility from the municipalities also took place even down to the level of the elected hospital board.[12]

ENABLING, CONTRACTING, MONITORING AND EVALUATION

The issue of the evaluation of programmes and initiatives is a notoriously difficult exercise but one which is a core function of modern government. It is not one which is always well performed according to the reports of the Audit Commission. For example, in 1994 it was reported that health and local authorities were spending up to £1,000 per day on management consultants but were often failing to ensure value for money. Local authorities, in particular, omitted to evaluate 70% of their products and the Commission found that poor project management meant that consultants were not being used efficiently or effectively. Fewer than 40% of the projects examined had payment linked to successful completion of the task and 30% had no written agreement of any form. Seventy per cent of NHS projects studied and 35% in local government had not been subject to competitive tendering. Failure to follow simple tendering regulations risked allegations of corruption and sometimes the spirit of competition was breached by tendering for an initial project and then awarding further work. In one case, an authority tendered a contract for £25,000 and then subsequently paid the same firm almost £200,000 in fees for related works.[13]

The 'enabling' state has highlighted problems about monitoring and evaluation as part of the arts of government which went substantially unaddressed in the past. The Treasury and Civil Service Select Committee, in its 1994 Report, commented upon evidence it had received concerning the evaluation of the policy process and remarked that all was not as well as it might be. Criticisms were made from several quarters, not least from former Permanent Secretaries, which led the Committee to recommend piecemeal reform. In particular, it urged that the policy tasks of an agency be specified in annual performance agreements and that they should be subject to evaluation other than by the parent department. It

---

12 Oonagh McDonald *Swedish Models: The Swedish Model of Central Government* (IPPR, 1992) pp 15, 18.

13 Audit Commission *Reaching the Peak – Getting Value for Money from Management Consultants* (HMSO, 1994).

also suggested the establishment of project teams within government for policy implementation and that policy project work should both be encouraged and monitored by the Office of Public Service and Science (OPSS) to ascertain the extent to which agency principles can be applied effectively to parts of the policy process. It also argued for a search for improved methods of auditing policy implementation.[14]

Exhortation such as this ought to be regarded as the minimum. There is an acute need for reinventing the doctrine of the separation of powers. Contract can assist this by clarifying what government expects from service providers in pinpointing responsibility and thereby improving accountability. Instead of distinguishing between legislative, executive and judicial functions, there is a need to concentrate on separating out purchaser and provider functions. But public law 'contracts' will often have to be different from the commercial variety and to embrace constitutional values in terms of formation of terms, pricing and dispute resolution. Public law contracts will often need to be based on common values which are difficult to express. In defining the best form of service delivery, there is a need to avoid the failures and the evasions of ministerial responsibility. Contract can be used for the pursuit of political objectives through individual rights and freedom of choice. Yet in making decisions about what to produce and in ensuring efficiency in the process of supply, the commercial-style contract will have to be re-examined for constitutional fit.

It is doubtful whether the present system of public law could deal easily with the transition to more marketised public services. The point has been raised in another jurisdiction by a judge of the New Zealand Court of Appeal, Sir Ivor Richardson, who has expressed the view that the model of administrative law which seeks to control the welfare state in a largely regulated economy is nowadays inappropriate. A more market-oriented state has rendered it in part obsolete. However, as Professor Mike Taggart has responded:

'The fundamental values of public law – openness, fairness, participation, impartiality and rationality – not only provide a yardstick against which to measure the activities of privatised enterprises with market power but should be embodied in the design of institutions and regulatory schemes at the outset. In

14 TCSC, 'The Role of the Civil Service', Fifth Report (HMSO, 1994) paras 205–211.

speaking up for these values, administrative lawyers perform their most important role.'[15]

The contract state needs to be charted with more definition and empirical detail before it is possible to blueprint a revised administrative law, but the time for such work seems manifestly overdue. There is a great deal wrong with administrative law in the UK and it is highly unlikely that the judiciary can come to terms with the changes being discussed without legislative support. This is perhaps evidenced by a (technically defensible) decision of the Divisional Court relating to the tendering process for court reporting services for the Lord Chancellor's Department. Although there was clear evidence of unfairness, the court held that since this was based upon the common law of contract rather than a regulatory statutory framework, the allegations lacked a sufficient 'public law' element to ground a successful application for judicial review.[16] This suggests that urgent attention needs to be paid to the legal and constitutional incidents of the contracting out process.

This belief is strengthened by the evidence of the Comptroller and Auditor-General to the Nolan Committee on Standards in Public Life to the effect that the spread of contracting out and market-testing had meant that a large number of public work contracts handed out to the private sector were no longer under the scrutiny of the National Audit Office.[17] Some legal systems of course recognise the special nature of contracts with a public element, perhaps most notably France, though the powers of the New Zealand Ombudsman or Information Commissioner represent another attempt to address similar problems. It is difficult to know the precise terms of contracts entered into between the government and private parties and therefore difficult to know how far the public interest is being adequately protected by the terms of such contracts. Until some method of casting light on these matters is devised it is probably premature to argue for a specifically public law jurisprudence, on the Continental fashion, but clearly there is a need to readdress these issues in the light of current developments, since the present position is by no means satisfactory.[18]

---

15 Mike Taggart, 'The Impact of Corporatisation and Privatisation on Administrative Law' (1992) 51 Australian Journal of Public Administration, September.

16 *R v Lord Chancellor's Department, ex parte Hibbit and Saunders* [1993] COD 326.

17 *The Guardian*, 2 February 1995.

18 Colin Turpin *Government Procurement and Contracts* (Longman, Harlow 1989).

Once more the jurisprudence of the Union of India seems to be more acceptable. In the recent *Cellular Telephones Case*[19] the Supreme Court laid down parameters for the scope of judicial review in commercial contracts. While restating the ancient wisdom that a reviewing court was not an appellate court, it nevertheless made it clear that it was entitled to act where there was evidence of arbitrariness or favouritism. The decision was based on art 14 of the Constitution of India which asserts equality before the law.

It is possible to envisage much of the government of the future as a network of contracts, or perhaps more properly compacts since legal enforcement may not always be possible or desirable. These must meet the requirements of customers but it must be remembered that citizens are more than mere customers. They require a quality of public life and guarantees of debating the terms of that public life. Then they are truly customers. It will be necessary to concentrate hard on policies and strategies, to judge what the market will bear and what it will not; to guard against unnecessary monopolies and to protect the public purse by making profits where possible and imposing charges where they make sense. All this, however, requires an organising framework and a new legal settlement whereby adequate machinery for monitoring, for evaluation and standard-setting are put in place.

Many of the problems, as well as the opportunities, presented by 'government by contract' have been outlined elsewhere, although a few reminders might be timely.[20] As to the contents of contract, there will need to be provision to include specifics of service price and quality, provision for monitoring or inspection, for regular reporting back, provisions for penalties, arbitration, complaints mechanisms for citizens not party to the contract and the role of ombudsmen, to say nothing of a revised role for the courts. In any event, because the contractual relations under discussion will often be long-term, there is a need for distinctly 'constitutional' doctrine to deal with the inevitable complexities. This is the separation of powers in a modern garb, but of course traditional conventions will not serve here. Contracting out in sensitive circumstances provides an illustration – with prison management being a particularly timely example. Not only does government have the responsibility for setting out the original policy framework under which contracting terms are set, but it will retain a responsibility for crisis

19 (1994) *The Times of India*, 5 August.
20 Norman Lewis *How to Reinvent British Government* (European Policy Forum, 1993).

intervention when things go wrong. Governing relations are not easily containable in traditional contract terms; a new settlement is required.[1]

An evaluation technique is needed which can be regularly if not routinely applied to questions concerning service initiation, continuance, amendment or expansion. The strengths of privatisation, contracting out, franchising, vouchers, user fees, public–private partnerships etc need to be considered as a set of general principles and then applied to particular delivery systems once policies have been determined. This should happen in conjunction with users, carers, professionals of all sorts in quality action groups or whatever form of citizen involvement seems appropriate, bearing in mind the commitment to 'hard looking' the decisions ultimately taken. The users of services should be regularly consulted on their views of the service with a commitment to change either the service itself or the delivery system where appropriate. Where public bodies deliver services, comparators can be used with other public bodies delivering similar services. There is a great deal to be done in all of these areas, not least since the deliberative machinery for taking decisions is inadequate. It is almost certainly the case that legislative support for some of these sentiments would reinforce commitment to them. In particular, a statement of competition policy whereby the public and the private can compete evenly should be adopted.

Relatively little has been said on the specifics of regulation though the claim has been made that since choice/human rights is the lodestar then the primary justification for regulation must be to put human beings back in touch with the choosing context where otherwise power configurations produce dislocations which inhibit genuine choosing. The Citizen's Charter proposals take developments further than before but there remain serious flaws in the nature of the regulatory regimes in spite of the fact that modern accounting techniques and the greater availability of management information allows regulation to be more robust than formerly. Two points in particular stand out. The first is that it is probably unwise for a regulator to act in the capacity of both regulator and ombudsman and the second is that the regulatory process is not institutionally structured to encourage an effective national debate. It has been said by a leading commentator that:

> 'A regulatory system without a clear rationale and without any clear legal structure in which it operates has inevitably

1 *Ibid* pp 27–28.

assumed what is probably the most frequently criticised regulatory characteristic in the post-privatisation U.K.; highly personalised regulation.'[2]

This stands in marked contrast to the regulatory commissions familiar from the USA so that dependence on the personal qualities of the regulator has led to a neglect of the development of fair procedures and the defining of regulatory principle to guide the regulators. As Prosser has acutely observed, the technical expertise of the regulator becomes his source of legitimacy instead of constitutional principles of fairness and rights holding centre stage, even though in early 1995 the courts had been prepared to grant an order to the competitor of a privatised industry by challenging the regulator.[3] It is clear that these matters need urgent reassessment, a matter again which could be best entrusted to a Standing Administrative Conference.[4]

Market mechanisms alone, presently characterised by inadequate information and an emphasis on cost, are, of themselves, unlikely to solve the problem of producing equitable, high-quality and more efficient public services. The use of contract has a valuable role to play, but within a broader constitutional and legal framework which encourages a more open and considered set of consultative practices throughout policy and management processes. Structured competition cannot be regarded as a substitute for reasoned policy and planning. To ensure resources and objectives are properly matched, further consideration needs to be given to financial, management and information schemes. All the objectives espoused here can be significantly affected by the quality of developments in law as well as the exigencies of economics and politics.

---

2 Tony Prosser, 'Privatisation, Regulation and Public Services' (1994) Juridical Review 7.
3 *Financial Times*, 10 February 1995.
4 Though see Cento Veljanowski *The Future of Industry Regulation in the UK* (European Policy Forum, 1993); Cosmo Graham and Tony Prosser *Regulating the Privatized Industries* (Oxford University Press, 1991); and Norman Lewis, 'Markets, Regulation and Citizenship' in Roger Brownsword (ed) *Law and the Public Interest* (Franz Steiner, Stuttgart 1993) especially at pp 26–30.

Chapter 9

The social market economy and the constitutional framework

It is too early to know how the hybrid constitutions of the Eastern and Central European countries, reformed out of recognition since the fall of communist rule, will develop. It will be instructive to see how they cope with the tensions between a system based on open markets and property rights and one committed to a social state which seeks to nurture the material and cultural needs of pluralistic groups. In the years to come the legal systems of these countries will need to manage the balancing acts necessary to rank the different levels of rights and to calibrate the different generations of rights. To some extent, of course, the German Constitution has already had to grapple with a number of these issues.

The principal features of the social market economy have already been described. The framework of that economy includes the rights of property and inheritance, freedom of choice in the exercise of a trade and profession, freedom to form or join economic or trade associations, freedom of commerce and industry flowing from the general right to personality and the principle of the social welfare state. As well as Germany and many of the new democracies the Committee on Security and Co-operation in Europe (CSCE) adheres to similar values by not only proclaiming a commitment to democracy as the only system of government and the enumeration of human rights and fundamental freedoms to be guaranteed, but also by a commitment to economic liberty and free market economics.

Although pluralism and experiments in living are widely acclaimed, not a great deal of distinctly constitutional thought has gone into the implications of these claims or of those for free participation in social and cultural life. Yet the German Constitution and its attendant jurisprudence signals the potential of constitutional claims to secure these ends. Articles 1 and 2 are the most significant. The former states that 'the dignity of man is inviolable. To respect and protect it is the duty of all state authority.' The latter

provides that 'Everyone shall have the right to the free development of his or her personality' but only 'insofar as he or she does
not violate the rights of others or offend against the constitutional
order or the moral code'. Taken together, these two provisions are
the heart of the German Constitution. Article 1 has been taken to
mean that the concept of human dignity includes a morality of
duty that may limit the exercise of a fundamental human right.
The image of man in the Basic Law according to the Federal
Constitutional Court is not that of an isolated sovereign individual:
rather it favours a relationship between individual and community
in the sense of a person's independence and commitment to the
community, without infringing upon a person's individual value.
Furthermore, the 1982 Declaration of the Council of Europe
comes close to spelling out some wide-ranging implications of freedom of speech and expression. It assumes not only participation in
political life but also in social life.[1]

Whatever the levels of disagreement, it is now clear that just as
freedom is the basis for markets, so it is also the basis for certain
levels of welfare provision. For, although markets may be highly
efficient mechanisms for controlling the production of goods and
services, their impact on welfare is frequently uneven. In other
words, civil and political rights have vital implications for markets,
regulation and the incidents of citizenship. So does a minimal level
of social and economic protection which must be constantly examined to ensure its adequacy. These are early days but, for example,
the constitution of Albania is interesting in stipulating that
although 'The country's economy is based on the diversity of ownership, the free initiative of all economic subjects and the regulatory role of the state', nevertheless 'economic initiative of juridical
and physical persons cannot develop contrary to the social interest
and should not impair the security, freedom and dignity of man'.
This distinctly regulatory form of words has enormous potential
and in the hands of an enlightened judiciary could prove to be far-
reaching.

Most of the classic constitutions of the world, although often full
of ringing declarations, have not usually sought to attach legal significance to the dignity of man and to the generic right to equal
concern and respect. This is especially true in that of the UK, which
embodies the belief that law should operate at the margins, that it
should be the interpreter of political promises rather than the
great interpreter of the pattern of politics. More generally, it is not

1 And see also the Preamble to the International Covenant on Civil and Political
Rights 1966.

difficult to see why many regard social and economic rights as non-justiciable since the boundaries of the separation of powers are in issue. But it is precisely those boundaries which have been contested since the end of the Second World War, when the rediscovery of human rights portended a more active role for the world's judiciary than many had formerly been willing to concede. The expansion of human rights is bound to cause the precise nature of the separation of powers to be re-examined and that is no bad thing.

At issue here is the very contribution which the legal system can make to the art of governance. The *gesellschaft* tradition dies hard in many countries, not least in the UK, where resistance to progressive developments can be expected to be strong. There are clearly limits to the role and the rule of law which need to be carefully defined and defended, and it is in this area that the greatest challenge to the world human rights movement can be expected in the years to come. If there is controversy over the role of the judiciary in the social and economic rights arena, how much richer is the possibility for judicial invention when faced with interpreting a constitution which proclaims 'the full development of personality and human dignity' (Albania), 'the right to free self-realization' (Latvia), 'respect of human personality and dignity' (Slovenia), 'humanism' (the Preamble to the Albanian constitution), 'dignity' and the 'unlimitability' of rights (Czech Republic), 'the inviolability of person' as one of the highest values (Russia) and so on. These expressions may be seen as merely illustrative or aspirational but the jurisprudence of India has shown that once the judiciary begins to take such sentiments seriously, the implications can be momentous.

For instance, the centrepiece of Gewirth's celebrated PGC or principle of generic consistency is the necessity of 'freedom and well-being'.[2] Few would oppose the underlying force of this expression but in the hands of a master-logician cum moralist the concept has transformative power; the power to transform both law and politics. Sentiments such as freedom and well-being actually embedded in a statement of constitutional values could have enormous transformative potential, even on a case-by-case basis.

The world community appears to be revising traditional concepts of the rule of law upwards. Just as, for example, the Hungarian Constitution of 1989 speaks not only of the rule of

---

2 Alan Gewirth *Human Rights: Essays on Justifications and Applications* (University of Chicago Press, 1982).

international law and the inalienability of fundamental human rights, so it updates the rule of law to take account of its social obligations:

> 'The Republic of Hungary is an independent democratic con-
> stitutional state where the achievements of both Western-type
> democracy and democratic socialism prevail.'

Even as far back as the Vienna meeting the CSCE was speaking not only of the dignity of the human person in general but the development of protection in the field of civil, political, economic, social, cultural 'and other human rights'.

> 'The participating States recognize that the promotion of eco-
> nomic, social, cultural rights as well as of civil rights is of para-
> mount importance for human dignity and for the attainment
> of the legitimate aspirations of every individual. They will
> therefore continue their efforts with a view to achieving pro-
> gressively the full realization of economic, social and cultural
> rights by all appropriate means, including in particular the
> adoption of legislative measures. In this context they will pay
> special attention to problems in the areas of employment,
> housing, social security, health, education and culture.'[3]

Whatever uncertainties have been registered previously about the contribution of the legal order to the strengthening of markets and market economics, the mood is changing. Even in the USA, there is active discussion of a constitutional amendment to require a balanced budget, which if not precisely about markets, is about a certain philosophy of market economics. The convergence criteria of Maastricht should also be seen in this light, quite apart from what the Protocol has to say about social and economic protec-tions. A general commitment to a mixed economy is emerging, which chimes well with the celebration of choice and experiment. The 1991 Bulgarian Constitution, while committing itself to mar-ket economics, also embraces the mixed economy:

> 'The economy of the Republic of Bulgaria shall be based on
> free economic initiative.
>
> The state shall establish and guarantee equal legal conditions
> for economic activity to all citizens and corporate entities by

3 Concluding Document, Cm 649 (HMSO, March 1989).

preventing any abuse of monopoly status and unfair competition and by protecting the consumer (it is also committed to international trade by extending protection to foreign nationals).'

But it also states:

'A state monopoly shall be establishable by law over railway transport, the national postal and telecommunications networks, the use of nuclear energy, the manufacturing of radioactive products, explosives and powerful toxic substances.'

Whether such a balance can be maintained as the global economy develops is open to question. More intriguing still are two articles of the Albanian Constitution. Article 10 provides that the country's economy is based upon the diversity of ownership, the free initiative of all economic subjects and the regulatory role of the state. This is perfectly consistent with, if not four-square with, the arguments for economic activity being grounded in human rights. The article continues by insisting that the economic initiative of juridical persons must not be allowed to develop contrary to the social interest nor should it impair the security, freedom and dignity of man. To this end, it will be fascinating to watch any unfolding body of jurisprudence which seeks to grapple with these complex balances and to watch the response of the political elite should they believe the judiciary to be trespassing upon their preserve. Furthermore, although committed to a version of free market economics, the later provision in art 13 concerning the taxpayer's obligations to support the social state is bound to be contested by many politicians of a minimal state persuasion.

The Constitution of the Russian Federation displays many similar tendencies, although the somewhat robust politics being pursued at the time of writing suggests that the judiciary may well be put on hold for some little time. Be that as it may, the constitution is firmly committed to health, social protection, housing etc and is embedded in a social market context where economic freedom must be harnessed 'to the public good'. Chapter 7 of the constitution, which is concerned with property, labour and enterprise, is riddled with high-sounding and potentially tension-ridden sentiments.

Germany, however, was the most instructive juridical personality prior to the events of 1989. Unlike the Anglo-American or common law tradition which emphasises the importance of natural rights possessed by the individual against the state, the German tradition assumed that law and justice could be achieved only within and under the protection of the state. The Basic Law, after all, in art 20 set up a 'democratic and social federal state' with both the executive and the judiciary being bound 'by law and justice'.

Many of the world's newer constitutions seek to embody the principles of the European Social Charter (ESC) with varying degrees of commitment, while often going beyond and tempting the judiciary into embarking on exercises in political philosophy which must sorely stretch the nature of judicial autonomy over the longer term. The Slovenian Constitution, for example, proclaims a 'social state' and provides very strongly worded entitlements and duties in the field of health and general social insurance (parents incidentally are enjoined to exercise the 'duty to maintain, educate and bring up their children', thereby producing what looks at first sight to be a polarisation between New Right economic and moral philosophy and social democracy/provision). It would be easy to multiply examples but the central fact remains that many of these new constitutions are the product of historical and social conjunctions which are uneasy in terms of ruling political assumptions. Markets have re-established themselves for the most part against the claims of centralist control-and-command political systems but there is a reluctance to abandon the concept of community and fellowship, of social provision and a floor of welfare. A new breed of judges will be needed to perform the role of the philosopher-king of ancient Greece.

The time is ripe to argue that the legal order can be arranged in at least three layers. The first is the constitution proper; the second, a set of sub-constitutional principles invested with a special status, and 'ordinary' laws. Precisely which set of rights/expectations most properly fall within which category may be contested.

There is distinct constitutional movement even in the official ranks of the British Labour Party reflected in its 'Commission on Democracy'. Its commitment to human rights is expressed in a document which recommends a two-stage advance. The first stage consists of a commitment to the passing of a Bill to incorporate into British law the civil and political rights of the European Convention on Human Rights (ECHR). The second is for an all-party Commission to deliver to Parliament within two years a home-grown Bill of Rights which, as well as updating the civil and political rights found in the ECHR, would also include social and economic rights. The extended civil and political rights would include freedom of information, data protection, disability and discrimination. The passage of the first Bill would include the establishment of the

Commission which would be asked to produce a new Bill within two years. The extension to economic and social rights would take the ESC as its starting point and the document states that 'Labour would want economic and social rights within a British Bill of Rights to be speedily enforceable and *ultimately justiciable*'. Consideration would be given to the supplementation of the ESC with additional rights. Seeking to address the difficulties of the changing shape of the doctrine of the separation of powers, the document goes on to say:

> 'A British Bill of Rights would be a statement of aims and values. It would be a guide to interpreting law and formulating new law easily understood by M.P.s, judges and above all the citizen [though] ... the specific levels of social provision should remain the province of Parliament which, when it was willing to pass precise legislation, would have to commit the appropriate levels of resources ... '

and further states:

> '... there is a compelling argument for confining the British Bill of Rights to the establishment of rights as underlying principles against which government could be judged, rather than enforceable entitlements to specific forms of provision.'[4]

Some of the enforcement mechanisms may be a little under-developed but what is most refreshing is the commitment to the legal order as some kind of guarantor of the larger compass of rights which a freely choosing individual should have available. It is at this point that there is a need to develop the argument about sub-constitutional principles or 'directive principles of state policy' as the Constitution of India would have it.

It would not be right to leave this line of argument without reference to the so-called 'Social Chapter' of the Maastricht Treaty of the European Union.[5] Article 1 proclaims that:

> 'The Community and the Member States shall have as their objectives the promotion of employment, improved living and working conditions, proper social protection, dialogue between management and labour, the development of human resources with a view to lasting high employment and the

4 Graham Allen MP *Labour and Rights, Stage 2 – A British Bill of Rights* (October 1994).
5 Treaty on European Union 1992, Appendix 1.

combating of exclusion. *To this end the Community and the Member States shall implement measures which take account of the diverse forms of national practices . . . and the need to maintain the competitiveness of the Community economy.*' (emphasis added)

With a view to achieving the objectives of art 1, art 2 says that the Community shall support and complement the activities of the Member States in a number of areas including the information and consultation of workers, the collective defence of the interests of workers, and co-determination. In so doing the EU Council may adopt by means of directives minimum requirements for gradual implementation and shall act unanimously on a proposal from the Commission after consulting the European Parliament. The Commission shall also, under art 7, draw up a report each year on progress in achieving the objectives in art 1.

Slips there no doubt will be twixt cup and lip, but this constitutes a serious attempt to constitutionalise the social market economy within one of the world's most important regional associations. It will be watched with interest even though the UK is presently not formally signed up to the Protocol. That this is the case is clearly in conflict with the philosophical analysis of choice unless the British government intends to honour the spirit of the Protocol rather than the letter. Presently this does not seem to be the intention.

SUB-CONSTITUTIONAL PRINCIPLES

Leaving aside the 'technical' problem of entrenchment within the UK legal system, there are clear difficulties in making social and economic rights as specific as first generation rights but there is no reason why a body of principle which is agreed across the political spectrum and which rises above politics should not be proclaimed within a foundation document, even if it is not as clearly justiciable as other parts of a constitutional framework would be. This would represent a sensible approach in a constitution drawn up in a green-field fashion in the late twentieth century.

The Indian Constitution is again something of a precedent, but in a different way American administrative and constitutional law have become *de facto* locked together in juridical symbiosis. Take, for example, Title 5 of the United States Code – the Administrative Procedure Act. The guiding sentiments have been around since at least the 1930s and, in something resembling their present form, since 1946. They are now culturally embedded in the jurisprudence of Federal America and although it is not inconceivable that the legislation could be repealed, such a move would meet enormous opposition. It has not been formally added to the constitution for a number of reasons, not least the difficulties inherent in the amendment formula, but there is no doubting its resonance as part of the legal settlement. The 'New Administrative Law' of the Commonwealth of Australia, although only going back to the 1970s, invites comparison. If a tailor-made constitution for the times were introduced in the UK there would be no inhibition on giving it an unaccustomed flexibility with principled 'rankings' a central feature, as may well turn out to be the case in the Central and Eastern European democracies.

Let us return briefly to the Constitution of India. Although a number of the directives might be unappealing, it would be difficult to reject art 38(1) which reads:

> 'The State shall strive to promote the welfare of the people by securing and protecting as effectively as it may a social order in which justice, social, economic and political, shall inform all the institutions of the national life.'

According to one of the leading judicial figures in the promotion of Social Action Litigation, these principles constitute the most important and creative part of the constitution and proclaim social justice to be the central feature of the constitutional order.[6]

Despite potential disagreement, there are a number of obvious candidates for inclusion at some level of constitutional entrenchment. A pollution-free atmosphere, for example, is being increasingly demanded and is bound to make strong claims for a place in a revised settlement, even though it would necessarily act as an impediment to the rule of unfettered market forces. Choice necessitates certain physical features which a poisoned environment is bound to deny, to say nothing of preserving entitlements for the unborn. In fact, the European political 'Right' has argued for environmental impact statements to be written into any emergent EU Constitution while also seeking to make it clear that, at least within the EU, power rests with the people and is delegated upwards. It is difficult to see how such sentiments could be consistently rejected within the UK itself.

---

6 See Sri Khrishna Agarwala, 'The Legal Philosophy of PN Bhagwati' (1987) 14 Indian Bar Review 136.

'On the other hand, there is much to be said for the view that the market provides a more effective mechanism than political processes for individuals to realise their unique preferences and human aspirations. Political processes have a legitimate role in attempting to redress market failures and in providing collective support for those who do not succeed in a market setting. There should consequently be established institutional arrangements to ensure competition as part of the concept of respect for the rule of law and political pluralism in a democratic framework. At the level of the European Union it has been argued that a constitutionally established Community Competition Authority should adjudicate by means of public hearings and should publish its findings and all evidence pertinent to those findings, subject to commercial confidentiality alongside consumer representation. Member states would agree to have in place mechanisms within their own markets to ensure free competition.'[7]

COMMUNITY AND VOLUNTARY ASSOCIATIONS

The fashionability of partnerships in current political thinking has been noted, but so far in its primarily economic overtones; its social, one might say its more purposive, aspects have been marginalised. These aspects now need to be re-examined with a view to identifying their appropriate status.

The rights of organised labour, although retaining a powerful universal resonance, have yet to find an acceptable form in today's global markets. The European Union is inching towards a solution to these problems while the present US Administration is also concerned to ensure that the rights of labour are not submerged beneath the flurry of financial movements across the globe. The UK has international obligations to respect, in particular, the freedom to associate and to form workers' associations and it has been suggested that such institutions may be capable of reinvigorated welfare functions which might slim down the state's responsibilities in this area. A genuine commitment to these rights would be reflected in the directive principles of the constitution, leaving successive governments, with judicial assistance, to work out the most appropriate means of securing them.

7 'A Proposal for a European Constitution', Report by the European Constitutional Group (European Policy Forum, London, December 1993).

Some of the 'new' constitutions have attempted to give constitutional form to a few of these concerns. Thus the Constitution of the Russian Federation includes the following:

> 'Voluntary associations, political parties, trade unions, youth associations, national-cultural societies and other voluntary organizations, mass movements and religious and other associations, are formed and operate freely in the Russian Federation. The conditions of the registration of voluntary associations or their statutory instruments are determined by law.'

In similar vein, the Constitution of Latvia establishes the rights of everyone to establish 'social or other types of non-profit organizations' and to participate in their work. These are large statements, espousing a great deal more than labour associations. There is, embedded in these sentiments, a theory or sub-theory of government in that they speak to a community where the state is merely the representative of the people and as such acts against their interests when it produces alienation or *anomie*. This amounts to a rejection of both the centralising state and the atomising of individuals into pure market-appetites; it represents nothing less than the third angle of the virtuous triangle. As has been argued earlier,[8] social capital, and such things as trust, common standards and networks can improve the efficiency of society by facilitating co-ordinated actions, for example, at the level of a city, fostering partnerships of various sorts, workers organisations and the like.

It has been noted that many of the great mutual institutions were Victorian responses to untrammelled industrialisation which frequently tore apart human rights as they are now understood. Building societies, housing associations, co-operative enterprises, trade unions, credit unions, such organisations as the Open Space Society and the National Trust all emerged through collective, non-governmental effort. Elements of local government, from libraries and museums to parks and town halls, arose through a combination of public subscription and private donation. They were motivated by a notion of common public benefit; general ownership rather than either private or state ownership. It is interesting that once more credit unions capable of developing

---

8 See Chapters 5 and 6 *passim.*

community banks which have as their aim support for small businesses in the community are beginning to emerge.[9]

British history is replete with examples of the rejection of a centralised state interfering in community affairs. A conspicuously pluralistic commonwealth has characterised British social and political history at numerous points in the nation's development but has waned of late. A properly federal constitution would draw institutional competences between the various arms or levels of the state and the third corner of the triangle.

A further word needs to be said about the voluntary or third force sector which is increasingly performing public functions. This sector requires regulation to ensure adequate standards, adequate information and transparency and satisfactory accountability methods, both to the general public and internally within the organisations themselves.[10] However, beyond this, there is an obligation upon the state in its duty to provide choice and freedom to *encourage and support* voluntary organisations which seek to improve the quality of life, to encourage comradeship and so on. The state's theoretical duty can be delivered through any number of mechanisms but the community group delivery mechanism fits naturally with the obligation to let society flourish.[11]

Government at the centre needs to readdress its relationship with intermediate bodies of all sorts, both strictly governmental, voluntary and associate, and community. This is more than merely delivering services through community agencies. It gives such agencies a special standing with the state at all levels; a status which recognises their role in fulfilling vital public functions as a new form of para-state force. Nor should it be surprising if, in time, some of these groupings adopt more evidently political attitudes, not least in the form of lobbying for change.

The relative autonomy of voluntary and community bodies has diminished over recent times. Their identities have been increasingly defined in terms of the dominant state partner so that even innovation and change, let alone radical initiatives, have been confined to the centralised state and its natural partner, the private sector. This is not consistent with arguments for choice, freedom

---

9 See eg Dick Atkinson *The Common Sense of Community* (Demos, White Dove Press, London 1994) p 36.

10 Norman Lewis *How to Reinvent British Government* p 28.

11 And see Norman Lewis, 'Markets, Regulation and Citizenship' in Roger Brownsword (ed) *Law and the Public Interest* (Franz Steiner, Stuttgart 1993) p 134.

190   *The social market economy and the constitutional framework*

and democracy, and thought must now be given to affording a constitutional status to associations whose actions ought not to be trimmed to avoid giving political offence. Associative action tends, in the natural course of things, to develop from the purely charitable and supportive to the more active role of promoting ideas and advancing causes without becoming part of the classically political fabric itself.

Most commentators now believe that the 'one size fits all' model is outdated and that no single agency is likely to be able to satisfy demands in a society characterised by market preferences, heightened individualism and a firmly-rooted belief in choice. It may even be that 'solutions' create new problems and that change and aspiration will move forward dialectically. If this is right, then it would appear to reinforce another belief of the New Right: viz that the politics of paternalism should be jettisoned; that it is unsatisfactory for important decisions to be conducted by a handful of activists when the alternative is to re-enfranchise the citizen as consumer or neighbour.

As the advanced world appears to be moving into an era of regional groupings to contest the uncontrolled energy of the global markets, so the city is re-emerging as the focus of expression and concern. In Europe alone, more than 20 urban networks have been created to share experiences, best practices and to initiate joint projects. They have begun to by-pass capitals and to focus on 'the business of business'. The former ports of Barcelona, Marseille, Glasgow and Genoa often appear to have more to say to each other than they do to their state capitals about their plans to shape their economic futures. The need to make cities more sustainable requires creative, 'holistic' planning, yet in the UK this is severely hampered by the fact that the cities control only an estimated 16% of their expenditure. In world terms they are labouring under enormous disadvantages where cities as distinct as Milan and Melbourne retain a large measure of fiscal and political independence.

The creativity of these cities is only partly about infrastructure; it is also about the environment, about creating networks of voluntary and community organisations, about linking institutions of higher education with the city's inhabitants.[12] Frug observed that local and community politics are subject to considerable legal restraint while private corporations, being by nature 'private',

12 See Charles Landry and Franco Bianchini *The Creative City* (Demos, London 1995).

deserve legal protection.[13] Of course, the modern corporation is private only if language is stretched to its limits and a reassessment of institutional competences may be overdue. Whatever changes to company law may be thought necessary to ensure that footloose oligarchies do not impede citizen choice, it is clear that local politics needs to be greatly extended while encouraging linkages with business organisations for the benefit of the citizenry at large.

At the community level there are many illustrations of potential innovation. For example, there are the newly-emergent Birmingham Community Development Trusts which have arisen to satisfy local needs, in part by concern with regeneration in partnership with other voluntary organisations and with the public and the private sector.[14] Again, school 'clusters' are emerging which pool part of their budgets and undertake a number of joint initiatives. In the welfare field, experiments are appearing through housing associations, housing co-operatives and housing action trusts with neighbourhoods capable of performing numerous functions currently operated by either the public or the private sector once given a degree of ownership and resources. The fact that many local authorities resist such developments suggests that their legal responsibilities need to be refashioned.

As Atkinson has said:

> 'It is not sufficient to devolve finances and managerial control out to schools and to community agencies. Parts of the political process itself must be devolved. The emergent self-governing urban village needs its own non-party political voice and a degree of control over its own affairs.'[15]

Neighbourhood councils or forums ought, on this analysis, to be encouraged with members elected or co-opted from other local agencies such as schools and development trusts. A neighbourhood officer, often seconded from local government in experiments during the 1960s and 1970s, could be funded either by a precept on the rate or by pooling a part of the budget of local self-governing agencies. Although these bodies should be able to handle and run many of the services which they need, one of the neighbourhood officer's functions could be a lobbying one with the appropriate level of government. Atkinson sees such people as

13 Gerald E Frug 'The City as a Legal Concept' (1980) 93 Harv LR *passim.*
14 See eg Dick Atkinson *The Common Sense of Community* (Demos, White Dove Press, London 1994) pp 13–14.
15 *Ibid* p 42 and *passim.*

professional 'social entrepreneurs'. Together these developments
need not constitute another layer of government but ought in
many instances to replace the 'over-intrusive city machine'. In tune
with everything that has been said in the preceding chapters of this
book, Atkinson argues:

> 'As a consequence the Town Hall can concentrate its efforts
> less on trying to run everything and thus failing to do anything
> well, but on enabling and resourcing others to achieve excel-
> lence.
>
> Because so many of the tasks once undertaken by the Town
> Hall can readily and more effectively be discharged within
> each village it is necessary to reduce its size and change the
> way it is organized. Most of the Town Hall's departments can
> be slimmed down or merged in order to meet new func-
> tions.'[16]

This scenario envisages a new community-sensitive department
which takes neighbourhoods as the basic building blocks from
which towns are constructed, the departments not being organised
on hierarchical lines but as a series of sub or neighbourhood
departments which deployed the levers of local government for the
benefits of each area or locality. The scaled-down Town Hall would
liaise with the grass-roots neighbourhood forum. Atkinson makes
one more telling point:

> 'The array of quangos and trusts have been rightly criticised as
> unaccountable to their local communities. But reconceived to
> embed them in the area they serve, with clear lines of account-
> ability and clear rights for local communities to remove those
> that don't perform, new self-governing agencies have the
> potential to be much more responsive and entrepreneurial
> than when they were locked into the monopoly of local gov-
> ernment.'[17]

The details matter less than the principle. This is where traditional concepts of subsidiarity meet community. A more
autonomous local government would have both the resources and
the obligation to enable the community to engage in acts of self-
expression. Not everyone will wish to take advantage of these

16 *Ibid* p 46.
17 *Ibid* p 49.

opportunities, but where they do they should have the right to do so.

There is little point in spelling out the standard constitutional formulae with which most will now agree. The first generation human rights are common currency while some system of checks and balances necessitating parliamentary and electoral reform must command broad support if the logic of choice and experiment is to be pursued. These are matters which need political finesse rather than intellectual analysis although it needs to be stressed that freedom of speech requires a particularly strong formulation if the power of the media to undermine individual expression is to be countered. The threadbare quality of claims of ministerial responsibility to vindicate the nature of democracy clearly needs to be recognised and modern accountability mechanisms based in part upon a revised system of administrative law ought for most to be uncontroversial. Other issues of constitutional reform are less commonly remarked upon.

Little time has been spent on mechanisms for the redress of individual grievances. This is not because they are unimportant; rather it is because most people now accept them to be important and proposals for reform are not difficult to find.[18] However, the one reform of a middle-range nature needed above all others is the Standing Administrative Conference or equivalent to which regular attention has been drawn. It threatens no constituency in itself, is inexpensive but would add enormously to the stock of public information and debate on the workings of the machinery of government. The only surprise is that it has not attracted more attention than it has amongst the welter of proposals for constitutional reform, especially given the record of similar experiments elsewhere.

As to the system of public law more generally, and in particular the role of the courts, little needs to be said in any doctrinal sense. The necessary reforms to 'constitutional' arrangements are bound to radicalise both the judiciary and the total system of public law through both a process of constitutional textual exegesis and the revised expectations of openness, consultation and a rights-based legal regime. That is as it should be and would bring the UK more into line with contemporary notions of the appropriate balance of powers in a revised polity. However, there are several important matters which still merit further consideration.

18 See, in particular, Norman Lewis and Patrick Birkinshaw *When Citizens Complain: Reforming Justice and Administration* (Open University Press, Buckingham 1993).

Analysis has led to the conviction that matters should be decided by those most affected by the decisions and that those decisions should, wherever possible, be pushed downwards, not just to ensure greater choice for locally elected politicians vis-à-vis Westminster but also so that those same politicians encourage the maximum opportunities for community empowerment and, whenever possible, self-management. To some extent this must be guaranteed by a constitution which is genuinely federal and under which the power of local and regional government cannot be eroded by simple primary legislation. However, going beyond this to the community level probably requires something resembling the directive principles of state policy.

At this point another word needs to be said on the issue of the governance of industry and the role of company law. It is worth beginning by saying that there is no point in pretending that the limited liability company or the constellation of institutional arrangements which are the City of London are genuinely 'private' in the same sense that each person has undisputed rights to personal privacy. Their actions are made possible by a combination of legal protections and other facultative devices which make it abundantly clear that the state facilitates their conduct. They are not simply players in a natural market-place but frequently are favoured players in a constructed market-place. If this is correct, then the state has the right to remake the terms and conditions of operation in the market to reflect the human rights which the state is established to protect.

It is here that the argument about stakeholders is bound to re-emerge. The state cannot regulate the global economy and, that being the case, the state must have obligations to its citizens to ensure that they are not left in the lurch by sudden and surprising movements of fleet-footed capital. Both the rights of citizens and the needs of the economy require that the system of corporate governance reflects codes of duty as well as of rights. This is demanded of citizens; no less entitlement should be expected of collectivities. In particular, there are undeniable basic rights for workers, including the right to work at levels of pay which reflect the social and economic conditions in which they are compelled to make their lives. And even the crudest arguments for labour markets require that workers receive the levels of information about the fortunes of the firms to which they are, at any given time, committed. This is being increasingly recognised in the European Union and elsewhere.

Furthermore, there are stakeholders other than the shareholder: customers, consumers, suppliers, citizens often habitat-dependent upon the fortunes of certain large corporations. It cannot be right to grant autonomy and more than autonomy to configurations of capital with the power to destroy careers and communities and to pretend that all citizens are equally invested with choice in any real measure. A benign system of company law would reflect these concerns, whether such a code was comprised by primary legislation or something somewhat better entrenched. It may be thought that, like the proposed Administrative Procedure Act or Code of Administrative Law, a special status ought to be given to the rules which govern the financial and industrial base. Be that as it may, the directive principles also have a potential role to play.

The important point to stress is that these crucial concerns, some of which will need at any given time to be afforded a ranking order, are genuinely constitutional concerns. Protecting the rights of human beings within a social setting of their own or their predecessors' creation is a task pre-eminently for the constitution.

ONCE MORE TO THE DIRECTIVE PRINCIPLES

The Indian experience suggests that directive principles of the constitution are capable of doing a great deal of work, especially if the Preamble to the constitution was committed to equality, natural justice, freedom and well-being and the right to participate in political and social life.

The right to life is bound to be at the centre of any revised human rights document and once its atomic crystals have been broken open will lead to the development of a sub-set of rights and expectations. It is fitting that the judiciary should interpret this basic right in the light of developments and expectations engendered in the conduct of the nation's affairs. Similarly with the right to equality before the law. The Indian *Cellular Telephones Case*[19] affords a valuable illustration of how such a basic claim can generate unexpected results. The right not to be discriminated against in a tendering process is merely one example of the potential sweep of such a consensual commitment, but the possibilities are many and dramatic and would absorb race, gender, sexual inclination, age, disability, religious and political persuasion and so on. The right would imply equality in the face of state activity whether as an employee or mere citizen, it would embrace the prohibition of

19 (1994) *The Times of India*, 5 August.

discrimination on the basis of life-style (often so important in the past in areas such as social security entitlement) and comprises what is in fact 'irrelevant considerations' writ large but capable also of grinding exceeding small. Irrelevant considerations is a well-established ground of judicial review at common law but it has never developed the broader sweep of which it is capable. As a clearly enunciated constitutional principle it could make a substantial contribution towards the liberation of human capacity.

An associated commitment is to 'natural justice'. As an unlimited sentiment this commitment would enjoy a broader range than the contested art 6 of the ECHR. Due process, which is the American expression of the sentiment, amounts to treating each individual as of the same worth. It is part of freedom and well-being to act upon interests as individually perceived in a framework of mutuality. Choice is embedded in the concept of action and natural justice allows an individual to represent their own interests, their version of events, their concept of freedom and well-being to those who would impact upon it. Granted that citizens concede, through a procedure for moderating collective freedom and well-being, decisions on the merits to the political/administrative process, they do not forfeit the right to participate either vicariously or, depending on the nature of the impact, directly or *in personam*. These ideas, jointly and severally, expressed with some measure of prominence, are capable of contributing to human rights development in a way not generally understood. Yet arguably more significant still is the right to 'participation in government and civil society'. Choosing and participation are inextricably linked and ought to be seen to be the centrepiece of constitutional arrangements.

HOLDING AN UMBRELLA OVER SOCIAL AND POLITICAL ACTION

Let the right to form associations and groups and to engage in social action as part of interactive nature be ceded. The state then has a duty to encourage action in and rights within voluntary organisations, but there is a need to go further and argue for the right to participate in civic, social and industrial association. Choice, action and participation are generic concepts and can be limited only by special justification. No doubt the right to participate in social and industrial action can be played out pragmatically in line with cultural developments and expectations but of special significance is the right to participate in political action at all levels, including that of the community. This has implications for administrative law, for ombudsman systems and the like and has enormous regenerative potential in political settings.

Choice, to reiterate, involves pursuing chosen actions in social settings. There is no brooking this inevitable linkage; it is, to paraphrase, 'the state we're in', the way things are. Furthermore, state institutions are institutions for vicariously exercising some of those choices. They belong to the people who are entitled to participate in them. This goes beyond due process or natural justice in the grievance or individual concern case and on into participation in the political process; consultation, rule-making, the corporate planning of state institutions; 'due process writ large'. It is for these reasons that a constitutional provision is required, preferably in the Bill of Rights, to graft on to the polity the right to participate at the systemic level.[20] This goes with the grain of devolved government and will have implications for life in the city, for the government of schools, the health services and the like. Of course such authorities or agencies would enjoy considerable leeway in how they encouraged participation; again there is the need to encourage innovation and competitive experimentation to engender best practices and revised or heightened expectations but all this would be set against the constitutional duty to foster participation backed by both the ombudsman system and, ultimately if rarely, the courts. They, no doubt, will occasionally be called upon to deliver Himalayan judgments which can be expected to mark out the boundaries of civic rights and to bring aberrant political players back on side.[1]

PARTICIPATION IN SOCIAL AND INDUSTRIAL LIFE[2]

This claim may meet some resistance but it should come as no surprise by now. It should be clear that isolation is not the natural

20 As to Parliament itself, the constitution could be specific and require, eg post-First Reading public hearings (subject to a waiver) or leave Parliament to determine its own procedures *through a specific mechanism.*

1 The courts could profitably be accorded Indian-style powers to appoint commissions of investigation to undertake what has been called the 'social audit' function of law through eg interim orders and other measures which are not restricted to traditional sanctions; there is a need to unchain ourselves from the past.

2 This may be seen against the background to the Social Protocol of the Treaty of Union, of the European Social Charter, a persuasive protocol to a UK Constitution covering social and economic rights etc.

condition and that there are clear existential linkages between being human and engaging in associative conduct. No unreasonable – that is to say non-mutual – impediment should impair the right to choose in concert with others whose aims are shared. Not only must the state not inhibit such associative conduct but it must create or nurture the conditions for associative possibility. The right, already discussed, to participate in or form provident bodies or credit unions on non-discriminatory terms would represent an obvious illustration[3] as would the right to establish independent schools or health bodies, though the equality provision might be called upon occasionally to pull in two different directions.

As to industrial participation, it is important to remember what has been said about dignity and choice and markets which bargain 'signal to signal' in order to seek a genuine free market in labour. The present situation produces too much compulsion for freedom to operate. So again the Social Protocol and directive principles on social rights will naturally link in to this primary right. If the constitution were to speak of the state duty to encourage participation, then an ombudsman or court could find in any given context that not enough had been done and Indian-style remedies might well be brought into play. By all common and standard measures of human rights and choice, individual citizens must be able to demand not only dignity (which needs unpacking but which clearly partakes of various International Labour Organisation standards) but also the right to extend to one's choice feeding into the collective (ie the firm) choice procedures, although it is inescapable that the operation of capitalism does not represent a true consent procedure. Even if there is tacit consent to 'pure' market forces, then since capitalism is scarcely ever that, it must follow that regulating the rights of labour into existence must be legitimate.

Furthermore, it is clear that there must be a right to join labour associations which do not deprive others of their rights since to associate with others is a fundamental entitlement. The White Paper on Competitiveness, on the other hand, is muddled, confused and less than consistent in this area. Competition must be 'fair' (no analysis), the government 'supports Treaty objectives for social, environmental and consumer protection', it 'welcomes action by companies ... to promote effective involvement of employees and the sharing of experience', it welcomes the Royal

---

3 There would, it will be recalled, also be a Competition Authority empowered to act broadly.

Society of Art's 'Tomorrow's Company', Interim Report 1994, including the desire to 'create a sense of shared identity with all stakeholders ...' and accepts that 'Regulation is an essential responsibility of the Government'. No consistent philosophy can be detected; there is no attempt to work through the logic of respect for mutual choice in capitalist relations and, of course, no deeper inquiry into the preconditions for choice to reign in the workplace or the market-place. All of this makes it the more necessary for the constitution to provide the opportunity for ensuring that, as a nation, the implications of choice and human rights in all aspects of life are worked through. Giving the rights to ombudsmen and the courts to interpret the meaning of promises we make to ourselves can only enhance the likelihood of a genuine spirit of nationhood and shared community emerging. They will not necessarily behave like their predecessors but, with a new set of procedures and sanctions available, they may well be able to force the pace on moving towards the creation of a genuinely choosing society.

British political history has many achievements to its credit, not least a record of unparalleled social stability, most clearly illustrated in times of national crisis. However, times have changed and the sense of identity is no longer as secure as it once was. What is at base a fair society is in danger of fragmenting. A restoration of national instincts and sentiments is called for in circumstances where raw politics must learn to accept second place. The legal order now needs to re-assert itself as a unifying force which relegates factions to the function of engaging in civilised debate.

The government accepted the accolade offered by a *Times* leader which claimed that 'Statecraft is becoming a major British export, just as privatisation was in the 1980s'.[4] If this is so the nation may be best employed seeking to repatriate it in clear constitutional terms. True statesmen have always accepted that it is their duty to rise above politics.

---

4 *Competitiveness: Helping Business to Win* Cm 2563 (HMSO, 1994) para 14.13.

Chapter 10
Conclusions

This book has attempted to bring together things which are ordinarily kept apart. In doing so, it has offered a new agenda, a new set of materials and a new set of challenges to traditional legal and constitutional scholarship. It opens up possibilities for the legal order which are rarely acknowledged by non-lawyers, especially in the UK where law, lawyers, and legal processes are considered to be part of an insensitive establishment unconnected to social, economic or political problems. In particular, a clear divide is normally asserted between the legal and the political by the establishments of the respective professions' practitioners. This is profoundly mistaken and the UK is almost isolated in failing to understand the necessary relationships between constitutions and politics and a broad concept of law's potential contribution to political debate and change and, more importantly, to the liberation of individual and social needs.

On reflection, many things which people regard as important but unrelated have a necessary, deeper, level of connection than meets the eye. The lawyer who understands only the law fails even to understand the law; such is the saw. The political scientist who forgets that law is ultimately more important than politics forgets his Aristotle and much else besides. British political and social history has made such amnesia understandable to some extent but amnesia it remains. That law has many sides, many levels and many variants and these have not been sufficiently explained over the years by generations of lawyers and legal scholars. Their failures are lamentable and make it easier for others to claim not to understand the virtue and versatility of the legal order.

This partly accounts for the unarguable disregard in recent times for some of the humanistic tenets which most people hold dear. Although there are many other examples, this is especially obvious in the case of labour. Across the world, industrial man has been continuously subordinated to the needs of production and finance, yet not only are these processes not products of a pure, unconstructed, market model but they have been producing random results; results not mandated by the general will. Naturally, it is easier to identify such shortcomings than to remedy them or even to identify with certainty what a remedy would look like. Yet unless reality is confronted with a reaffirmation of basic beliefs, there will be no map to point the way towards improvement and reform. These beliefs and needs must be given a constitutional status so that the nation keeps at the forefront of its thinking the celebration of choice and the possibilities for being free and expansively human.

The legal firmament has concentrated on the traditional civil and political rights to the relative exclusion of the material, psychic and associational. Responses have been, for the most part, reactive rather than analytic at the level of the total individual personality. A revised legal and political order will, in contrast, strike a more expansive note which is not limited to public institutions but which addresses the whole social order. Nonetheless, it is important to stress that a reformed system of law and politics must be unprecedentedly flexible; revised parliamentary processes, improved participative machinery for the policy process, an expanded role for administrative law, new tasks for ombudsmen and courts with the power to order investigations and potential programmes for delivering on constitutional rights are all required. And, not least, a Standing Administrative Conference is needed which has, as its primary remit, the oversight of the machinery of government. The function of these institutions is to produce a politics of participation, inquiry and circumspection informed by first principles and entitlements.

It has been argued that a revised compact should comprise both a Preamble affirming a statement of beliefs, in very general terms, of primary constitutional rights, albeit more extensive than normally envisaged and including equality, natural justice, civic participation etc and a layer of directive principles, following the Indian example. Over a period of time, these principles could be expected to play a crucial role, elaborating on the primary rights under changing conditions and in the context of the needs of the times, the pace of social movements and so on. Furthermore, if the assumption that courts or other legal institutions are only suitable for determining simple rights/duties formulations is abandoned, then it is possible to see how constitutional expectations could unfold gently and, hopefully, consensually. Participation may serve as an example. If an ombudsman or court had found that it was not being adequately advanced in any particular context it might order fuller investigation and inquiry in the way that the Indian courts have sometimes done. It would be for the court ultimately to determine the remedy and whether the response was satisfactory. It would be a grave error to believe that either ombudsmen or courts would seek confrontation and flex institutional muscle. On occasion firmness would be required but that is already the position. This proposal, after all, would make real the life which the constitution reached for; a situation which reflects the aspirations of the nation and not a faction.

Constitutional scholarship needs to expand to address the realities of deep-grained, systemic choice which embraces reform of the total set of fiefdoms: industry, the City and much else besides. There will be a need for labour and company lawyers to join forces with public lawyers to present layers of analysis and varied menus currently unimagined. Equally, the logic of experiments in living supports pushing decision-making in like-minded groupings down to the lowest level where choice can effectively occur, drawing upon mutual experience and the dynamic processes of human interaction to create new realms of opportunity and to allow space in which to express existing forms of association.

It will be objected that international, global markets will increasingly inhibit the powers of nation states to determine their own affairs. That is as may be, but the response will be likely to be the expansion of regional groupings of nation states each needing their own statement of constitutional principles which will surely differ little from what is being suggested here. In any event, countries such as the UK will not wish to abandon all vestiges of sovereignty and there will remain a great deal of work for national constitutions to perform. It should be reasserted too that 'ought' implies 'can' not only in relation to philosophical argument but in the struggles of the living law. Abandonment of basic beliefs is a poor response to the fact of circumscribed autonomy.

A testament is needed for this generation and for those yet unborn. It is time to establish a constitution which proclaims the importance of people's lives across the years and to ensure an adequate measure of support which allows those lives to be lived to the full. These matters are too important to be left to politicians, who must be held to account for upholding the covenant which allows them to practise their trade in the first place. The constitution must go beyond statements of the obvious and must attempt to shade in the sensibilities, to encourage methods of dialogue and new instrumentalities to enable politics to learn new ways of delivering on settled expectations. There are currently too many parts of government which citizens cannot reach: the potential of the legal order needs to be tapped in order to make them accessible.

That being said, it is worth stressing that what is presented here is a menu and not a blueprint. It would be naïve to expect national affirmation of the whole analysis but a valuable purpose will have been served if it has become clear what the nation would be missing if it failed to take up the challenges posted here. Above all, it should by now be apparent that legal and constitutional scholarship needs to be broader and deeper than heretofore. The legal order needs to assume its share of responsibility for liberating our choosing natures.

Index